Alternative Schooling and Student Engagement

Nina Bascia · Esther Sokolov Fine
Malcolm Levin
Editors

Alternative Schooling and Student Engagement

Canadian Stories of Democracy within Bureaucracy

palgrave
macmillan

Editors
Nina Bascia
Department of Leadership, Higher and
Adult Education
Ontario Institute for
Studies in Education
Toronto, ON, Canada

Malcolm Levin
Ontario Institute for Studies in
Education
University of Toronto
Toronto, ON, Canada

Esther Sokolov Fine
York University
Toronto, ON, Canada

ISBN 978-3-319-85354-3   ISBN 978-3-319-54259-1   (eBook)
DOI 10.1007/978-3-319-54259-1

Cover image: © Cultura Creative (RF)/Alamy Stock Photo

Printed on acid-free paper

This Palgrave Macmillan imprint is published by Springer Nature
The registered company is Springer International Publishing AG
The registered company address is: Gewerbestrasse 11, 6330 Cham, Switzerland

In memory of
Bob Davis
Ursula Franklin
Murray Shukyn
Roger Simon

FOREWORD

This book presents a world where students actually thrive. Alternative schools blossomed in the late 1960s and 1970s during a time of progressive reform in mainstream education. In Ontario, the Hall–Dennis Report—*Living and Learning*—sparked a great deal of this activity along with broader changes in the culture. Today, schools exist within a climate where students are constantly measured. Given this, alternative schools are needed more than ever to help demonstrate what education can and should be. In general, alternative schools focus on the development of the whole person, democratic decision-making, and self-directed learning.

This book describes the history and reality of life in schools, mostly within the Toronto District School Board. Many of them started in the 1970s and have continued despite the pressures of "accountability." The journey for many teachers in these schools is not without struggle. In their chapters, we hear their voices calling for a more humane education and showing some of the ways it can be achieved. We also hear the voices of students who have attended these schools. For example, one student comments:

> I learned not to take for granted given truths, I learned to ask a lot of questions and decide what the truth is for myself. I learned there are a lot of different opinions in the world and that I need to be aware of them. I learned that people have different learning styles and ways of being, and that these differences should be embraced by the systems we learn and

work within. People kept asking me what I thought at such an early age, and though it took some time, eventually this forced me out of excruciating shyness. I learned I really had to speak up for what I believed was right (Kim Simon, in the final chapter).

This is the kind of learning and growth that we wish for all students. Education needs a much broader vision than that currently offered by Ministries and Departments of Education. This book describes schools where students' well-being is nourished. It also encourages all educators to reflect on the purposes and meaning of education.

Professor Jack Miller
Ontario Institute for Studies in Education
University of Toronto
Toronto, ON, Canada

CONTENTS

About the Editors

Nina Bascia is Professor and Chair of the Department of Leadership, Higher and Adult Education and at the Ontario Institute for Studies in Education (OISE) at the University of Toronto. She is the founding director of the Collaborative Program in Educational Policy, also at OISE. She has published a number of books, including *The Contexts of Teaching in Secondary Schools: Teachers' Realities, Unions in Teachers' Professional lives, The Sharp Edge of Educational Change, and Teacher Unions in Public Education.* She currently is working on a study of how teachers and students negotiate curriculum in secondary alternative schools in Toronto.

Esther Sokolov Fine is Professor Emeritus and Senior Scholar at York University in Toronto, Canada. Prior to her work in the York Faculty of Education, she was an elementary teacher with the Toronto Board of Education, where she taught in downtown public housing communities and alternative programs. Her latest book, *Raising Peacemakers* (Garn Press, 2015), tells the story of her 22 years of research with a community of students at a small alternative public school, beginning when they were very young and interviewing them as they grew up. Her research has been funded by Social Sciences and Humanities Research Council of Canada (SSHRC). Research interviews filmed by Roberta King can be seen at www.childrenaspeacemakers.ca.

Malcolm Levin was a founding parent of MAGU, Toronto's first public alternative elementary school, and later served as the parent representative on the Toronto Board of Education's committee on Alternative and Community Education. Before coming to OISE as a faculty member in 1968, he was a doctoral student, researcher, and supervisor of student teachers at the Harvard Graduate School of Education and a member of the editorial board of the Harvard Educational Review. At OISE, he taught courses in program organization, history, philosophy, and sociology of education and alternative education, and co-edited a series of classroom booklets on Canadian Public Issues. Later, he served as Academic Assistant Director of OISE, Director of the University of Toronto's Institute for Child Study, and Principal of the University of Toronto Schools, a university-affiliated secondary school for gifted and talented youth. He has been a freelance jazz pianist since his teens and continues to play in retirement.

Introduction

Toronto's Public Alternative Schools: An Overview

In the early 1970s, long before schools of choice, magnet schools, and charter schools became the favorites of educational reformers across North America, a small cluster of public alternative schools made their appearance within what were then the cities of Toronto, North York, Etobicoke and Scarborough. The first was SEED, launched in 1968 as a summer enrichment program before becoming an alternative high school under the Toronto Board of Education. SEED was followed by MAGU, a multi-age grouped elementary school established by the North York Board of Education in 1970. In 1971, the Toronto Board established ALPHA, an alternative elementary school similar in philosophy and organization to MAGU. In the same year, alternative high schools were started in Etobicoke (SEE) and North York (AISP). The Scarborough Board launched its own alternative elementary school—Scarborough Village—in 1973 and an alternative high school (ASE) 2 years later. Toronto created two additional alternative high schools in 1973— Contact and Subway Academy. Only one of these alternative schools— Subway—was initiated by central administration. The main impetus came from teachers, parents, and students who lobbied and gained the support of sympathetic trustees and school administrators.

These events unfolded in a distinctive climate characterized by a revival of child-centered progressive educational philosophy and practices and a rejection of traditional mainstream institutional schooling.

They were animated by a level of socio-political activism not seen since the 1930s. The revival of child-centered progressive education was fueled by the Ontario Ministry of Education's publication of "Living and Learning," called the Hall–Dennis Report, co-authored by a prominent judge and an elementary school principal. The report drew upon a range of historical progressive education sources from the USA, the UK, and locally from the University of Toronto's own Institute for Child Study (ICS) Lab School.

The Hall–Dennis Report called for a major overhaul of Ontario's public school system from the Ministry of Education down to the classroom. Its overall thrust was to radically decentralize program development and administration. Individual school boards were to assume responsibility for tailoring their programs to the needs of their students within a broad flexible framework. At the high school level, in particular, mandatory courses and examinations were to be replaced by more flexible course offerings under a "credit system" based on hours of instruction.

The report recommended replacing the existing lock-step programs with a more individualized curriculum, taking into account the differing needs and interests of students. It also recommended the establishment of school–community councils to encourage the collaboration of parents and teachers in meeting the needs of students. It called for a more student-oriented curriculum with responsibility for program development delegated to school boards, individual teachers with input from parents and students. The role of the Ministry of Education was to change from top-down inspection and enforcement to establishing flexible guidelines, providing advice and ultimately approving or rejecting submissions from individual boards of education.

The progressive spirit of Hall–Dennis opened the doors to ungraded primary classrooms, new schools with open area designs, new high school courses designed by teachers, and elimination of standardized province-wide examinations at the high school level. While some teachers, administrators, and school trustees welcomed these changes, others felt unprepared to take on the challenges of a decentralized system and felt that the new approach would undermine academic standards and quality. A "Back to Basics" backlash gained momentum with support from Minister of Education Thomas Wells, who spoke of the need to "maintain standards" and "accountability."

Nevertheless, Living and Learning had let the progressive education genie out of the bottle in which it had been corked for decades. Wells' pronouncements were pounced on in an issue of Interchange, a new academic journal of education published by the recently (1965) established Ontario Institute for Studies in Education (OISE) by previous Minister of Education Bill Davis. In addition to the present writer, Murray Shukyn of SEED and Roger Simon of ALPHA led the attack.

In 1968, Shukyn and a small group of high school teachers launched SEED as a summer program for Toronto high school students, housed in rented space in the downtown YMHA Community Center. Two years later, the Toronto Board approved SEED as a year-round alternative high school, along with ALPHA, a progressive elementary school spearheaded by a group of activist parents. Both ventures were supported by recently elected young trustees linked to the rising left-wing New Democratic Party of Ontario. These trustees—notably Fiona Nelson, Gordon Cressy, Dan Leckie and Bob Spencer—emerged as prominent figures in a "reform caucus" at the Board.

Meanwhile, in North York, a predominantly middle-class suburb of Toronto, a group of activist parents who called themselves "parents for a Hall–Dennis School" were meeting with Mel Shipman, a sympathetic trustee, and a school superintendent, Claude Watson, to promote the establishment of a non-graded elementary school modeled after those in Leicestershire in the UK. The group included well-connected professional and business people, notably two professors who had left the USA to take up positions at recently created York University. Mildred and David Bakan had elementary school-age children who they wanted to be educated in a modern progressive public school directed by parents and teachers. In 1969, the North York Board approved a "Multi-Age-Grouping Unit" (MAGU) to be housed in one of the Board's elementary school buildings. Thus, MAGU became Canada's first public alternative elementary school.

These public alternative schools came into being as a consequence of collaboration and negotiations between activist parents, teachers and students, and a few supportive school administrators and trustees who supported the spirit and recommendations of the Hall–Dennis Report. In this respect, the change process was both bottom-up and top-down. The growth and development of alternative and community school initiatives thrived mainly in the city of Toronto, where politicians favoring community involvement in education and other social services were dominant. The Toronto Board created a School–Community Relations Department and an Alternative and Community Programs Committee to establish procedures and vet proposals for new initiatives. Dale Shuttleworth, an experienced school–community relations administrator, was recruited from the North York Board to lead the new department and guide its work.

During the 1970s and early 1980s, middle-class parents took advantage of the opportunity to propose new alternative elementary schools across the city (e.g., Beaches, Downtown, High Park, Mountview) and in neighboring Scarborough (Scarborough Village). In addition, a trio of teachers from Deer Park Senior School, located in an affluent area of north Toronto, started the city's first Grade 7/8 alternative—Spectrum—in a local elementary school building.

New high school alternatives were also launched in the 1970s and early 1980s. The Toronto Board created two independent study alternatives modeled on Philadelphia's "school-without-walls." Parkway Program. Subway Academy One and Subway Academy Two were set up along Toronto's main east-west subway line to provide flexible study arrangements for high school students. Students were expected to work independently and arrange to meet with their teachers at regular intervals.

However, many high school students from poor and working-class families lacked the skills and discipline for self-directed learning but were not being well-served in mainstream high schools. In response to this need, Toronto teacher Harry Smaller and a group of like-minded teachers launched Contact in 1973, soon to be followed by West End and Oasis.

Three independent (private) alternative schools that were experiencing financial difficulties—Hawthorne Bilingual, Inglenook, and Wandering Spirit Survival School—requested and were also granted public school status under the Toronto Board.

The proliferation of public alternative schools continued in the 1980s. Three new grade 7/8 schools—Horizon, Delta, and Quest—and two more high school alternatives—City School and School of Life Experience (SOLE)—opened their doors to students. In addition, the Etobicoke and North York school boards launched performing arts schools.

The efforts of Toronto teachers, parents, and school trustees, supported by a temporarily permissive Ministry of Education, created an institutional process for establishing new public alternative schools and programs across the Greater Toronto Area (GTA) which continues to this day. However, the political and economic environment within which public schools operate today has changed dramatically. Accountability, Assessment, and Austerity have replaced Diversity and Innovation as the central concerns of provincial educational policy. Alternative schools, along with mainstream schools, have had to make adjustments to this turnabout.

In 1990, in the midst of a recession evoking calls for reduced government spending, a three-way provincial election contest resulted in Ontario's first left-leaning New Democratic Party (NDP) government under the leadership of Bob Rae. The results surprised everyone, including Rae and his fellow New Democrats, who found themselves inheriting a substantial budget deficit left behind by the defeated Liberal government. Rae responded by calling for all public-sector employees to take a 5% wage cut. Public sector workers and their unions were furious, especially teachers, who had supported the NDP and felt betrayed.

The next provincial election in 1995 resulted in a sharp swing to the right as a hard-line Conservative party led by Mike Harris from North Bay swept to power with a mandate to curb the powers of local school boards, public service unions, and municipal governments. The Harris Conservatives launched what they called a "common sense revolution" that reversed what the conservatives in the 1960s had started. They re-centralized power at all levels. The Ministry of Education now decided how much each local school board could spend based on province-wide formulas, regardless of local needs. The City of Toronto and its school board was merged with the other five metropolitan boroughs. Toronto was viewed by the Harris Conservatives, whose power base was in sub-urbia and small town Ontario, as a breeding ground for what they called the "tax and spend" Liberal and NDP parties. While alternative schools continued to operate, they no longer received additional staff resources they had been previously allocated to meet the needs of their students, particularly in high schools such as Contact, West End, and Oasis. The new Toronto District School Board (TDSB) had to operate under the same funding formulas as Harris's rural town of North Bay.

CONCLUSION

Nearly all the pioneering public alternative schools in Metropolitan Toronto continue to operate today with healthy student enrollments; in 2014, there were 19 elementary level alternative schools and 21 high school alternatives listed on the TDSB Web site. New schools continue to be proposed and established under the administration of the TDSB. What began as a bold innovation in public education in Toronto in the 1970s has become an integral part of the public school system in the GTA in the twenty-first century. The chapters in this book are an effort to re-capture the history and dynamics of this mini-revolution in public education from the perspectives of many who participated in it and helped shape it as well as some who are presently working in alternative schools.

Malcolm Levin

PART I

Local Democracy Within Bureaucracy: Critical Perspectives

Curriculum Development in Alternative Schools: What Goes on in Alternative Schools Stays in Alternative Schools

Nina Bascia and Rhiannon Maton

Alternative schools allow school systems to meet the social, emotional, and physical challenges of children and youth that are not addressed by mainstream schools. The major features that distinguish many alternative schools from their mainstream counterparts are democratic practices involving students and teachers, and small school and class sizes that allow for personalized relationships among staff and students (McLaughlin et al. 1990; Raywid 1994; Te Riele 2007). Many alternative schools experiment with different modes of organization that encourage curricular innovation (Raywid 1994). Often, teachers and students take an active role in designing original courses and programs (Bascia and Fine 2012).

That public alternative schools are able to develop innovative programs is a remarkable feat given the bureaucratic, top-down school systems in

N. Bascia (✉)
University of Toronto, Toronto, Canada

R. Maton
University of Pennsylvania, Philadelphia, USA

© The Author(s) 2017
N. Bascia et al. (eds.), *Alternative Schooling and Student Engagement*,
DOI 10.1007/978-3-319-54259-1_1

which they operate (Darling-Hammond 1997)—the same systems that promote standardized programs at mainstream schools that alienate some students (Wehlege 1989). What is it that buffers alternative schools from the currently prevalent educational practices that constrain teachers' work (Ball 2003)? How does teachers' work in alternative schools mediate the effects of bureaucratic educational systems in order to maintain innovative programming that is responsive to students' interests?

This chapter focuses on curriculum development in secondary alternative schools in the Toronto District School Board. It uses the concept of organizational "loose coupling" to describe how alternative school teachers and students actively select and craft courses and programs within the context of the school board and Ontario's provincial policy constraints. The concept of loose coupling helps explain alternative school teachers' abilities to innovate, as well as the limits of their influence beyond their own schools, and thus limiting curricular cross-fertilization. Research on teachers' careers helps us discern the continuities between teachers' lives and their work.

The data that inform this chapter come from interviews conducted as part of an exploratory study that focused on the work of five teachers. The five schools these teachers worked in reflect the diversity of secondary alternative schools in Toronto. They included academically oriented schools, schools geared to the education of working-class students, schools emphasizing student accessibility, and "transitional" schools for students who have left mainstream schools and may wish to return. Interviews revealed how teachers came to work in the school, how they determined what and how to teach, their working relationships with students and colleagues, school administration and governance, and the challenges and opportunities posed by their work.

A hallmark of many Toronto alternative schools is the extent to which staff (and students) experiment with different modes of organization and participate in curricular innovation. Several courses and practices that are now part of Toronto's and Ontario's official curriculum were developed and delivered first or early in alternative schools; some examples include gender and women's studies, holocaust and genocide education, and peace-making and conflict resolution (Bascia et al. 2014). While new courses and programs are also developed in mainstream school settings, Toronto's alternative schools are a rich source of teacher- and student-driven curriculum innovation. But because alternative schools tend to operate in a sphere separate from mainstream schools, these curricular "gifts" only rarely enjoy broader dissemination.

ALTERNATIVE SCHOOLS AS LOOSELY COUPLED ORGANIZATIONS

The concepts of loose and tight coupling were developed by organizational theorist Karl Weick (1976) to describe the organizational structure of schools in the United States. According to Weick, a tightly coupled organization is managed by a set of mutually understood rules enforced by an inspection and feedback system. In tightly coupled organizations, supervisors know exactly what employees are doing and can coordinate all the activities of different departments according to a central strategy. In contrast, in loosely coupled systems, there is a minimal coordination or regulation and several means might produce the same ends. Loose coupling allows more self-determination, local adaptation, and the development of creative solutions.

School systems are believed to be tightly coupled (Louis 1990; Meyer and Rowan 1977). Many educational practices are assumed to be uniform across public school systems and schools: for example, sorting students by age and presumed academic ability, dividing the curriculum into subjects and grades, the nature of student–teacher and teacher–teacher relationships, and fidelity with officially prescribed curriculum policy (Miles and Darling-Hammond 1998; Siskin 1994). These assumed regularities produce what Mary Metz (1989; also Hemmings and Metz 1992) has termed "real school," and what Tyack and Tobin (1994) call the "grammar of schooling."

Metz writes that expectations for "real school" are easily fulfilled when students "accept the staff's agenda as worthwhile" (p. 87), but when students do not keep up as expected or are disengaged from school, these expectations are more difficult to meet. Educators may respond to such challenges by developing distinct programs within schools (e.g., special education, ESL, vocational programs) that act as add-ons or pullouts to the "regular" academic program without seriously challenging its primacy (Miles and Darling-Hammond 1998). In this way, schools may resort to loose coupling to cope with the students who do not conform to system expectations.

School systems require public schools and educators to comply with system rules and expectations for "real school" with at least the appearance of tight coupling (Meyer and Rowan 1977). But some school systems may use alternative schools to help manage the dissonance that arises when they are confronted with diverse populations of students. In a sense, the existence of alternative schools reduces the pressure on regular schools to accommodate diverse students' needs and interests.

In order to maintain unique programs while ensuring their continued existence in public school systems, alternative schools may challenge some—but not all—of the expectations for "real school." In our study, alternative school teachers acknowledge the school board and province's expectations for "real school," but they also understand that teaching in an alternative school requires something more and different from "real teaching."

Loose Coupling and Alternative Schools

In the Toronto District School Board, there was a tension "between the diversity required for innovation and the standardization assumed by the normal operating procedures of the Board of Education" (Darling-Hammond et al. 2002: pp. 665–666). A special superintendent for alternative schools operated at the school board level. From the school district's perspective, coordination, and communication were managed efficiently—even though alternative schools maintained unique educational programs (Bascia and Fine 2012). Alternative schools were nominally headed up by principals, although many of these principals have responsibility for multiple schools. A lead teacher (or "curriculum leader") may have handled daily decision making, and teachers might experience greater autonomy than in traditional school settings. This enabled small alternative schools to maintain a system-required student–administrator ratio while also serving to loosen organizational coupling by reducing administrative oversight. To accommodate provincial student–teacher ratios, Toronto's secondary alternative schools had small teaching staffs, with each teacher typically responsible for multiple grades and subjects.

Secondary alternative schools' small size meant that most subject areas had only a single teacher—and teachers most often taught more than one subject. For example, one teacher at a highly academic school asserted that he was the only philosophy teacher in the school and did not need to work with other teachers, did not have to coordinate the same tests, and was able to customize class reading lists every semester. At another school that emphasized student accessibility, a teacher noted the absence of overt external control over teaching, saying that there were no "curriculum police" at the school. The relationship between what teachers did in their classrooms was only loosely coupled with what occurred at the school or school board level.

While many teachers reported working independently, the philosophy teacher described how two teachers at his school collaborated to develop a year-long course on "Mathematics in Art," thus providing students with credits in two distinct courses. He believed that the school's small size, autonomy and absence of bureaucracy that came with working at an alternative school made such innovative courses possible. A teacher at another school described how he and two other teachers provided a physical education course in response to students' expressed interest. A three-teacher team taught the course: one teacher's knowledge of yoga and alternative health practices dovetailed with another teacher's addressing health issues such as body image and gender awareness. In this case, three out of the six teachers at that school delivered a course for which students would get physical education credits.

In the secondary alternative schools where the five teachers worked, students and teacher participated in democratic practices, thus playing a significant role in shaping course content, activities, assignments, and assessments. Teachers described how student input helped shape the choices of subjects offered. Teachers followed provincial curriculum guidelines but, at the same time, they tailored what they taught under the aegis of provincial courses based on student survey responses. By teaching new courses much of the time, based on student interests, they did a fair amount of curriculum development. For example, one teacher, who had taught in an alternative school for a number of years, reported that she had to work without a textbook and was always bringing in new articles and materials. Being responsive to student requests clearly required lots of continuous work.

One kind of curriculum innovation the teachers engaged in was thematic teaching that connected various subject areas. In some schools, several teachers, or the whole staff, agreed to focus on a common theme across courses. Because of the intense nature of their workloads, teachers sometimes also organized their courses around themes, different each year, in order to allow them to recycle some of the same content across the several subjects they taught. For example, one teacher described how she used the theme of carbon footprints to focus on water as a human right in a Grade 11 World Issues class and ethics about the earth's resources in Grade 11 Philosophy. In this way, she said, although she taught four courses per semester, she did not have to overextend herself in terms of her own knowledge base, and students got a variety of different subject-based perspectives on a given theme or topic.

Minimal administrative oversight, small size, demanding teaching schedules and involving students in decision making together created a situation where significant authority was located at the school and classroom level, and where curricular innovation was the norm. But teachers had to walk a fine line between the priority of delivering curriculum that students found engaging and ensuring that students earned the credits required to graduate from high school and be admitted to college or university. For this reason, innovative curriculum was offered under the aegis of regularly approved courses. For example, courses on gender and women's studies (which were not yet part of the official provincial curriculum) were listed on students' academic transcripts as fulfilling requirements for Grade 11 Philosophy. At one school, an entrepreneurship course fulfilled provincial Business Studies course requirements.

CONTINUITIES AND RUPTURES

Some of the teachers we interviewed had spent their entire teaching careers in alternative schools, sometimes only in their current school. Two teachers had started teaching in mainstream high schools; both said they would never teach in mainstream schools again.

Alternative schools in Toronto existed in a kind of bubble. The curricular inventions created within them did not typically find their way into general circulation in mainstream schools. Teachers' comments suggested that this could be due to the constraints on their opportunities to interact with teachers beyond their own schools. Given the time and energy they put into working with students, several teachers in the study said they rarely attended teacher union or subject area organization meetings.

One teacher said she believed alternative school teachers had less influence outside their schools than teachers from mainstream schools. Alternative school teachers were not typically invited to participate in official school board or provincial curriculum development. Nor, she said, did they have the opportunity to provide professional learning sessions for other teachers. Loose coupling between alternative and mainstream schools might serve to inhibit the spread of innovation.

IMPLICATIONS FOR THE SPREAD OF CURRICULUM INNOVATION

Drawing on interviews with five teachers in the Toronto District School Board's secondary alternative schools, this chapter has explored the structural factors and work of teachers that enable curricular innovation, as well as those factors that inhibit the expansion of innovation beyond alternative schools. Using the notion of loose coupling, it described the contradictory relationship that exists between school board and provincial policy expectations and actual curricular practices in alternative schools. On the one hand, teachers and students created or modified courses by using the school board or provincially approved course expectations as scaffolding to ensure students earned the credits they needed for academic advancement and graduation from high school. On the other hand, student and teacher interests were major drivers in developing course content, activities, and assignment practices.

The chapter has identified several features of alternative schools (the small size of staff and student cohorts, minimal administrative oversight, and teachers' heavy workloads) that support curricular invention. Yet, these same factors may serve to limit the spread of innovation to mainstream schools by limiting the access (and therefore the influence) of alternative school teachers to educators beyond their own school walls.

The teachers' comments suggest that structural features of mainstream secondary school programs also make it unlikely that alternative schools' innovative curricular practices could be adopted there: Their large size and their organizational division into academic departments, with teachers' work more tightly coordinated within, and weaker bounds between, subjects (Little and Siskin 1994; Siskin 1994); greater anonymity among teachers and students due to the large cohort size and lack of spatial proximity (Hargreaves 1994); greater administrative scrutiny given the hierarchical relations between teachers, department heads, and school administrators. Mainstream and alternative schools exist at different points along a continuum between innovation and prescription, with limited opportunities for curricular cross-fertilization. Loose coupling serves to enable innovation within alternative school boards even while it inhibits the spread of innovation to other schools.

AUTHORS' BIOGRAPHY

Nina Bascia is Professor and Chair of the Department of Leadership, Higher & Adult Education at the Ontario Institute for Studies in Education (OISE) at the University of Toronto. She is the founding director of the Collaborative Program in Educational Policy, also at OISE. She has published a number of books, including *The Contexts of Teaching in Secondary Schools: Teachers' Realities, Unions in Teachers' Professional lives, The Sharp Edge of Educational Change*, and *Teacher Unions in Public Education*. She currently is working on a study of how teachers and students negotiate curriculum in secondary alternative schools in Toronto.

Rhiannon Maton, Ph.D. is an educational researcher and faculty member in the Critical Writing Program at the University of Pennsylvania. Her research focuses on how educational stakeholders understand and enact agency— with particular attention to teacher and community activism, teacher inquiry groups, and the potential for critically engaged action within school structures and systems.

CHAPTER 2

Alpha Alternative School: Making a Free School Work, in a Public System

Deb O'Rourke

I think my ideal world would have a million little ALPHAs in it. Each one small and kind of different.

This was the reflection of one of ALPHA's original students, interviewed about his experience 40 years later. Growing up in caring places with strong teacher/parent partnerships, many alternative school alumni might feel the same. The Toronto School Board's first alternative school policy called this the *Toronto Experience*:

> Alternative school programs in the City of Toronto may be unique in North America because in almost every instance they were initiated by groups of parents, teachers, students and other interested persons who approached the Board of Education for support of experimental programs within the system. (TBE 1978, *Re: General Policy for Alternative School Programs.* p. 3)

D. O'Rourke (✉)
York University, Toronto, Canada

© The Author(s) 2017
N. Bascia et al. (eds.), *Alternative Schooling and Student Engagement*,
DOI 10.1007/978-3-319-54259-1_2

11

OISE professor Malcolm Levin maintains that Toronto's alternative schools were originally "seen by many as free schools by another name" (1984, p. 7). In the international *free school movement* of the 1960s and 1970s, thousands of these grassroots schools were created, most outside of school systems.

Allen Graubard called A. S. Neill's Summerhill the "grand-daddy of free schools" (1972: 112). Neill's 1960 book *Summerhill: a Radical Approach to Child Rearing*, gave hope to people far beyond the UK. In 1969, I was a student activist in a Calgary organization that, in communication with the students of SEED in faraway Toronto, created a summer free school. The Calgary initiatives did not last. But 15 years later, I was able to enroll my child in a public free school in Toronto. ALPHA later became my place of employment and the subject of my master's thesis. This chapter is drawn from my M.Ed. research, which included interviews with alumni parents, teachers, and students.

WHAT IS A FREE SCHOOL?

Founded in 1921, the private English boarding school Summerhill is described by its founder Neill as "a self-governing school, democratic in form." Its students are free to play, and lessons are optional. But its motto is *freedom, not license*. Children are held responsible for actions that affect others: "Everything connected with social, or group, life, including punishment for social offenses, is settled by vote at the Saturday night General School Meeting ..." (Neill 1969). Summerhill had been operating for 39 years when A.S. Neill wrote that it was no longer an experiment but a "demonstration school, for it demonstrates that freedom works" (Neill 1960: 4). But he never allowed his or Summerhill's name to be used in the schools they inspired, explaining: "If a school is set up simply in imitation of Summerhill, that is wrong ... No school, Summerhill included, is the last word in education" (Snitzer 1972: 13).

Schools inspired by Summerhill each survive on their own terms. Teaching in African-American communities for decades, Jonathan Kozol practiced and wrote about urban free schooling. He found that the key to the acceptability of a free school to low-income and minority parents was the "great debate concerning basic skills."

> I found myself aligned with those who argued for a policy of undisguised, sequential, and intentional skill teaching. The haphazard, libertarian

approach of many of the counterculture schools disturbed me greatly. I was convinced that they would shortchange children and drive away poor people. I also feared that they would inevitably drive away large numbers of black parents who were otherwise devoted to the moral and aesthetic aspects of the Free School. (Kozol 1982: 2–3)

Kozol wrote, "Free school, as the opposite of public school, implies not one thing but ten million different possibilities" (1972: 56). Chris Mercogliano and Jerry Mintz of the Alternative Education Resource Organization hold annual courses to help parents and educators to "grow" their schools in the soils of their communities.

A "MOMENT OF POSSIBILITY"

In Ontario in the late 1960s, this soil was unusually fertile. Jonathan Kozol (1972: 5) named Toronto as a locus of the Summerhill-inspired international free school movement. ALPHA's oral history participants agreed that "*This Magazine is About Schools* [the most prominent of a number of Toronto-based education magazines] and the Hall-Dennis [provincial education] Report, combined with a generation that was just having children that had gone through the sixties as a formative part of their identity" were "major factors in the developing context for the Alternative School movement." These factors fostered "the sense that citizens could … initiate policies that best meet their needs." They motivated people "to think about going to the public system for the creation of alternative forms of education for their kids." One co-founder recalled: "I think people thought it was a moment of possibility."

The press identified ALPHA's co-founders as economically diverse, including "people in public housing and in the hip counterculture, as well as middle-class professionals" (*The Globe and Mail*, Sept 24, 1971). Historically and today, most free schools are independent of public systems. But ALPHA's founders did not want their school to be "available only to a small and relatively privileged part of society. They wanted a publicly-funded school, hoping to use their political influence to set a precedent for other parents…" (Golden, April 1973: 22). They identified with Toronto's *Community Schooling* movement, embracing its fundamental goal to "improve the educational system through a process of decentralizing decision-making" (Martell 1970: 76). Community Schooling activists advocated local control of neighborhood schools, so that "teachers, parents, and older students" could organize curricula that taught the basics, built meaningful "social sciences programs that relate directly" to the neighborhood, and drew on local residents as resource people (1970: 48). Alternative school founders differed from some community schooling activists in their conviction that it was also necessary to start new public schools with pioneering pedagogies, to give different models a chance. Structurally different schools were seen as necessary, to directly address what Ron Miller (2002: 39) described as "a deeply felt sense that the established system of schooling as such was an oppressive institution that thwarted young people's social, educational, moral, and even intellectual development."

RESISTING THE HIDDEN CURRICULUM

Radical education critics, often dismissed as romantic, saw the authoritarian, graded structure of public schools as a hidden curriculum, retained and lived when content is long forgotten. Charles Silberman articulated in *Crisis in the Classroom*, "What educators must realize, moreover, is that how they teach and how they act may be more important than what they teach..." (1970: 9). A vocal anti-fascist, Neill felt that coercive schooling prepared students to submit to all forms of totalitarianism, overt and disguised. He argued that the Earth's and humanity's salvation were tied to their emotional health: "let the kids be themselves, and in a few generations, the world will become healthy and happy."

ALPHA: A GROUP CREATION

In notes hand-written in 1971 by an ALPHA co-founder, the "hidden curriculum" is number one under the penciled question "Alternative to what?" *The A.L.P.H.A. Experience*, the proposal approved by the Toronto Board of Education in December 1971, committed to foster "competence" in literacy and arithmetic, "knowledge of the society of which one is a part," the ability to coordinate and cooperate with others, initiative, and self-respect. Parents wanted their school to "reflect and nurture the values of" cooperation, diversity, freedom of expression, autonomy, and social responsibility. As in the free school movement in the United States, such goals expressed fundamental values of the greater society (Miller 2002: 62). The main difference from the mainstream was that free schools determined to walk their democratic talk, not just "teach" it within a structure that enforced a hidden curriculum of hierarchy and compliance. ALPHA's parents took this responsibility by specifying that their school would be governed by a "staff-community council" (The ALPHA Community 1971).

ALPHA's co-founders argued for their school on the basis of the 1948 *United Nations Universal Declaration of Human Rights*. They felt "some pause about what we were doing" when they saw that a "homophobic right-wing minister" and a teacher who was a "right wing public voice for education for years through the seventies" were proposing "a parent-run, extremely right-wing program, under the same logic that we were going for..." This is an oft-stated concern, but the solution lies right in the text of the UN Declaration. Article 26 states, "Parents have a prior right to choose the kind of education that shall be given to their children." Article 29 specifies: "These rights and freedoms may in no case be exercised contrary to the purposes and principles of the United Nations."

It was a tough start. Suddenly charged with the care of nearly a hundred frisky, fearless children, ALPHA's parents described the first year as chaos. In their "interminable" meetings, "We ended up really with these two factions fighting and very much the issue really was over ... how free should a free school be." This argument was shared with many other alternative schools (Novak 1975: 44–50; Mercogliano 1999: 6; Deal 1975). During its self-named year of chaos, ALPHA's enrollment halved and its teachers left. But the School Board allowed the remaining parents to continue the struggle. No one involved in ALPHA's early years takes credit for founding it: All insist it was a group effort. But parents name a teacher hired right after that first year as essential to its survival. I call Susan Garrard ALPHA's *foundational* teacher: Hired in 1973 and remaining until retirement in 1996, she was an island of stability around whom a staff and parent team was able to coalesce.

"Meeting": "Does Anybody Have Anything to Say?"

Susan Garrard recalled that Summerhill-style weekly meetings were not effective, with over 60 students under 13. The solution was "short, sweet daily meetings."

> Being kids, they all had to have their turn. So, we always kept a list of who had had a turn as chairperson, and they would choose the next

chairperson. Later on, it got to be that if you were a little kid you'd have to choose a big kid, or if you were a girl you'd have to choose a boy ...

They found they also needed a kind of sergeant-at-arms, called the "separator." Working together, an experienced kid paired with a small one, the older helped the younger to focus. A parent explained that Meeting was "key to how that place worked."

> **Parent 1980–1991**: All the dynamics got played out there, and approaches to problems got played out there and it was fundamentally important. So how that got shaped was really everything. ...It was their meeting and they chaired it, and made it work.

At Meeting during ALPHA's second year, adults and students together worked out a system for dealing with behavior problems.

COMMITTEE: "WHAT'S HAPPENING?"

With kids moving about, opportunities for conflict arise: so do opportunities to teach conflict resolution. An ALPHA intervention often begins with the blame-free question "What's happening?" From there, the parties each take turns saying their piece without interruption—a common approach to mediation. For situations that, in other schools, can lead to the Principal's office, ALPHA developed *Committee*, a rotating group of five students balanced by age, gender, and experience, listen to the problem and, if the parties cannot resolve it, often decide on a consequence for an offender. All students have a chance to serve on *Committee*.

Freedom to move and student-paced learning help the integration of lively children who might have trouble in mainstream schools, but not always. The 1982 *Alternative Schools, A General Policy*, noted:

> Alternative schools are under increasing pressures from social service agencies to take students who have difficulty or who have dropped out of regular school ... Because the schools tend to be small and less impersonal than regular schools, many students adapt well. On the other hand, because of their size, alternative schools face the danger of having to absorb too many "difficult" students too quickly. (The Board of Education for the City of Toronto 1982: 7)

Personal relationships with teachers and direct feedback from peers offered by *Committee* can be effective at helping lively children to learn to self-regulate. But the collaboration of staff, parental, and administrative is sometimes necessary to access therapeutic resources for children with deep emotional challenges.

TEACHING AND LEARNING

In an ungraded school, developmental stages are very visible. On their own, ALPHA's students coalesced into two groups on either side of a developmental watershed that appears at about the age of nine. They are called, simply, the Littlekids (K-3) and Bigkids (grades 4–6). Each has several rooms on separate floors, where they often move about quite freely. Teachers program both independently and collaboratively. Curriculum is often emergent, coming from the children's interests. Much teaching is holistic, organic, and arts-based, but students can also be found working on times tables and math books. Allowing students to choose activities and responding to their successes enables staff to address learning styles quickly and directly. Diagnosis and labeling are required only where a perceptual challenge or a serious behavioral problem indicates a need for extra support.

Free schooling, like any schooling, requires due diligence. A complete free agency to decide when and if they want to be taught seems to work for the private school students of Summerhill and Sudbury Valley (Gray 2008; Lucas 2011). But Kozol argues that proactive literacy teaching is vital in schools with diverse, mobile, and often oppressed populations. Though many kids pick up reading as organically as they learn to speak, Kozol (1972: 30–31) observed: "for as many as one quarter or one-half of the children in a Free School situation, it is both possible and necessary to go about the teaching of reading in a conscious, purposeful and sequential manner." But he also noted: "Twelve years of lockstep labor in the field of math or language arts are manifestly wasteful of a child's learning energies and learning hours. Freire teaches basic literacy in forty days" (pp. 39–40). John Holt argued that children could "gain what we have come to think of as five or six years' worth of ability in reading in a matter of months. They might not all do this when were six years old, but what difference would that make?" (1972: 76). At ALPHA, literacy is approached carefully and proactively, responding to a child's trajectory while resisting faddish assumptions about what students should be doing at particular ages.

Evaluation: The Tail that Wags the Education Dog

Until 1996, ALPHA had no report cards. Then, the Ontario Ministry of Education forced its teachers to spend many hours preparing them. They are filed in a drawer. Parents may ask to see their child's report, but they rarely do. A petition to the Director of Education in 18 January 1996, signed by every ALPHA family of that era, stated:

> A non-competitive atmosphere is the core of our philosophy. We believe that young children should explore, make mistakes, take risks, and challenge themselves. Comparative grading and standardized testing undermine this learning process and for this reason we firmly oppose these strictures.

American educator Debra Meier would agree:

> Learning happens fastest when the novices trust the setting so much that they aren't afraid to take risks, make mistakes or do something dumb. Learning works best, in fact, when the very idea that it's risky hasn't even occurred to kids … No one is sorting or ranking us, and we are not confronted with much that is out of our family's control, stuff that is arbitrary and could hurt us. (Meier 2002: 18)

ALPHA's traditional evaluation: a family conference, often child-led, is still how the home and school team work out where the student is, where they want to go, and how to help them. The time teachers spend filling out report cards is a drain on the school's small resources, one example of how alternatives are weakened by Board structures.

Students Evaluate ALPHA

Periodically, alumni are invited to give feedback on how their transition to subsequent schooling went and how well they feel ALPHA prepared them. This collection of quotes is from such a gathering in March, 1987:

> I learned a natural respect for other people.

> I learned patience because I had freedom.

> I learned to chair meetings …

> Because ALPHA is a smaller school I learned to get closer to people.

I gained more than I knew at the time. Most kids have a narrow band of knowledge. I can look at issues from different angles.

I learned to motivate myself when I really want to.

I learned how to relax in school. I do not form mental tension …

I learned to use my common sense.

I learned to work at my own pace.

I developed social skills here that enabled me to approach high school teachers and say, "I'm scared, I can't cope. (The ALPHA Community 1987: 27)

Jerry Mintz of Alternative Education Resource Organization (AERO) pointed out that people involved with democratic schooling "have a different set of criteria" to define success:

We care how happy they are. We care if they know how to get along with other people … We care if they're creative: we care if they can take responsibility. We have standards: those are … [our standards]. Another standard is: Does your kid like this school? How about the most basic thing: is the customer satisfied?

The Family/School Partnership: *Sharing Education*

ALPHA's founding parents "wanted to be a part of their [children's] lives" and felt "it was a much more holistic and a much more natural way of educating our kids." So, ALPHA's motto is *Sharing Education*. Volunteerism is also the only way to alleviate the brutal adult/child ratios in public schools, which Dewey referred to as the "mechanical massing of children" (1900/1990: 34). One of ALPHA's alumni recalled "having a lot of comfort knowing that everybody … was somebody's mom or dad even if they weren't your mom or dad…" But the close collaboration has challenges. Like any school, ALPHA attracts every kind of family, including, on occasion, deeply dysfunctional ones. The School Board tends to deal with this by herding parents into committees and tasks far from the classroom. But ALPHA's commitment to the vital home/school link resulted in years of work on *The ALPHA Alternative School Community Code of Conduct*, to clarify what parent participation does and does not mean. It was finally adopted in 2012 (The ALPHA Community 2014: 42).

COMMUNITY SCHOOL CONSENSUS GOVERNANCE

A 1979 Board-published brochure declared unequivocally "Parents run ALPHA." After a decade of trying out formats for a *staff-community council* (informally called the "Parent Meeting") that satisfied their "horizontal" vision of egalitarian governance, parents with experience in the Quaker community and in peace movements introduced the solution: all-community consensus governance. ALPHA's open monthly meetings invite all to participate. The only officers are the Finance Committee, who account for the money raised and budgeted by the community. The minute-taker and chair are chosen from those present at each meeting. Issues are talked out until agreement is reached. According to Susan Garrard, democracy is ALPHA's secret of survival: "If ever that broke down, then everything broke down. I think the fact that people were able to stick to that all through those years is why it's still going."

RELATIONSHIP WITH THE BUREAUCRACY

The relationship between public school administrators and alternative schools has always been delicate. ALPHA's initial proposal did not include a principal, but it was "forced to accept at least minimal supervision by a certified principal" (Lind, May 23 1972: 5). Within a bureaucracy that often resorted to "foot-dragging" and information "withheld" (Murray, April 1972: 4) to slow down innovation, there were a few visionaries. Early parents fondly recall Mike Lennox, a superintendent who was temporarily ALPHA's "principal of record," reassuring that "anything that was educationally desirable was administratively possible." Administrator Dale Shuttleworth was "our man in a clutch" who "defended us in that culture." Sometimes, defense was urgently needed. But often ALPHA got lucky with "arm's length" principals shared with (and primarily preoccupied with) a neighboring school, but willing to defend ALPHA when necessary. Parents from the 1980s remember "autonomies: space—physically and metaphorically ... we were really left on our own. So for a free school that's a blessing..." (p. 275).

Unfortunately, even during that "blessed time," systemic progress was not made in policy. The reverse happened: The 1986 *Provincial Review Report* ... was "generally impressed with the level of commitment and the quality of curriculum delivery in the majority of alternative schools and programs" (Ontario Ministry of Education, p. 14) but then recommended that the structures that fostered these "trusting learning environments" be replaced by "greater congruence of practice (*sic*) with existing legislation and policies" (p. 24). Since then, in tandem with an international neo-liberal globalization and austerity movement, the centralization agenda has strengthened. Administrators encountering alternative schools are often shocked about their lack of compliance to the rituals and methods that most people equate with schooling, and reflexively move to "correct" them. Schools that resist are often labeled *elitist*. Thus, schools tend to lose their identities, not through open debate about methods, but by being forced—regulation by regulation—into conformity with the mainstream. Since ALPHA's inception, parents have found that much of their volunteer time must be devoted, not to helping students, but to grappling with issues that come from the administration. Many are initially grateful to the system that offers this school. But as they spend wearying amounts of their volunteer time struggling for their model's survival, their broken trust and stress sometimes grow into anger and cynicism.

MODELS FOR DEMOCRACY

In the words of current community members, ALPHA's democratic structure *is* its pedagogy: not a hidden curriculum but a conviction openly stated and freely chosen by its families, that expresses its society's core values. By its nature, democracy cannot be imposed. An alternative educator's strategy is as democratic as their conviction: to effect change through debate and modeling, instead of imposition. In its first approach to the Toronto Board of Education in 1971, the *ALPHA Community* proposed:

> It is our belief that in order to obtain any educational or other form of social progress, new programs should be created on an experimental basis within the system. It cannot be done all over the system at one time. To this end we will be an educational experiment for Toronto schools ... (The ALPHA Community, 1971, *Brief for the Management Committee*, p. 6)

This should not be confused with experimenting *on* children. The most draconian experiments—such as family and cultural deprivation, and long hours of physical and emotional restraint for the very young—continue to be imposed, not by families and teachers, but by powerful institutions. Alternative and community schooling proponents argue that family and community, not far away authorities, have the greatest stake in the vitality of their children and, as Debra Meier contends, should have "sufficient authority to act on its collective knowledge of its children" (2002: 4).

It is difficult to sustain an "authentic" model, with resource levels set by the mainstream and pressures to conform to its ideologies. A parent whose children attended ALPHA as the 1990s neo-liberal education movements climaxed, noted that even as Canada embraces the inspirational myth of democracy, its culture owes much to a different paradigm:

> I remember actually understanding ... we strive for democracies and cooperatives and sensitivities and sensibilities, but in fact we live in hierarchies and that's the structure. And the leader is the moral head who sets the tone ...

But struggle and compromise do not invalidate the model. American researcher Ann Swidler witnessed organizational and cultural innovations in free schools that she felt both reflected and affected the society at large.

> Watching teachers and students in free schools, I became convinced that culture, in the sense of symbols, ideologies, and a legitimate language for discussing individual and group obligations, provides the crucial substrate on which new organizational forms can be erected .... Organizational innovation and cultural change are continually intertwined, since it is a culture that creates the new images of human nature and new symbols with which people can move one another. (Swidler 1979: viii)

Henry Giroux argues, "Schools are one of the few sites within public life in which students, both young and old, can experience and learn the language of community and democratic public life" (1988: xiii). Alternative schools—including free schools with deep structural differences from the mainstream—support a range of possibility. Diversity, fostered instead of fought, could create generous public systems that leave no one out. Inheriting a struggle to bring up children who are "at once individuals and community persons" (Neill 1992: 5), free schools are historic institutions whose very existence engages us in vital confrontations with dilemmas around choice, freedom, community, responsibility, and authority. They bring to a contemporary context a search for ways to authentically share with our children, society's deepest democratic aspirations.

REFERENCES

Deal, Terrence E. 1975. *An Organizational Explanation of the Failure of Alternative Schools.* Stanford, CA: Stanford Center for Research and Development in Teaching.

Dewey, John. (1900/1990). *The school and society.* Chicago, IL: University of Chicago Press.

Giroux, Henry. 1988. *Schooling and the Struggle for Public Life.* Minneapolis: University of Minnesota Press.

Golden, M. 1973. "alpha-bits." *Community Schools,* (April, 1973): 21–24. The Community Schools Workshop of Toronto.

Graubard, Allen. 1972. *Free the Children: Radical Reform and the Free School Movement.* New York: Pantheon Books (Random House).

Gray, Peter. 2008. Children Educate Themselves IV: Lessons from Sudbury Valley. *Psychology Today* (blog). https://www.psychologytoday.com/blog/freedom-learn/200808/children-educate-themselves-iv-lessons-sudbury-valley. Accessed 4 Jul 2016.

Holt, John. 1972. *Freedom and Beyond.* New York: Dell Publishing.

Kozol, Jonathan. 1972. *Free Schools.* New York: Houghton Mifflin. Republished in 1982 as *Alternative Schools.* New York: Continuum.

Kozol, Jonathan. 1982. *Alternative Schools.* New York: The Continuum Publishing.

Levin, Malcolm. 1984. And Now for Something Completely Different: What's 'Alternative' About Toronto's Alternative Schools? *Mudpie* 5 (7): 7.

Lind, L. 1972. Experimental Schools: A Motherhood Issue, 5. Toronto: *The Globe and Mail*, May 23.

Lucas, H. 2011. *After Summerhill: What Happened to the Pupils of Britain's Most Radical School?* Bristol: Herbert Adler Publishing.

Mercogliano, Chris. 1999. A Profile of the Albany Free School. *Paths of Learning: Options for Families & Communities* 1 (1): 8–13.

Martell, G. 1970. Community Control of the Schools—Toronto and New York. *This Magazine is About Schools* 4 (3): 7–49.

Meier, Deborah. 2002. *In Schools We Trust: Creating Communities of Learning in an Era of Testing and Standardization.* Boston: Beacon Press.

Miller, Ron. 2002. *Free Schools, Free People: Education and Democracy after the 1960s.* Albany: State University of New York Press.

Murray, E. 1972. Report from the Board: Who Makes Decisions? *Community Schools,* April, 4–5.

Neill, Alexander Sutherland. 1960. *Summerhill: A Radical Approach to Child Rearing.* New York: Hart Publishing.

Neill, Alexander Sutherland. 1969. *Summerhill: A Radical Appoach to Education.* UK: Victor Gollancz.

Neill, Alexander Sutherland. 1992. *Summerhill School: A New View of Childhood,* ed. Albert Lamb. New York: St. Martin's Griffin.

Novak, Mark. 1975. *Living and learning in the free school* 88. McGill-Queen's Press-MQUP.

Parents' Group Seeks New Kind of Education. 1971. *The Globe and Mail,* September 24.

Snitzer, Herb. 1972. *Today is for Children: Numbers Can Wait.* New York: The Macmillan.

Swidler, Ann. 1979. *Organization Without Authority: A Dilemma of Social Control in Free Schools.* Cambridge, MA: Harvard University Press.

The ALPHA Community. 2014. *The ALPHA Parent Handbook.* Vol. 2.

The ALPHA Experience. 1971. http://alphaschool.ca/about/history/. Accessed 22 March 2011.

The Board of Education for the City of Toronto. 1982. *Alternative Schools, A General Policy.* Toronto: Office of the Director of Education.

Toronto Board of Education (TBE). 1978. *Re: General Policy for Alternative School Programs.* Toronto: Office of the Director of Education.

AUTHOR BIOGRAPHY

Deb O'Rourke is a freelance writer and educator with a Masters in Education from York University and has published journalism, essays, and poetry with NOW Magazine, Rabble, and various fine art and literary publications. Her MEd thesis was a history of ALPHA Alternative School. Her relationship with alternative schooling began in Calgary in 1969, when she created a summer free school with fellow students. It continued with various roles at ALPHA Alternative School from 1985 to the present: as a parent, visiting artist, researcher, staff member, and volunteer.

CHAPTER 3

Tracing Tensions in Humanization and Market-Based Ideals: Philadelphia Alternative Education in the Past and Present

Rhiannon M. Maton and T. Philip Nichols

Public schools tend to have some autonomy from the rest of the public education system (Bascia and Maton 2016), affording them space to construct and refine their values over time. They strive to responsively flex to transforming social, cultural, and political ideals and to reflect such values within their mission, structure, and curriculum. The past 40 years have seen varied framings and foci on humanizing and market-based principles within alternative education—two ideas that sit in uneasy tension within the larger aims of public schooling.

Education as a force for humanization means striving for enhanced humanity as an end goal of schooling and educative processes. Freire (Freire 2004) described how a transformative education should endeavor

R.M. Maton (✉) · T.P. Nichols
University of Pennsylvania, Philadelphia, USA

© The Author(s) 2017
N. Bascia et al. (eds.), *Alternative Schooling and Student Engagement*,
DOI 10.1007/978-3-319-54259-1_3

to create opportunities for growth in critical awareness, challenging worldviews, and movement toward a more radical and humanized society. In contrast, market-based discourses and ideologies frame education as providing opportunity for students to achieve economic mobility and secure national economic stability (Apple 2004a, b; Hursh 2004). Market-based reforms strive for enhanced efficiency in the implementation of education and prioritize privatization of formerly public resources—such as counseling services for students, after school programs, standardized testing development and implementation, and even public schools themselves—in the pursuit of enhanced system efficiency (Harvey 2005; Larner 2000).

In this chapter, we ask: What are the different ways that ideological trends toward humanization and the market are framed and enacted by alternative school leaders in the past and present?

We examine the interplay between democratic and market impulses by comparing the landscape of Philadelphia public alternative schools over time, with particular attention to how alternative school discussions engage discourses of humanization and the market. In this chapter, we explore how public alternative schools are shaped by these competing histories and ideological influences and provide a view into how public districts today understand the work of alternative schools amidst the bureaucratic order of market-based reform efforts. Through specifically examining the case of Philadelphia, we show that there is an essential tension between human and market-based aims that continually plays out within public alternative education in North America.

THE PHILADELPHIA CONTEXT

This section maps the context of alternative public schools in Philadelphia by presenting two snapshots of its shifting educational landscape. The first is set in 1975—one year after the school district created its first Alternative Programs Office; the second, in 2015—one year after the newly formed Office of New School Models opened its first three alternative public schools. Our purpose in pairing these snapshots is not to draw evaluative comparisons across the 40 years that separate them; nor is it to fit each into a tidy narrative of incremental progress or decay. Instead, we position these portraits side by side in order to make legible the continuities and discontinuities that underpin the tenuous interplay of humanizing and market-based ideals in one district over time.

PHILADELPHIA IN 1975

The history of Philadelphia's alternative schools is perhaps best understood in the larger context of American "progressive" education—a fragmented pedagogical movement loosely organized around principles of humanizing, experiential, democratic learning (Zilversmit 1993). Though the conventional historiography suggests the movement's momentum in the early 20th century tapered off amid postwar critiques of its relative rigor (Cremin 1961), its legacy can be seen in the proliferation of alternative and experimental school models that surfaced in the 1960s and 1970s: open classrooms, free schools, small schools, "deschooling," and "unschooling" (see Mercogliano 1998; Ravitch 1983). While some of these approaches operated outside of formal public schools, many school districts worked to integrate such innovative designs into the system itself. Arguably, the most expansive and sustained effort to do so in the United States was the School District of Philadelphia.

With the founding of the Alternative Programs Office (APO) in 1974, the School District of Philadelphia (SDP) solidified its established commitment to alternate ways of organizing the school experience to better serve elementary and secondary students. Leonard Finkelstein, the program director, and Harriet explicitly referred to the APO as "a response to the recognition that a large segment of the pupil population is composed of alienated, capable but bored, disruptive and/or indifferent students who have not been successfully educated within the confines of traditional programs" (p. 82). By 1975, the APO boasted more than 60 alternative programs within the school district—the highest in the nation. Many of these were modeled directly on 1960s innovations such as open classrooms, schools without walls, mini-schools, and schools-within-schools (Finkelstein and Pollack-Schloss 1975). Some emerged from close identification with particular neighborhoods, such as the West Philadelphia Free School. Others focused on flexible forms of vocational education, such as the Urban Career Education Center. Still others linked progressive schools across district borders through networks such as the Alternative Schools Project (Glatthorn 1975).

Perhaps the most famous alternative school within the APO was Philadelphia's Parkway Program, hailed by Time Magazine in 1970 as "the most interesting high school in the United States." The Parkway

Program was a school without walls, which meant that classes, assemblies, and administrative offices were distributed across the varied resources of the city. Students enrolled in a journalism class, for example, would meet at a local newspaper office. Students engaged in lessons about U.S. legal history would meet in a courthouse. This allowed the school to offer not only the conventional subject matter instruction, but also the experiential learning opportunities not ordinarily available to high school students. Further, the school provided a daily tutorial period to support academic and interpersonal coherence across this array of offerings (Finkelstein and Pollack-Schloss 1975).

The impetus for this design was to bring about a more humanizing form of education. According to John Bremer, the program director,

> Learning is not something that goes on only in special places called classrooms, or in special buildings called schools; rather, it is a quality of life appropriate to any and every phase of human existence; or more strictly, it is human life itself. (quoted in Miller 2002: 87)

This vision was supported at other tiers of district oversight: not only did Finkelstein and Pollack-Schloss (1975) and the APO argue that "humanization of education is the vital ingredient underlying the achievement of any alternative program" (p. 82), but Superintendent Mark Shedd had made it the goal of his term to "humanize" public education in Philadelphia (Miller 2002).

Such programs provide insight into how humanizing ideals worked in tandem with district bureaucracy at this time. For Finkelstein and Pollack-Schloss (1975), the aim of the APO was not to craft a one-size-fits-all alternative to traditional schools, but rather to provide an array of schooling options to match students to an "ideal" learning environment, rather than "mold [them] to an unyielding educational program" (p. 90). With this vision in mind, the APO systematically collected detailed information about all of its alternative programs, prepared reports, and coordinated with central offices to provide measurable, positive changes for alienated students. This process helped legitimize what was viewed as a controversial reform effort. And it often managed to do so in a way that honored alternative programs on their own terms—for instance, in allowing the Parkway Program to select an evaluation team based on "humanizing" principles (Wofford and Ross 1973). But on the other hand, the tenuous relationship between humanization and district oversight also produced a "creative tension" (Wofford and Ross 1973: 74) between school and system—one that, according to Finkelstein and Pollack-Schloss (1975), could only be mediated through a continuous process of self-reflexivity and patient re-adjustment (p. 84).

PHILADELPHIA IN 2015

Market-based logic emphasizes accountability and efficiency, and frames innovation, choice and competition as means to achieving these aims (Harvey 2005; Larner 2000). Market-based logic has been applied to education through emphasizing the ways in which education can be made more efficient, with schools and education workers such as teachers and administrators made accountable to the state through testing, and evaluation measures threaded through school, district, and state accountability structures (Apple 2004a, b; Hursh 2004; Ravitch 2010; Supovitz 2009). Over the years, the School District of Philadelphia (SDP) has increasingly instituted market-based rhetoric and policy. This is made apparent through both explicit policies leading to a shrinking district and expansion of privately managed charter schools (see Fine 2013; Kerkstra 2014; Popp 2014; Raywid 1996), employing a market-based language, including references to families as "customers" and its increased focus on "innovation" (see School District of Philadelphia 2016).

The district currently hosts two offices for alternative schools and programs. The first is the Office of New School Models, which acts as a network of innovative schools and features five small alternative programs espousing design- and project-based curriculum and pedagogy (for more on connections between project-based learning and early progressive education principles, see Pecore 2015). The second SDP office dedicated to alternative schools and programing is named The Opportunity Network: Alternative Education and offers programs to students "who are in need of education options which go beyond the constraints of the regular classroom" (The Opportunity Network 2016).

These schools primarily focus on meeting the needs of students seeking re-entry after dropping out or expulsion, or those students with special socio-emotional needs. For the purpose of this paper, we are primarily concerned with alternative schools associated with the first, the Office of New School Models, as this network most explicitly grapples with and exemplifies the complexities of humanization and market-based thinking in alternative schools today.

The Workshop School (WS) is an initiative of the Office of New School Models that initially opened its doors for the 2013/2014 school year. According to the SDP Web site (2016), the school has grown from 91 students in its first school year to over 200 in March 2016. Its student population is primarily African-American and all students are considered economically disadvantaged. WS hosts a Web site separate from that of the SDP, and there describes in some detail its innovative curricular and pedagogical approach. The Web site also features a short video describing its structure as well as a list of extensive media coverage, suggesting that journalistic media coverage seems to act as a significant marketing source.

WS centers on design-based thinking and innovative program design (The Workshop School 2016; Windle 2016). It maintains central foci on "real world problem solving" and authentic learning that strives to bridge the "real world" with school learning (Flick 2014; The Workshop School 2016), as well as efforts to nurture a creative and democratic community for both staff and students (Windle 2016). The school's short video highlights teacher goals centered on helping students learn to "treat this school like a job" (Flick 2014). WS also provides students with extra counseling and support, and some students state that the school community of staff and students feel like a "family" (Windle 2016).

This brief examination of one of SDP's featured alternative schools draws attention to some of the ways in which humanization and market ideals interact to shape the form and intended functions of contemporary alternative schools. Alternative schools take up creative—and "innovative"—forms as they strive to prepare students for professional careers where they will work in the "real world" to solve workplace problems. They reinforce a notion that the purpose of schooling is to prepare empowered individuals who will enact entrepreneurial and innovative professionalism within their future workplaces (see Brown 2015; Friedman 2007).

Yet, alongside these market-based goals coexists the careful attention to how the school might support the humanization of its students by fostering a "democratic" environment with socio-emotional supports and nurturing a sense of "family" in the school community. The curricular and pedagogical focus of the WS also reveals how Freire's (2004) notion of praxis is put into motion in new ways that emerge from a combination of humanization and market-based ideals. Through striving to nurture the praxis-oriented relationship between reflection and action, the school asks students to engage in a recursive learning process of classroom-based thinking/reflection and project-based action. Freire's notion of praxis has been altered from its original revolutionary ideals to explicitly center on achieving market-based outcomes and metrics, rather than enhanced student humanization.

Discussion

Reading across these snapshots of alternative education in Philadelphia, it can be tempting either to romanticize the valence of "humanization" that characterized 1970s APO or to vilify the market ideals that underpin the contemporary emphasis on job preparation and "entrepreneurship." However, such responses fail to account for the tangled interplay of both humanizing and market impulses across time. In this section, we consider the continuities and discontinuities that span these configurations of alternative education, paying particular attention to their broader cultural context, stated purposes, and common ideological tendencies.

From a contemporary vantage point, Philadelphia's APO and its emphasis on "humanizing" education can appear as a "radical" and expansive effort to counter the rigid order of American schooling—and in many ways, it was. But it was also an outgrowth of a particular constellation of factors shaping the discourse of alternative education in the 1960s and 1970s: the lingering influence of progressive pedagogy, the Black Power movement (e.g., Countryman 2006), the rise of New Left activism concerned with school reform (e.g., Goodman 1960), the publication of A.S. Neill's *Summerhill* (1960/1992), and the circulation of new alternative methods (e.g., Kohl 1969; Postman and Weingartner 1969). By 1970, many of these "radical" efforts had been accepted even within mainstream educational policy and planning. In 1970, *Fortune* editor Charles Silberman conducted a Carnegie-funded study of U.S. schools that positioned open classrooms as humanizing alternatives to the "mindlessness" of traditional schooling. Likewise, in 1972, the Association for Supervision and Curriculum Development (ASCD) featured a themed issue of *Educational Leadership* on the subject of "humanizing" school. In this way, the APO might be understood less as a clean break from an established system and more as an extension of a culturally situated discourse of alternative teaching and learning.

In the same way, the present reforms through the Office of New School Models might be understood as an outgrowth of a particular constellation of cultural factors: discussion of standards and accountability in the wake of *No Child Left Behind* and *Race to the Top* policies, shifts toward privatization and charter schooling in urban districts (Ravitch 2010, 2013), national efforts to increase science, technology, engineering, and mathematics training (White House 2011), and relatedly, calls for K-12 schools to produce entrepreneurial "innovators" (e.g., Wagner and Dintersmith 2015; Honey and Kanter 2013). In this new configuration of alternative education, "humanization" is not gone, but rather reconfigured in service of emergent cultural concerns. For example, the emphasis on the family-like conditions at the Workshop School pairs an ethic of care and humanization with the larger discourse of job preparation and competition—all without calling attention to the internal conflicts these discrete aims have historically shared (see Labaree 2012). In this way, we might trace the discontinuity between our snapshots not as a directional line from "humanizing" to "market ideals" but rather as a layering process where the rhetoric of humanization forms a foundation on which market-based concerns with job preparation and entrepreneurship are constructed.

Recognizing this interplay also makes legible the ways these two impulses frame the notion of "choice." Perry (2009) points to the potential of public school choice for realizing democratic ideals through supporting diverse "educational pathways" (p. 440) that are responsive to student and family needs. From this perspective, alternative schools accommodate a wide range of learning needs and thus enhance the opportunities for humanization—a characterization that aligns with Finkelstein and Pollack-Schloss' (1975) vision for the APO to match students with programs that best suit their needs. On the other hand, Fabricant and Fine (2012) point out that the current "discourse of choice and public education has been appropriated almost entirely" to focus on privatized solutions to public education (p. 7). In this view, the current emphasis on "school choice" underlying alternative school options represents an inclination toward economic competition, both among schools in the local public school system and with outside charter and private schools. This is illustrated in the proliferation of media coverage surrounding the Workshop School, which operates not only as an advertisement for the program but also as evidence of success that can be leveraged for securing and maintaining philanthropic support (see Brown

2015). In this way, while both models invoke "choice" as a principal concern, they do so by drawing on diverging notions of humanizing and market-based ideals.

In framing such divergences, we must also avoid oversimplifying the interplay of market and humanization impulses in order to reveal both models' shared tendency toward individualism. Bannerji (1995) points to a contemporary tendency to frame people as "unconnected and autonomous" (p. 18), composed of a self and consciousness that is independent of the world and its social and ideological structures. Whether alternative schools espouse ideals of offering students educational choice to realize their humanistic or economic potential, either framing reveals the tendency to position students as autonomous agents who have free reign to move across social class and opportunity at will. Such a stance not only risks overstating the agency of those within institutions and systems structured by inequity, but also heightens internal tensions in the purposes those institutions serve. Labaree (2012), for example, argues that school models shaped by individualism have historically failed to distinguish private concerns (e.g., social mobility) and public interests (e.g., job preparation) from the collective, democratic aims of schooling that are not easily reconcilable with individualism. In this way, the market-based and humanizing ideals invoked under the rubric of "choice" in alternative schools are not so much discrete categories as they are entangled ideologies that place competing demands on teachers and students. These ideals problematize the notions of autonomy, agency, and individuality that often underlie discussions of "choice" in education.

Conclusion

In this chapter, we have shown that the current drive toward market-based values and outcomes shaping Philadelphia public alternative education is historically situated and cannot be isolated from long-term humanization ideals. Culturally situated policy foci shape how Philadelphia public alternative schools position and articulate their values and mission. We find that an economic focus coexists alongside the enduring and visible persistence of historical progressive and countercultural models of alternative schooling and that these entwined values adopt a common individualistic framework. What does this description of alternative education in Philadelphia suggest about the varied impact of humanization and market ideals on public education today?

First, our research shows that historical policies persist in shaping the structure and practice of schools in ways that extend over time. Like Bascia (2001), we argue that school change and structure are governed not just by current policy trends and frames, but also by the ideological forces shaping policy and popular thought in the past. Current curricular trends emphasizing students' product development and "innovation" might be understood as fundamentally bound up in historical emphasis on creativity and a humanistic personal expression, just as framings of families as "customers" might be understood to be informed by an historical emphasis on the civic rights of communities to access a sound and responsive education. Policymakers and alternative school educators will do well to bear in mind the complex ways in which ideological forces take shape and continue to exert potency over time.

Second, this portrait of Philadelphia alternative schools provides a long-range view of how broader shifting values are reflected in the changing nature of education over time. Market and humanization ideals have always existed in tension within alternative education, but the current climate of high stakes testing, privatization of public schooling, and global economic competition have privileged a pragmatic market-driven orientation (see Apple 2004a, b; Fabricant and Fine 2012; Hursh 2004). Philadelphia's Workshop School highlights the current potency of market forces in shaping alternative school form and function—the school explicitly emphasizes job preparation and an entrepreneurial mindset throughout curriculum, pedagogy, stated values, and desired student outcomes.

This poses a notable contrast to Philadelphia alternative schools of the past, such as the Parkway Program, which espoused an explicit focus on humanizing ideals steeped throughout all aspects of students' lives. While market forces have a long history of fueling and informing education policy, the present configuration of structures, values, and discourses of schooling seem to provide unprecedented latitude for these ideological forces to exert their influence on the practice of teaching and learning.

Finally, we would like to emphasize that humanization should not be seen as something attached to a single structure of schooling, or enshrined in a particular curriculum or pedagogy. Philadelphia's Workshop School shows that even when market-based values explicitly shape curriculum, pedagogy, and values, humanizing principles still deeply infuse local school climate and the care with which teachers approach their work with students. Humanization is less a static category than it is a process—something negotiated through the lived interactions of teachers, students, administrators, as well as the spaces and materials that constitute the learning environment. From this perspective, even alternative schools explicitly structured by the logic of market ideals can be seen as sites of possibility and transformation as students, parents, and other invested participants mobilize the existing structures and resources to enact their own goals for humanizing education.

REFERENCES

Apple, Michael W. 2004a. Creating Difference: Neo-Liberalism, Neo-Conservatism and the Politics of Educational Reform. *Educational Policy* 18 (1): 12–44.

Apple, Michael W. 2004b. *Ideology and Curriculum*, 3rd ed. New York: RoutledgeFarmer.

Bannerji, Himani. 1995. *Thinking Through: Essays on Feminism, Marxism, and Anti-Racism*. Toronto: Women's Press.

Bascia, Nina. 2001. Pendulum Swings and Archaeological Layers: Educational Policy and the Case of ESL. In *The Erosion of Democracy in Education: From Critique to Possibilities 2001*, ed. John P. Portelli, and R. Patrick Solomon, 245–268. Calgary, Alberta: Detselig.

Bascia, Nina and Rhiannon Maton. 2016. Teachers' work and innovation in alternative schools. *Critical Studies in Education*, 57 (1) : 131–141.

Brown, Amy. 2015. *A Good Investment?: Philanthropy and the Marketing of Race in an Urban Public School*. Minneapolis: University of Minnesota Press.

Countryman, Matthew J., and Up South. 2006. *Civil Rights and Black Power in Philadelphia*. Philadelphia: University of Pennsylvania Press.

Cremin, Lawrence. 1961. *The Transformation of the School: Progressivism in American Education: 1876–1957*. New York: Random House.

Fabricant, Michael, and Michelle Fine. 2012. *Charter Schools and the Corporate Makeover of Public Education: What's at Stake?*. New York: Teachers College Press.

Finkelstein, L.B., and H. Pollack-Schloss. 1975. The Alternative Program Movement in Public Education: The Philadelphia Experience. In *Educational Innovation: Alternatives in Curriculum and Instruction 1975*, ed. Arthur D. Roberts, 82–93. Boston, MA: Allyn and Bacon, Inc.

Flick, Lauren. 2014. Open Education Philadelphia – The Workshop School. *USA: The Workshop School, Philadelphia School District*. http://www.workshopschool.org/our-approach/.

Freire, Paulo. 2004. *Pedagogy of the Oppressed*. New York: Continuum Intl Pub Group.

Friedman, Thomas. 2007. *The World is Flat: A Brief History of the Twenty-First Century*. New York: Picador.

Glatthorn, Allan. A. 1975. *Alternatives in Education: Schools and Programs.* New York: Dodd, Mead & Company.

Goodman, Paul. 1960. *Growing Up Absurd: Problems of Youth in the Organized System.* New York: Vintage.

Harvey, David. 2005. *A Brief History of Neoliberalism.* New York: Oxford University Press.

Honey, Margaret, and David E. Kanter. 2013. *Design, Make, Play: Growing the Next Generation of STEM Innovators.* New York, NY: Routledge.

Hursh, David. 2004. Undermining Democratic Education in the U.S.A.: The Consequences of Global Capitalism and Neo-Liberal Policies for Education Policies at the Local, State and Federal Levels. *Policy Futures in Education* 2 (3–4): 607–620.

Kerkstra, Patrick. 2014. Philadelphia's School Crisis: A City on the Brink. *Phillymag.com,* 1–14. http://www.phillymag.com/articles/philadelphia-school-crisis-city-brink/?all=1. Accessed 30 Jan.

Kohl, Herbert. 1969. *The Open Classroom: A Practical Guide to a New Way of Teaching.* New York: New York Review.

Labaree, David. 2012. *Someone Has to Fail: The Zero-Sum Game of Public Schooling.* Cambridge, MA: Harvard University Press.

Larner, Wendy. 2000. Neo-Liberalism: Policy, Ideology, Governmentality. *Studies in Political Economy* 63 (1): 5–25.

Mercogliano, Chris. 1998. *Making It Up as We Go Along: The Story of the Albany Free School.* Portsmouth, NH: Heinemann.

Miller, Ron. 2002. *Free Schools, Free People: Education and Democracy after the 1960s.* Albany: State University of New York Press.

Neill, Alexander Sutherland. 1960. *Summerhill: A Radical Approach to Child Rearing.* New York: Hart Publishing Co. Inc.

Neill, Alexander Sutherland. 1992. *Summerhill School: A New View of Childhood,* ed. Albert Lamb. New York: St. Martin's Griffin.

Pecore, John. L. 2015. From Kilpatrick's Project Method to Project-Based Learning. In *International Handbook of Progressive Education 2015,* 155–171. New York, NY: Peter Lang.

Perry, Laura B. 2009. Conceptualizing Education Policy in Democratic Societies. *Educational Policy* 23 (3): 423–450.

Popp, Trey. 2017 Doomsday in the District. *The Pennsylvania Gazette.* February 27. http://thepenngazette.com/doomsday-in-the-district/.

Postman, Neil, and Charles Weingartner. 1969. *Teaching as a Subversive Activity.* New York: Delta Books.

Ravitch, Diane. 1983. *The Troubled Crusade: American Education, 1945–1980.* New York: Basic Books.

Ravitch, Diane. 2010. *The Death and Life of the Great American School System: How Testing and Choice are Undermining Education.* New York: Basic Books.

Ravitch, Diane. 2013. *Reign of Error: The Hoax of the Privatization Movement and the Danger to America's Public Schools*. New York: Vintage Books, Random House.

Raywid, Marry Anne. 1996. Taking Stock: The Movement to Create Mini-Schools, Schools-Within-Schools, and Separate Small Schools. *Institute for Urban and Minority Education*, no.108.

Supovitz, Jonathan. 2009. Can High Stakes Testing Leverage Educational Improvement? Prospects from the Last Decade of Testing and Accountability Reform. *Journal of Educational Change* 10 (2-3): 211–227. doi:10.1007/s10833-009-9105-2.

Wagner, Tony, and Ted Dintersmith. 2015. *Most Likely to Succeed: Preparing Our Kids for the Innovation Era*. New York: Scribner.

Windle, Greg. 2016. The Art of Teaching and Learning at the Workshop. *The Notebook Philadelphia*. http://thenotebook.org/articles/2016/03/07/art-of-teaching-learning-workshop-school. Accessed 7 Mar.

White House. 2011. *A Strategy for American Innovation: Securing Our Economic Growth and Prosperity*. Washington. http://www.whitehouse.gov/innovation/strategy.

Wofford, Joan, and Joanne Ross. 1973. *Philadelphia's Parkway Program: An Evaluation*. Philadelphia, PA: Philadelphia Parkway Program.

Zilversmit, Arthur. 1993. *Changing Schools: Progressive Education Theory and Practice, 1930–1960*. Chicago, IL: University of Chicago Press.

The Opportunity Network: Alternative Education. 2016. *School District of Philadelphia*. http://webgui.phila.k12.pa.us/offices/r/alternative. Accessed 3 Mar.

The Workshop School. 2016 http://www.workshopschool.org/. Accessed 3 Aug 2016.

AUTHORS' BIOGRAPHY

Rhiannon M Maton Ph.D. is an educational researcher and faculty member in the Critical Writing Program at the University of Pennsylvania. Her research focuses on how educational stakeholders understand and enact agency——with particular attention to teacher and community activism, teacher inquiry groups, and the potential for critically engaged action within school structures and systems.

T. Philip Nichols Ph.D. is a candidate in Reading/Writing/Literacy at the University of Pennsylvania, where he also earned an M.A. in History and Sociology of Science. His research examines how the ways we practice, teach, and talk about literacy are entwined with larger histories of technology and scientific knowledge production.

CHAPTER 4

Alternative Schooling and Black Students: Opportunities, Challenges, and Limitations

Carl E. James and Julia A. Samaroo

The consistent call for education that is responsive to the diverse needs, interests, and aspirations of students—especially racialized students—suggests that today's public schools have been failing these students. The growing disengagement of many Black students from their educational processes contributes to their poor academic performance, low achievement, and high dropout rates (Toronto District School Board 2010)—all of which have motivated parents, educators, and students to advocate for alternative and culturally relevant schooling. While alternative public school programs have existed for decades, such programs have yet to remedy the disparities in Black students' educational experiences and achievements.[1] The questions we aim to explore in this chapter are: (1) Why has the existing alternative schooling structure not been able to address the schooling needs of Black students? (2) What must be done differently if alternative schools are to effectively address their needs? and (3) What cultural, social, and educational adjustments must be made for

C.E. James (✉) · J.A. Samaroo
York University, Toronto, Canada

© The Author(s) 2017
N. Bascia et al. (eds.), *Alternative Schooling and Student Engagement*,
DOI 10.1007/978-3-319-54259-1_4

alternative schools to be responsive to the needs, issues, and concerns of Black students and parents?

Codjoe (2001) asserts that, "If we are to address the chronic academic underachievement of Black students, teachers, parents, and school administrators must tackle aggressively the issue of racism and the negative thoughts associated with it" (p. 344). We use critical race theory (CRT) to examine the schooling and educational situation of Black students, noting ways in which race and racism operate in their lived experiences. We reference a 40-year study of the Africentric Alternative School (AAS), a public elementary alternative school in the Toronto District School Board (TDSB) to explore the possibilities, challenges, and limitations of this school and its program in terms of how the existing alternative school structure and policies of the school board mediate its effectiveness in educating Black students.

ALTERNATIVE SCHOOLING IN ONTARIO: SETTING THE CONTEXT

In Ontario, public alternative schools tend to be established to address the educational needs of youth whose parents deem the existing mainstream schooling structures inadequate. As such, parents play a significant role in the creation and ongoing operation of such schools. Parents who are most conversant with and knowledgeable about the schooling system tend to be best able to persuade school personnel to respond to their children's needs, interests, and aspirations. It is often middle-class parents who have the knowledge of teaching philosophies and learning, a sense of their entitlement, and an understanding of what to expect from the school system—in essence, those with cultural and social capital (Bourdieu 1977)— who are able to "ask for something different" from mainstream schooling programs. Such parents have been able to get their voices heard in discussions on how their children are being educated and the ways in which their education might be structured. Such parents are a decidedly different population from those advocating for an alternative approach to education where the impetus is grounded in experiences of overt and covert racism, discrimination, lowered expectations, streaming into special education, and deficit thinking (Brathwaite and James 1996).

In Toronto, for the most part, publically funded alternative schools tend to be program-focused (e.g., arts, drama, music, sports, environmental, democratic education, social justice, academic credit recovery, workplace experience) and/or identity-focused (e.g., boys, girls, students with physical and/or developmental disabilities, athletes, indigenous youth, teen mothers, and Lesbian, Gay, Bisexual and Transgender youth). The AAS can be considered "identity-focused"; however, in a society where "race" is used as a signifier of "foreign" racialized groups—in this case, African Canadians—such a school tends to be seen as contrary to society's "harmonious multicultural" color-blind narrative.

HISTORICAL CONTEXT OF THE EDUCATION OF BLACK STUDENTS IN ONTARIO

In Ontario, from 1850 to 1964 (114 years), it was mandatory for Black students to attend "separate" schools; this suggests that a form of "alternative" schools existed for them. However, this alternative to mainstream schools was certainly not the same as schooling that Black parents and community members demanded in the 1970s. These earlier segregated schools,[2] authorized by governments, were rooted in oppressive, racist, and deficit thinking about Black students. Black parents and community members advocated for school programs that took into account the histories, identities, and experiences of Black children. In fact, over the years, scholars have documented how the education of Black students has been questioned, interrogated, and debated with few or no changes (Dei et al. 1997; Brathwaite and James 1996).

In response to high dropout rates, low academic achievement, disproportionate numbers of Black students in special education, vocational programs and non-academic courses (Brown 1993; Cheng et al. 1987; Deosaran1976; Toronto District School Board 2010), and the discriminatory educational experiences of Black students (Dei 2008; James 2012), Black parents, educators, and community activists advocated for improving the conditions of the schooling process for Black students (Dei and Kempf 2013; Henry 1993). They mobilized, as Henry (1993) asserts, "to define their own educational agenda, and to seek alternative models and approaches for educating their children. They know that Canadian schooling is systematically failing Black youth" (p. 207).

Accordingly, numerous programs, projects, and initiatives,[3] as well as committees and associations,[4] were created to redress the negative outcomes and harmful effects of the education system for Black students.

Many research studies were conducted, some using interviews and focus groups with Black students, parents, and educators, and reports were published,[5] noting the poor educational outcomes and negative educational experiences of Black students. However, despite sharing their lived experiences, the assertions of students and families were dismissed as inconsequential—evidently not sufficient to challenge the prevailing hegemonic discourse sustained by the policies and practices within the system.

Throughout the 1970s and 1980s, deficit-based explanations of the underachievement of Black students placed blame upon students themselves and their families (Brathwaite and James 1996). Labeled as being slow learners, learning disabled, hyperactive, and/or suffering from attention deficit, many Black students were placed in special education classes where it was further perceived that their educational performance was a product of their abilities, capabilities, and social conditions rather than a consequence of an alienating system that many minoritized[6] students experienced. Not only did the Eurocentric curriculum content not reflect the lived experiences of minoritized students, but the hidden curriculum implied that the problem was within students themselves.

Throughout the 1990s and 2000s, calls for multicultural education, race relations, anti-racist education, and culturally relevant and responsive pedagogy gained momentum in the school boards and teaching faculties in universities across Canada (James 1995, 2011). Nevertheless, the programs that were initiated did not significantly change the high dropout rates and low academic achievement of Black students, since their disengagement, disenfranchisement, and drop-out ("push out") continued to be framed and interpreted in terms of their individual approach to the schooling process rather than a result of the ways in which the school system operates (Dei 2008; Dei et al. 1997).

Our brief discussion of the history of the education of Black students in Ontario highlights the lack of accountability of governments and the school boards to adequately support initiatives and programming to improve the schooling and poor educational outcomes of Black students, despite the longstanding, collective advocacy and the vast amount of work done by Black parents, educators and community members, and researchers. This persistent cycle, influenced by the political, social, and cultural discourse in Canada during each decade, is indicative of how Black and other minoritized students have been constructed within an education system through systemic racism.

CRITICAL RACE THEORY

We use critical race theory (CRT) as a lens to explore the schooling of Black students within a context of alternative education. The theoretical insights from this paradigm allow us to understand the nuances and ways in which the education system attempts and fails to be responsive to the needs, interests, and aspirations of racialized students. CRT gives attention to the endemic and ingrained nature of race and racism, the problem of color blindness, illusions of neutrality and meritocracy in society, centrality of experiential knowledge of racialized people, importance of utilizing their narratives and counter-narratives, and how white supremacy plays a role in maintaining the marginalization of racialized people (Dixson and Rousseau 2005; Gillborn 2006; Milner 2007). Solorzano and Yosso (2001) assert that CRT "challenges the dominant discourse on race and racism as it relates to education by examining how educational theory and practice are used to subordinate certain racial and ethnic groups" (p. 2). According to Gillborn (2015), in order "to understand how racism works, we need to appreciate how race intersects with other axes of oppression" (p. 279), in terms of race, class, gender, ethnicity, sexual orientation, and disability in different contexts and over time (Gillborn 2015).

While our examination of the Africentric Alternative School (AAS) foregrounds race, we understand that the experiences and desires of members of the school community are mediated by other identity markers. Hence, cultural diversity has to be recognized as inevitable in the culture of the school. This diversity and the power of Whiteness, we argue, is what needs to be recognized—thereby enabling an appreciation or imagination of the complexities, relationality, and nuances of how race and racism operate in the schooling of Black students, and their search for a space in which to learn about themselves in preparation for becoming full participating citizens within society. This learning is necessarily grounded in a constructivist paradigm that promotes a child-centered, active teaching and learning environment in which individuals construct meaning based on their own knowledge, ideas, and experiences, as well as through shared group experiences (Richardson 2003; Yilmaz 2008).

THE AFRICENTRIC ALTERNATIVE SCHOOL

Compared with other alternative schools, and arguably most schools, AAS has been contentious and has faced significant public debate both before and after its opening. Despite three other alternative schools[7] opening in the same year by the TDSB, "none of these new additions has been so controversial as the Africentric Alternative School" (Hammer 2009). In the early 2000s, motivated by the consistent failure of the education system to meet the needs of Black students, parents, community members, and their allies renewed[8] their longstanding demands—as noted earlier—for culturally relevant school programs, curriculum content, pedagogical approaches, and resources that were responsive to the educational needs of Black youth in Toronto.

But in a society that prides itself on being multicultural and race neutral, having a school or program that is populated with largely, or only, Black bodies was seen as inconsistent with the neoliberal ethos of colorblindness, racial neutrality, and cultural freedom and concomitantly, the objectives and principles of alternative schooling as an option for parents, even though there are existing TDSB schools with predominantly Black students. The establishment of the AAS was considered by many as segregationist—if not racist—and thereby problematic (Gulson and Webb 2013; James 2011; Levine-Rasky 2014). For instance, in 2008, the Premier of Ontario and the Minister of Education both voiced their opposition and disappointment with the TDSB's approval of the AAS, noting that making all schools' curriculum more inclusive was the solution to addressing high dropout rates of Black students rather than "separating" students (in Benzie 2008). The continued contradictory association of segregation with AAS suggests that there is a "reluctance to admit that race matters in Canada and, therefore, plays a role in the experiences of Black students ... acknowledging that racism operates as a barrier—both in the school system and the society generally—to students' participation in education and to their achievements" (James 2011: 202).

Lessons Learned: Understanding the Challenges, Limitations, and Opportunities

Using the AAS as a way to review the implications of alternative approaches to mainstream schooling for Black students in Ontario reveals the continued struggles facing Black students, despite the unique successes achieved by the school. We argue that while the establishment of the school was both timely and crucial, being conceptualized within the existing alternative school policy (TDSB 2012) presents particular problems with respect to the school's capacity to establish educational programs, curriculum materials, and academic "standards" that are responsive to its students.

Grappling with the Institutional Challenges

While establishing a school grounded in a culture of high expectations and with a focus on African-centered curriculum and teaching practices is quite a feat for the Black community and its allies—though not something entirely new[9]—there was a palpable renewed hope and aspiration that the school would significantly improve the education of its Black students. The perception that having school board approval would promote the school's success and ongoing operation may have overshadowed the implications of operating as an alternative school within a school board. The unforeseen reality is that the school has had to grapple with implementing Africentric pedagogy and curriculum within the very type of Eurocentric, Western framework, and structures of a school board that have been failing Black students in Ontario for decades. It is difficult to address inherent anti-Black racism within education and society when a school is trying to survive institutional barriers such as limited space, resources, and funding (James et al. 2015).

AAS is an alternative elementary public school currently in its eighth year of operation, serving approximately 120 students from Kindergarten through Grade 8.[10] While the school is located in a northwestern area of Toronto, its students do not solely reside in the surrounding neighborhoods, making issues of boundary, transportation, and mobility challenging (James et al 2015).

AAS operates within an existing elementary public school. Both schools' names are on the front of the building; however, the front entrance is used for the main elementary school. The entrance of AAS is off to the side of the school building. Morning routines include singing *O Canada*, the national anthem, and James Weldon Johnson's *Lift Every Voice and Sing*, commonly referred to as the Black national anthem. Students also recite the school's pledge. Once a week, the school begins the day with a morning assembly for all students and staff, which includes affirmations (e.g., positive or inspirational quotation of an influential Black person), drumming, reciting the Nguzo Saba principles, and morning announcements.

Because AAS operates within an existing junior public school, Clayton,[11] a student, pointed out that "Sometimes we don't have gym or something, but [it is because] Sheppard's using it." The "school within a school" model tends to place limits on the extent to which the AAS can easily and fully implement program, curricular, and pedagogical activities. Other factors such as limited funding (i.e., alternative schools receive less funding than mainstream schools), a lack of existing Africentric resources, and expectations of achieving "success levels" on provincial standardized tests and assessment measurements affect the school's ability to deliver the caliber of education desired by staff, parents, and community. Despite these challenges, AAS staff are committed to the success of their students and they work tirelessly to overcome these challenges and limitations by creating their own resources and translating the school board professional development to make it relevant to their students (James et al. 2015).

WORKING WITHIN AND THROUGH THE LIMITATIONS OF AFRICENTRICITY

The lack of clarity around, and having no singular definition of, Africentric education within a Canadian context has proved challenging. There are overarching objectives and various approaches to teaching within the school's mandate. But multiple perspectives of Africentricity, informed by different worldviews within the Black diaspora, combined with varying expectations of the school by parents, community members, and the wider public, are perceived by the staff and parents as challenging and in some ways limit the ongoing operation of the school.

AAS offers students the opportunity to learn the Ontario mandated curriculum infused with the histories, cultures, experiences, perspectives, and accomplishments of people of African descent. One example of such infusion is the use of the Nguzo Saba—the seven principles of Kwanzaa (i.e., *Umoja* [unity], *Ujima* [collective work and responsibility], *Ujamaa* [cooperative economics], *Kuumba* [creativity], *Imani* [faith], *Kujichagulia* [self-determination], and *Nia* [purpose])— to inform teaching, learning, and school practices.

Under the alternative school model, student transportation to and from school is the sole responsibility of parents, and financial resources collected through school fundraising cannot be used for student transportation. So even though Africentricity, as constructed by the AAS, is informed by *Ujima* and *Ujamaa*, the school is unable to help parents and students address transportation problems. Rebecca, a teacher at the school, clarified that:

> There's no free busing. So for [alternative] schools that have catchment areas from all around the city, that means that parents coming from working class backgrounds would have to be paying up to $1,000 a month for busing, which means they can't come here, basically.

The disconnect between Western and African pedagogies and schooling philosophies, coupled with the fluid and complex definition(s) of Africentric education, limits the transformative potential of the school. Christina (a teacher) explained that the school is hindered by the Western structures of the school board with its Eurocentric curriculum, which makes their work "Africentric-lite, because if we were to really go full force with it, we'd have to change up the structure. If Africentric means holistic and democratic and circle and all of that, then…our whole teaching practice [would be] changed."

OPPORTUNITIES TO HEAL THE SCARS

The AAS is regarded by many people as an appropriate response to the decades-long search for "something different" for Black students—an alternative to mainstream schooling that would address the high dropout rate of Black students which is partially attributed to demeaning and dismissive treatment, disengaging teaching practices, and culturally irrelevant curricula in mainstream schools. An AAS administrator described Black students and their parents as

> historically disenfranchised, marginalized and distrustful of the public education system … and the toxicity that actually comes with that … It's something that they have to grapple with and understand. So even though they are bringing this baggage into this space, fortunately for us, they know it's a safe enough space for them to do that.

The fact is, racism, inherent in the education system, is a common experience for many racialized students and families; yet, despite the evidence that attests to their negative experiences, no structural or systemic changes have been made. In theory, attempts to address the limiting effects of racism can happen at any school if there is a desire to affect such change. But it is at AAS where parents, students, educators, administrators, and community members perceive that attempts are being made to foster a positive Black identity and in the process to build students' self-esteem, cultivate a sense of pride, and encourage a strong sense of community through parental engagement (see James, et al. 2015). Monique (a student) used the popular concept of "the village" to describe the meaning and significance of the school to its students. "Everybody in the village is caring. We know each other … it's more home-ish. For a lot of Caribbean people…when you come to school you feel like you're home, and for us … it's a school of 17 different villages but we all know each other."

AAS educators stressed the importance of building the self-esteem and pride of Black students to prepare them to live and participate in an inequitable society. Wesley (a teacher) asserted that "I wanted who-ever sat in front of me to be proud of their heritage, be knowledge-able about it, be critical of it, to be transgressive, and to question and interrogate and challenge." Likewise, Wendy (another teacher) sub-mitted:

> I want them to have that strong sense of self because once you understand yourself you're more open to understanding others… Sometimes within our society, people don't always understand the importance of know-ing who you are, knowing that you're a contributor, [and] knowing that your history is tied in with other histories … when looking at the system, and having been apart of it, a lot of times you're like looking in on [what] somebody else has done.

CONCLUSION

Critical education scholars (e.g., Dei and Kempf 2013; Henry 1993; Levine-Rasky 2014) maintain that Ontario's education system was designed to serve, and still serves, the economic, social, cultural, and political interests of White, Western European elite Canadians. Consequently, working class, minoritized and immigrant students "who lack the necessary social and cultural capital and may resist assimilation, are less likely to succeed in the school system unless it is responsive to their educational needs, expectations, interests and aspirations" (James and Wood 2005: 93).

Positioned within the status quo education system, AAS as an alternative model of schooling is both an asset and an obstacle to the education of Black youth—in other words, a paradox. On the one hand, it gives specific attention and value to African Canadian historical contributions, worldviews, and knowledge which contribute to cultivating a culture of high expectations, nurturing a positive Black identity and high self-efficacy, preparing students to be critically aware of their social situation and building community support and educational assets. On the other hand, there is the perception that the school is limited and that the specific focus on African Canadians at the school makes the integration of information about the group into the standard provincial curriculum and into other schools irrelevant.

Some critics of the school suggested that integrating African history and pedagogy into the Ontario curriculum and across all schools within the TDSB would positively change educational experiences for all students. However, without substantial transformative education reform, the education of Black students will remain the same. Simply adding or subtracting particular items to education programs and curriculum and keeping all students in mainstream schools will be inadequate unless real efforts are made to address the enduring effects of structural inequities, racism, and discrimination in the education of Black students.

As often as reports are published outlining the educational failures of Black students, other reports celebrate the "higher" high school graduation and university attendance rates of "students," with assumptions that the education system is equitable, meritorious, and culturally responsive. The problem here might be that contradictory evidence is never interrogated using a "race lens." The color-blind ethos that undergirds the "we only see students; we do not see their color" approach to schooling means that no real and long-lasting reform in education is taking place. Indeed, for schooling to meet the needs, interests, and aspirations of students and their parents requires taking into account students' identities—their bodies, beliefs, and sense of belonging and community. The prevailing framework of alternative schools, coupled with the explicit mandate for a specific vision and philosophy for AAS, give rise to the understanding that more attention, effort, and time need to be allocated to developing strong relationships between students, educators, parents, and community members so as to enable students' educational success and individual growth.

Finally, in the case of the AAS, the Eurocentric middle-class ethos on which schooling and education in North America is predicated is likely to cast a "white shadow" (Peart 2010) over the Black bodies in the school. In other words, given the beliefs and claims of Torontonians—and Canadians generally—the school will not escape the scrutiny of and questions about its ability to really prepare students to live, work, and prosper in a Canadian society that is not race-neutral or color-blind.

NOTES

1. While we specifically focus on Ontario in this chapter, the issues and concerns discussed are not unique to this region of Canada. Similar experiences have been documented for Black students in Alberta, Manitoba, Nova Scotia, Quebec, and Saskatchewan (see BLAC 1994; Codjoe 2001; D'Oyley 1994).
2. In Canada, the last segregated school was closed in 1983 (Nova Scotia); Ontario closed its last segregated school in 1965.
3. Examples include: Afro-Caribbean Alternative Secondary School, Black Education Project, African Canadian Heritage Association, and Nighana Afrocentric Transitional Program.
4. Examples include: African Canadian Community Working Group, Congress of Black Women in Canada, Consultative Committee on the Education of Black Students in Toronto Schools, Organization of Parents of Black Children, National Council of Black Educators of Canada, and TDSB Africentric Advisory Committee.
5. See African Canadian Community Working Group, Consultative Committee on the Education of Black Students in Toronto Schools (1988), Lewis (1992), Royal Commission on Learning (1994).
6. We use the term minoritized to refer to all students who are marginalized in the school system. This includes immigrant, refugee, and working-class students. The term minoritized, like racialized, refers to a process in which members of non-dominant groups are treated in marginalizing ways, and as such, the discrimination that they experience contributes their negative social outcomes.
7. In 2009, TDSB also opened: da Vinci School (focused on Arts, Music, and Nature), Grove Community School (focused on environmental education, social justice, and community activism), and Equinox Holistic Alternative School (focused on Narrative-, Arts-, Inquiry-, Experiential- and project-based learning).
8. Variations of a separate public school for Black students were proposed by the African Canadian Community Group in 1992, and the Royal

Commission on Learning in 1994. Accordingly, in 1995 the Nighana Afrocentric Transitional Program for high school students was opened within the former Toronto Board of Education.

9. Previous initiatives in Toronto include the Afro-Caribbean Alternative Secondary School and Nighana Afrocentric Transitional Program.

10. AAS opened in September 2009 as a Kindergarten to Grade 5 School. Each subsequent school year thereafter, it added a grade to the school. Accordingly, since the 2012–2013 school year, the school has been a Kindergarten to Grade 8 School.

11. All the names of research participants are pseudonyms.

References

Benzie, R. 2008. McGuinty Turns Up the Heat on Trustees: Pressure School Board to Reverse Decision, Premier Tells Citizens. *Toronto Star*, February 1, A1.

Black Learners Advisory Committee (BLAC). 1994. *BLAC Report on Education: Redressing Inequality— Empowering Black Learners.* Halifax: Black Learners Advisory Committee.

Bourdieu, Pierre. 1977. Cultural Reproduction and Social Reproduction. In *Power and Ideology in Education 1977*, ed. Jerome Karabel, and Albert Halsey, 487–511. New York: Oxford University Press.

Brathwaite, Keren S., and Carl E. James. 1996. *Educating African Canadians.* Toronto: Our Schools/Our Selves & James Lorimer Ltd.

Robert, Brown S. 1993. *A Follow-up of the Grade 9 Cohort of 1987 Every Secondary Student Survey Participants.* Toronto: Research Services, Toronto Board of Education.

Codjoe, Henry M. 2001. Fighting a 'Public Enemy' of Black Academic Achievement—The Persistence of Racism and the Schooling Experiences of Black Students in Canada. *Race, Ethnicity, and Education* 4 (4): 343–375.

D'Oyley, V.R. (ed.). 1994. *Innovations in Black Education in Canada. National Council of Black Educators of Canada.* Toronto: Umbrella Press.

Dei, George J. Sefa. 2008. Schooling as Community: Race, Schooling, and the Education of African Youth. *Journal of Black Studies* 38(2):346–366.

Dei, George J. Sefa, and Kempf Arlo. 2013. *New Perspectives on African-Centred Education in Canada.* Toronto: Canadian Scholars' Press.

Dei, George J. Sefa, Josephine Mazzuca, Elizabeth McIsaac, and Jasmine Zine. 1997. *Reconstructing 'Drop-out': A Critical Ethnography of the Dynamics of Black Students' Disengagement from School.* Toronto: University of Toronto Press.

Deosaran, Ramesh A. 1976. *The 1975 Every Student Survey: Program Placement Related to Selected Countries of Birth and Selected Languages.* Toronto: The Board of Education for the City of Toronto.

Dixson, Adrienne D., and Celia K. Rousseau. 2005. And We Are Still Not Saved: Critical Race Theory in Education Ten Years Later. *Race Ethnicity and Education* 8 (1): 7–27.

Gillborn, David. 2006. Critical Race Theory and Education: Racism and Anti-Racism in Educational Theory and Praxis. *Discourse: Studies in the Cultural Politics of Education* 27 (1): 11–32.

Gillborn, David. 2015. Intersectionality, Critical Race Theory, and the Primacy of Racism: Race, Class, Gender, and Disability in Education. *Qualitative Inquiry* 21 (3): 277–287.

Gulson, Kalervo N., and P. Taylor Webb. 2013. 'Raw, Emotional Thing': School Choice, Commodification, and the Racialized Branding of Afrocentricity in Toronto, Canada. *Education Inquiry* 4 (1): 167–187.

Hammer, Kate. 2009. More Alternative Schools Opening than Ever in Toronto. *The Globe and Mail*, September 7.http://www.theglobeandmail.com/news/toronto/more-alternative-schools-opening-than-ever-in-toronto/article4290931/. Accessed Aug 2012.

Henry, Annette. 1993. Missing: Black Self-Representations in Canadian Educational Research. *Canadian Journal of Education* 18 (3): 206–222.

James, Carl E. 1995. Multicultural and Anti-Racism Education in Canada. *Race, Gender & Class* 2 (3): 31–48.

James, Carl E. 2012. Students 'At-Risk': Stereotypes and the Schooling of Black Boys. *Urban Education* 47 (2): 464–494.

James, Carl E. 2011. Multicultural Education in a Color-Blind Society. In *Intercultural and Multicultural Education: Enhancing Global Connectedness 2011*, ed. Carl A. Grant and Agostino Portera, 191–210. New York: Routledge.

James, Carl E., and Maxine Wood. 2005. Multicultural Education in Canada: Opportunities, Limitations and Contradictions. In *Possibilities and Limitations: Multicultural Policies and Programs in Canada 2005*, ed Carl E. James, 93–107. Black Point, Nova Scotia: Fernwood Publishing.

James, Carl E., Philip Howard, Julia Samaroo, Rob Brown, and Gillian Parekh. 2015. *Africentric Alternative School Research Project: Year 3 (2013–2014) Report*. Toronto, November 2015. http://ycec.edu.yorku.ca/files/2012/11/AAS-Research-Project-Year-3-Report.pdf.

Levine-Rasky, Cynthia. 2014. White Fear: Analyzing Public Objection to Toronto's Africentric School. *Race Ethnicity and Education* 17 (2): 202–218.

Lewis, Stephen. 1992. *Report on Race Relations in Ontario*. Toronto: Government of Ontario.

Milner, H. Richard. 2007. Race, Culture, and Researcher Positionality: Working Through Dangers Seen, Unseen and Unforeseen. *Educational Researcher* 36(7):388–400.

Peart, Raymond. 2010. Black Bodies/White Shadows: Examining the Colonial Legacy in Africentric Schooling. Master's thesis, York University.

Richardson, Virginia. 2003. Constructivist Pedagogy. *Teachers College Record* 105 (9): 1623–1640.

Royal Commission on Learning (RCOL). 1994. *For the Love of Learning: Report of the Royal Commission on Learning.* Toronto: Ontario Ministry of Education.

Solorzano, Daniel G., and J. Tara Yosso. 2001. From Racial Stereotyping and Deficit Discourse Toward a Critical Race Theory in Teacher Education. *Multicultural Education* 9(1): 2–8.

Solorzano, Daniel G., and Tara J. Yosso. 2001. From Racial Stereotyping and Deficit Discourse Toward a Critical Race Theory in Teacher Education. *Multicultural education* 9 (1): 2.

Toronto Board of Education. 1988. Consultative Committee on the Education of Black Students in Toronto School (CCEBTS). *Final Report of the Consultative Committee on the Education of Black Students in Toronto Schools.* Toronto: Ministry of Education, Toronto Board of Education.

Toronto District School Board (TDSB). 2010. *Achievement Gap Task Force: Draft Report.* Toronto. http://www.tdsb.on.ca/Portals/0/Community/CommunityAdvisorycommittees/ICAC/Subcommittees/AchievementGapReptDraftMay172010.pdf. Accessed Sept 2012.

Yilmaz, Kaya. 2008. Constructivism: Its Theoretical Underpinnings, Variations, and Implications for the Classroom. *Educational Horizons* 86 (3): 161–172.

Authors' Biography

Carl E. James teaches in the Faculty of Education and the Graduate Program of Sociology at York University where he is also the Jean Augustine Chair in Education, Community and Diaspora. His research interests include exploring questions pertaining to cultural identification in relation to race, ethnicity, class, gender, and citizenship; educational and employment opportunities and access; the possibilities and limits of equity policies and programs; and how multiculturalism as a state policy operates to essentialize, marginalize, and racialize individuals. Since 2010, he has been conducting research with colleagues on the Africentric Alternative School in Toronto. His recent publications include the following: *Life at the Intersection: Community, Class and Schooling* (2012), *Seeing Ourselves: Exploring Race, Ethnicity, and Culture* (4th Edition, 2010), and *Race in Play: Understanding the Socio-Cultural Worlds of Student Athletes* (2010).

Julia A. Samaroo is a doctoral candidate in the Faculty of Education at York University. Her research explores the intersections of community, identity, and education by examining the role(s) of community in the schooling of racialized students. She advocates for curricula and teaching practices to be informed by and reflect the identities and lived experiences of students and their communities. Her interests are focused on socio-educational issues as it relates to class, culture, ethnicity, and race, paying particular attention to the nuanced ways racism, marginalization, and discrimination operate in schools, as well as interrogating Canadian educational policies through a lens of social justice, equity, and inclusivity.

CHAPTER 5

Reverberations of Neo-Liberal Policies: The Slow Dilution of Secondary Alternative Schooling in the Toronto District School Board

Louise Azzarello

Education in Ontario, like most places, has undergone philosophical, political, and pedagogical shifts throughout its history. In the late 1960s and early 1970s, as a result of the Hall–Dennis Report, *Living and Learning*, the Ontario education system implemented progressive changes that promoted critical thinking, envisioned a more equitable notion of education, recognized that students should be active participants in their learning rather than passive vessels, and understood that it was imperative to consider not only what we teach but how we teach it. Work begun during this period saw transformations in educational thought, policies, and initiatives concerned with serving diverse communities while working toward enacting equity connected to race, gender, class, ethnicity, and sexual orientation. School boards and individual schools were able to enact the policies and programs that integrated

L. Azzarello (✉)
York University, Toronto, Canada

© The Author(s) 2017
N. Bascia et al. (eds.), *Alternative Schooling and Student Engagement*,
DOI 10.1007/978-3-319-54259-1_5

these new moves into education, thus directly benefiting and reflecting their communities.

It was at this time that Toronto's public alternative schools began to develop. Changes in the ways educators and policy makers understood the role and purpose of education, opened spaces for new, and sometimes radical, ideas of democracy and equity in education to thrive. Alternative secondary schools emerged in conjunction with progressive changes not only in educational thought but also in local politics and intensified community activism.

This political climate enabled the creation of a number of secondary alternative schools initiated by students and progressive educators, supported by communities, trustees, and Toronto Board administrators. Unfortunately, in the past 20 years, Ontario has experienced the dissolution of what was becoming a progressive educational system into a conservative, neo-liberal, hierarchical system where all aspects of education and schooling are to be measured, codified, and packaged.

A centralized education system, powered by neo-liberal ideologies and composed of restrictive authoritarian legislation and policies, has had a deep-seated impact on schooling at its core. Amalgamation of school boards, funding and staff cuts, standardized testing, homogenous curriculum development, and prioritizing mastery of employability skills over critical thinking skills have all altered the underlying foundations of local schools and boards, creating complex tensions among teachers and administrators in schools and at the board level. Inequitable fiscal constraints have been imposed by funding formulas; loss of teaching and non-teaching jobs and the elimination of programs and services increasingly put marginalized/racialized youth more at risk and limit their opportunities for success. Many in leadership positions no longer function as educators but rather as managers looking to impose a bottom line. "Student success" is repeatedly measured only in terms of credit accumulation, though it should include so much more. Work toward equity for all came to a standstill and more recently has been taken up as equality as the system reverts to a notion that providing the "same" education for all students equals equity.

Although these changes have had system-wide consequences in board management and politics, schools, classrooms, and students in the Toronto District School Board, this chapter will consider the particular ways this neo-liberal move has affected Toronto secondary alternative schools. Focusing on only a few of these changes, I consider how secondary alternative schools' independence, democratic practices, and their unique philosophies are dissolving within a system that has been stripped of its resources and has been forced to adopt domesticating, regulatory, and standardized practices.

THE NEO-LIBERAL SHIFT

The Progressive Conservative Party came to power in Ontario in 1995 under the leadership of Mike Harris, who had campaigned on a platform coined "the Common Sense Revolution," a capitalistic, market-based right-wing platform that would see reductions in taxes, debilitating cuts to public services such as welfare, health care, and education, attacks on unions, and the centralization of power. This right-wing government would introduce a number of bills that altered, and continue to have a negative impact upon, education, schooling, school boards, and schools in Ontario (Anderson and Ben Jaafar 2003; MacLellan 2009b; Sattler 2012).

The adoption of a neo-liberal agenda in educational policies and ideologies paved the way for a flood of reforms in education that allowed the Conservatives to dismantle any progressive actions that had been taken by the previous government. Specifically, they "shut down an Anti-Racism Secretariat created by the NDP, and its counterpart in the Ministry of Education, and took steps to remove references to pro-equity goals (e.g., anti-racism, gender) from future curriculum policy documents" (Anderson and Ben Jaafar 2003: 9). These changes continue to reverberate in Ontario schools today.

The two legislative measures introduced in 1996, Bill 160 (the *Education Quality Improvement Act*) and Bill 104 (*The Fewer School Boards Act*), enact a neo-liberal market economy model of education. Bill 160 aimed to centralize control over educational policies by transferring many decision-making powers in education from local school boards to the government. Veiled in a cry to reduce inequities and end the "crisis in education," Bill 160 resulted in loss of resources both material and physical by implementing a funding formula directly linked to enrollment numbers. Bill 160 also regulates and controls the distribution of monies, removes the local boards' powers to levy taxes to fund schools, increases class sizes, reduces curricular choice for students, strips principals and supervisory officers of their right to be members of teachers' unions, consequently creating a management class in schools, and regulates the number of trustees, with newly capped salaries. Bill 104 (*The*

Fewer School Boards Act) would see the amalgamation of school boards across Ontario, reducing the number of boards from 129 to 72. The Toronto educational system morphed into an unruly beast almost overnight. As six former school boards merged,[1] struggles over power and control of the organization ensued. It would take some time before the dramatic stripping down of resources and bureaucratic controls would come to alternative secondary schools. But come they did.

It is in the reverberations of this moment in the history of educational "reform" that this chapter is located. Situating an understanding of the slow dilution and the undoing of secondary alternative education and schools in Toronto, I examine a few ways the enactment of Bill 160, combined with the amalgamation of Toronto area school boards under Bill 104, have gradually eroded fundamental tenets of secondary alternative schools in Toronto.

Immersed in what seems like a never-ending fight for survival, alternative school educators are entrenched in an ongoing battle. Although I argue that these reforms have altered and damaged the possibilities of what alternative education can be in these neo-liberal times, it must be acknowledged that, despite 20 years of bureaucratic interference, there are educators who continue to re/create these spaces and re/imagine alternative education and schooling in this market-driven context. The burden on them is notable as they negotiate an ever-increasing restrictive system subjugated by a political agenda that does not value the contribution alternative schools make to the educational landscape.

"WHAT'S IN A NAME?"

Toronto's alternative schools were originally rooted in critical pedagogies, social justice, activism, and philosophies of equity and democracy. The majority were established and located in the City of Toronto, with a few scattered throughout the surrounding suburban areas. Common to all the Toronto alternative schools is a critical approach to upholding democracy in education, a commitment to critical pedagogy and an understanding that students have diverse experiences and needs and that the schools are theirs, for their learning, their education. These schools originally provided environments that were radically distinct from mainstream schools[2] regarding curriculum choices, involvement in community activism, and countering and challenging dominant ideologies.

Some schools worked closely with outreach and social workers to re-engage and support youth who were living in poverty, or who had been in conflict with the law or marginalized in mainstream schools because of their sexual orientation.[3] Other schools focused on community-based learning or aimed to create a university-like atmosphere through small classes. Each alternative secondary school was distinct and attracted particular students. They were/are not interchangeable—it was not a "one-size-fits-all" system. They did aim to simply reproduce a mainstream system in a smaller space; they were singular schools with a common understanding of alternative schooling as a critical approach to education that challenged the status quo, authoritarian systems of education, and worked toward developing democratic models of learning and teaching. It is these critical philosophical and pedagogical ideas that made Toronto secondary alternative schools alternative. But "what is in a name?"

In the new amalgamated board, the word "alternative" has been hijacked to describe programs for youth who are not attending school, suspended and expelled student programs, treatment programs, programs for students 18-21 who have dropped out of school and are returning to complete their high school diploma, programs for teenage mothers, and post-incarceration transition programs. Some of these programs had existed in some fashion in the six legacy boards but were not named or defined as "alternative" but now, in the amalgamated board, are characterized as "alternative."

Naming these programs thus demonstrates a system-wide lack of understanding of the history, philosophies, and functions of alternative education and schools. These other types of programs did not emerge from community activism, specific educational philosophies, or commitment to social transformation. Rather, they emerged from the system itself, as responses to outcomes of massive cuts, reactionary legislation, and bureaucratization. The main goals of these newly named "alternative" programs are control, compliance, and credit accumulation.

Why conflate these very different approaches to education under one name? This act of naming does not seem accidental. Language matters, names matter, so why, despite push-back from some board members, does this grouping exist today? It seems as if it was a deliberate erasure of history and progressive education. It diminishes and negates the uniqueness of each alternative school, marketing them as just another place to accumulate credits. As well, it makes it difficult for teachers, guidance counselors, social workers, and administrators trying to guide students to appropriate schools.

TAKING UP SPACE

By 1999, the new Toronto District School Board was beginning to adjust to amalgamation and dealing with huge financial cuts. The neoliberal assault on education instituted fiscal constraints through Bill 160 that would apply marketplace values linking resources to enrollment and quantitative performance data (Sefa Dei and Karumanchery 1999: 116). The new funding formula directly connected students to square footage—each student generates a dollar amount that determines the maintenance and operating budget of a given school. "Full-time Equivalent" (FTE) as defined by the funding formula for secondary students is based on the number of hours a student is in school each day and the number of courses they are registered in. This new method of counting students would not take into account, or allow for, the vast range of life experiences faced by many students attending alternative secondary schools in Toronto. Some students could not maintain a full course load due to their financial situations, if they were supporting themselves or helping provide for their families; some were dealing with mental health issues; and others were almost finished their courses and only needed a few credits. Although all these students were active participants, attending school daily, they did not generate the revenue of full-time students. This would alter the number of students deemed to be attending many of the alternative schools, thus reducing their operating budgets and eventually their teaching staff.

Positioning students as objects of revenue rather than diverse learners with specific needs and desires would force the newly amalgamated Toronto District School Board to "maximize" space. For example, the decision was made to relocate SEED. After 31 years in existence, for the first time in its history, SEED would be housed in an actual school building and removed from its central downtown location above Fran's Restaurant at Yonge and College Streets. The principal was committed to including staff in the decision to move; however, in the end, the board ignored teaching staff's input and chose a location that staff had adamantly declared inappropriate.

Yet another cost-saving strategy was the phasing out of the fifth year of high school, known at this time as OAC (Ontario Academic Credit), by the year 2003. This brought another blow to some of the alternative schools, such as SEED, that had previously focused on Grade 12 and OAC courses. This move forced SEED to initiate a full grade 11 program and begin to offer some grade 10 courses and caused similar disruptions and changes at some of the other alternative schools.

The relocation of SEED, combined with the new method of accounting for student numbers and the loss of OAC, all exacerbated and fueled the problematic relationships among staff in the early 2000s. SEED teachers felt as though the school and their own philosophies of education were being ripped out from under them. As often happens, the pressure turned inward and divided the staff. There were real issues to address at SEED; however, the centralization of power within the board and its disregard for teachers' past experiences, successes, and knowledge made it an environment where no structure remained to support staff moving toward a positive change. Some staff left, others were later forced out, and slowly the school almost disappeared, leaving the task of recreating it to a new generation of alternative educators.

DIVISIONS AND DYNAMICS OF POWER: WHO'S IN CHARGE?

Alternative schools had been the places where staff collaborated with students in governing the school. Weekly meetings where students created agendas, led discussions, posed questions, and challenged teachers were common. Students had a stake in running the school, and in some schools, they even participated in interviewing potential students. At SEED, with a staff member present, students ran the interviews explaining the school's philosophy to help interested students decide whether SEED was a place they would like to be and asked questions in order to ascertain whether the applicant understood the underlying philosophy of SEED and was committed to being an active participant in the school community.

Until 1999, students at SEED were even involved in the hiring process. When I was interviewed, the committee was composed of two students, two staff, and the principal, all with equal decision-making power. The students' opinions were valued and taken seriously. Prior to 1998, Heads of Departments (now known as Curriculum Leaders or Assistant Curriculum Leaders[4]) were part of the hiring process. This no longer happens, and the prospect that students and staff will ever be included in the hiring of staff looks bleak.

Today, in the majority of Toronto District School Board schools, principals and vice-principals interview and hire teachers without input from teaching staff. Bill 160's removal of principals and vice-principals from the teachers' bargaining unions positioned principals and vice-principals as managers and classroom teachers as workers, creating a split that encourages, supports, and reflects the devaluing of teachers' professional abilities and experiences. Most alarming is how ingrained and normalized this hierarchy has become. In the new regime, a great divide has been created between teachers and their school administrators.

As principals' and vice-principals' roles transformed from educators to management, a new environment ensued. For a group of alternative schools in the downtown area of Toronto, this meant shifting from having an off-site principal who saw their role as supporting the teaching staff, to first the addition of one, then two vice-principals, creating a management level within this group of alternative schools that had not existed before. Each vice-principal was assigned a number of alternative schools from this group and became much more involved in the actual day-to-day running of individual schools. This division countered and complicated the working relationships that had existed between staff and the principals in previous years.

Another phase of the centralization of power that would affect the structure and hierarchy throughout the Toronto District School Board and in alternative secondary schools was the implementation of Curriculum Leader positions that began in September 2003. This was yet another cost-cutting initiative that would weaken teachers' roles in the schools. These newly created positions would replace what had been subject-based Heads of Departments held by more experienced teachers. Curriculum Leaders now oversee mega-departments composed of a number of subject disciplines of which they only need expertise in one.

Although the alternative schools had no Heads of Departments to replace, there was an informal coordinator position. The coordinator's role was to work closely with the office administrator, overseeing and organizing budgets, school record keeping, and other administrative tasks. In some schools, two teachers shared this role, in some, teachers alternated the responsibility every year or two; in others, students voted on which interested staff member should take the role. In some other schools, the role was assigned to the same person for a number of years. However, in 2003, when Toronto District School Board restructured the

Positions of Responsibility model, it was decreed that each secondary alternative school would now have a Curriculum Leader.

The introduction of this position was inherently divisive as it comes with monetary reward and a sudden metamorphosis of the person in that position, in the eyes of the board and administrators. Whether one has been teaching for 10, 20, or just three years, this position holds authority, an assumption of knowledge, and is valued by administration over more experienced classroom teachers, in most cases without question. In some secondary alternative schools, this change did not have a noticeable impact on staff, while in others the divide was seen as interfering with fundamental philosophies underlying the process of running the school. Eventually, in some schools, this position would be used to assert power over classroom teachers, to impose administrators' ideas, establish new procedures without whole staff consent and, at times, could become a tool to bring into school teachers who would not resist or challenge the administration or to remove teachers that the administration found undesirable.

A hierarchical divide was instituted and encouraged during this administration's management and created tension and conflict between teaching staff in a number of the secondary alternative schools. In 2011, at a staff meeting for this particular group of alternative schools, the principal announced that teachers were not to contact the superintendent of alternative schools directly; all communications between teaching staff and the superintendent were to go through the principal. This edict clearly demonstrated the establishment of a managerial class and the principal's reinforcement and complicity in the perpetration of a hierarchical business model. No longer was this a community of educators working together for students, engaging in critical conversations about education and schooling, or modeling democratic and inclusive behavior. Rather, this was now a divided entity, a clear example of the impact made by managerial administrators leading alternative schools without critical philosophical understanding of the essence of alternative education.

"Less Staff Means Less Hope"[5]

Although staffing could often be stressful and problematic for alternative schools, pre-amalgamation issues were most often centered on the "bumping" process, a staffing practice that places teachers in specific teaching positions based on seniority, when they are surplus to a particular school. A teacher with more seniority than others in the board would be placed in a school and a more junior teacher could be "bumped" out either to a different school or out of a job. This process sometimes resulted in "bumping" staff into alternative schools who did not want to work in small democratic settings, who were not interested in alternative education, and who were not suited to these positions for a number of reasons.

Tensions and problems caused by these procedures would eventually work themselves out in a number of ways. Pre-amalgamation, long-established relationships among trustees, the teachers' union, and alternative school's teachers and principals often enabled solutions. This was, in part, due to the support from a number of senior board officials and trustees who acknowledged that alternative schools were providing essential educational spaces and opportunities for particular students and thus had different needs. They worked actively to support alternative schools, as they understood their importance to the educational landscape of the city.

A supportive climate did exist, and secondary alternative schools were usually supported when issues arose. There was the political will to support them, and their advocates understood their mandates and recognized their value. However, Bill 104 would cut the number of Toronto trustees from 74 to 20, and also reduced their salaries from $48,000 to $5,000 (Cash 2008). Their powers were limited, and their workload increased. Many trustees from the legacy boards did not run for office in the newly amalgamated board, and those who did were overwhelmed by the demands and confusions of creating a mega-board. MacLellan notes, "Of those that did run and were re-elected, they faced a governance structure that limited their ability to make decisions for the benefit of their students" (2009a: 14). This new barrier would make it difficult for those who supported alternative schools to exert any power within the bureaucracy of the board. It became much more difficult for trustees and board members to advocate for consistent and continued support of secondary alternative schools and, eventually, staffing issues would be more severe than the "bumping" process. Staff cuts were on the horizon.

We continue to live in a reductions-of-resources situation, as "The deeply flawed school funding formula for elementary and secondary education, designed by Mike Harris' Progressive Conservative government and inherited by the Liberal government when it was elected in 2003, has never been fixed" (Mackenzie 2015: 10). The Liberal government, despite promises to undo the damage created by the Harris government, has continued to support and add to the neo-liberal reforms that plague educational systems in Ontario. According to Noonan and Coral, "While the Liberal government, first elected in 2003, increased spending on education 24% between 2003 and 2008, they did nothing substantial to reverse the assault on the educational mission of schools." (2015: 60–61)

As the reduction in resources continued and the promised changes to the funding formula by the Liberal government did not appear, Spring 2011 would see a move by the Toronto District School Board to bring alternative schools and their staffing allocations more in line with main-stream schools. The downtown alternative schools, as a group, were slated to lose five teachers. Reducing teaching staff by one, in an alternative staff of nine or less, is a severe loss. One less teacher means six fewer courses. Teaching staff and students took political action to fight these major cuts, supported by community, parents, and a few trustees. Oasis Alternative Secondary School was one school marked to lose a teacher. Oasis is unique among the alternative schools, with three separate sites: Arts & Social Change, Oasis Skateboard Factory, and Triangle for LGBTQ youth. At that time, there were nine teachers across the three sites. Triangle was allotted three teachers, Skateboard Factory one, and Arts & Social Change five. Then, it was announced that one teaching position at Oasis' Arts & Social Change satellite would be lost in this round of cuts, and students were devastated.

As participants in a school where curriculum is centered on equity and social justice, students wanted to know what they could do—how could they take action? First, a number of students wrote letters to the Director and Chair of the Toronto District School Board. Then, working with Oasis' drama educator, they integrated these letters, along with letters from community council members, into their culminating theater piece entitled *Alternative Chances*. Students also joined teachers, community members, and staff from a number of alternative schools at a board meeting where they spoke out against the cuts, telling board members the important role the school played in their lives. They explained that cutting one staff member would destroy a whole program. Cut a teacher who provides a drama program, and suddenly the school has no drama program.

Activism and advocating was done through every possible channel and resulted in the reinstatement of two of the five teaching positions, with the understanding that there would be more cuts the next year. The two teaching positions were then assigned back to schools of the principal's choosing which did not include Oasis. Although Arts & Social Change students did not benefit directly from their activism, they learned that actions taken can make changes affecting the larger community.

Despite continued work to push the board to acknowledge different needs of alternative schools, the cuts continue. The board's stance is that staffing numbers must be brought in line with enrollment, as student numbers generate funding for teachers. There is no longer any real understanding of secondary alternative schools' needs, nor any concern for the schools' important contributions to the system at the board level. The cuts continue.

Now, forced to comply with neo-liberal business models, budgets, staffing, and resources must be divided equally rather than equitably. Value is not assigned by what you do, but by how many seats you fill. Success is measured not by what you teach but by how many students pass a standardized test. Difference is supposed to flourish in a system based on a one-size-fits-all structure. How does alternative education fit into this constrained notion of education where neo-liberal rhetoric hides, divides, and executes policies that undo the notions of equity rather than expanding them? Alternative schools represent the possibilities in education, the hope of what could be—something moving forward always changing, evolving, trying to get it right—not afraid to take risks and to try again. Although there are glimmers of hope, a heaviness weighs on educators committed to fighting to maintain the integrity of alternative education. The system is steeped in a contradictory reality where legislative discourse seems to dictate a liberating-equitable educational philosophy while at the same time stripping the system's resources. School practices are becoming standardized, with a disturbing focus on regulation and compliance. The implementation of these narrowing ideas of what education is, and what schools should be, puts at risk not only students, but progressive democratic educational thought and practices that have been the foundation of alternative schools in Toronto for decades.

Notes

1. The newly amalgamated board, The Toronto District School Board, was comprised of six other large boards from the Greater Toronto Area: the Toronto Board of Education, the Scarborough Board of Education, the

Etobicoke Board of Education, the North York Board of Education, the East York Board of Education and the Board of Education for the City of York.

2. For an in-depth account of a particular secondary alternative school prior to amalgamation, see Mary Beattie's *Narratives in the Making: Teaching and Learning at Corktown Community High School (2004)* (Beattie 2004).

3. Post-amalgamation outreach workers' jobs were cut and the number of social workers diminished, thus limiting the support for some of the most vulnerable students in the system.

4. Toronto District School Board altered its Position of Responsibility model for the start of the 2003–2004 school year. Department Heads and Assistant Heads would become Curriculum Leaders and Assistant Curriculum Leaders, and the number of positions would be cut almost in half (*Edu-Law, Human Resource Digest* 2003) (Tymochenko et al. 2003).

5. This phrase comes from a letter written in 2010 to the then Director of Education Chris Spence by a student from Oasis Arts & Social Change requesting that the Board not cut a teacher from the school.

REFERENCES

Anderson, Stephen E., and S. Ben Jaafar. 2003. *Policy trends in Ontario education* 1. ICEC Working Paper.

Beattie, Marry. 2004. *Narratives in the Making: Teaching and Learning at Corktown Community High School.* Toronto: University of Toronto Press.

Cash, Andrew. 2008. Matter of Trust. *NOW Magazine*, January 17. https://nowtoronto.com/news/matter-of-trust/.

Dei, George J. Sefa, and Leeno L. Karumanchery. 1999, Summer. School Reforms in Ontario: The 'Marketization of Education' and the Resulting Silence on Equity. The *Alberta Journal of Educational Research* XIV (2): 111–131.

Mackenzie, Hugh. 2015. *Harris-era Hangovers: Toronto School Trustees' Inherited Funding Shortfall.* Toronto: Canadian Centre for Policy Alternatives Ontario Office. https://www.policyalternatives.ca/sites/default/files/uploads/publications/Ontario%20Office/2015/02/CCPA-ON_Harris_Era_Hangovers.pdf.

MacLellan, Duncan. 2009a. Educational Restructuring and the Policy Process: The Toronto District School Board 1997–2003. *Academic Leadership Journal: The Online Journal* 7 (4): 76–87. www.academicleadership.org/emprical_research/Educational_Restructuring_and_the_Policy_Process_The_Toronto_District_School_Board_1997–2003.shtml.

MacLellan, Duncan. 2009b. Neoliberalism and Ontario Teachers' Unions: A 'Not-So' Common Sense Revolution. *Socialist Studies* 5 (1): 51–74.

Noonan, Jeff, and Mireille Coral. 2015. The Tyranny of Work: Employability and the Neoliberal Assault on Education. *Alternate Routes: A Journal of Critical Social Research* 26. http://www.alternateroutes.ca/index.php/ar/article/view/22312/18157.

Sattler, Peggy. 2012. Education Governance Reform in Ontario: Neoliberalism in Context. *Canadian Journal of Educational Administration and Policy.*

Tymochenko, Nadya, Bob Keel, M. Hubbard, and K. Ferreira. 2003. Boycott of New Positions of Responsibility Constitutes Strike. *Edu-Law Human Digest 1 (1).* http://www.keelcottrelle.com/assets/files/pdf/archive/human-resources/|2003-06-Digest.pdf.

Author Biography

Louise Azzarello is a Ph.D. candidate at York University. Her research proposes a notion of "looking otherwise" in order to question how we might come to differently understand and enact our obligation and responsibility regarding (looking at) the cruelty we inflict on each other through the examination of specific artworks and iconic news photographs that reference unjust violence, hostility, and death. Her M.A. thesis, *Spectacle & Discipline: Regulating Female Bodies through Dance*, explored the notions of spectacle and body regulation in Western Theatrical Dance from a feminist perspective. A secondary school educator at the Toronto District School Board, Louise's teaching practices are located in interdisciplinary and equity frameworks. She has worked closely with the Toronto District School Board's Aboriginal Education Centre on a number of initiatives and has presented workshops and papers on critical pedagogy, equity, media, art, and interdisciplinary curriculum.

PART II

Historical Perspectives

CHAPTER 6

Private to Public: Alternative Schools in Ontario 1965–1975

Harley Rothstein

ROMANTIC AND PROGRESSIVE EDUCATION MOVEMENTS

The emergence of alternative schools during the 1960s was a transformative development in Canadian educational history. Drawing on the Progressive ideas of John Dewey and the Romantic[1] educational tradition in England, alternative schools were a reaction against the rote learning and 'one-size-fits-all' practices that characterized the public school system well past 1960. Hundreds of Progressive schools or "free schools," as they came to be known by the mid-1960s, sprang up all over Canada and the United States.[2] They offered a child-centered or humanistic education with an emphasis on freedom for children in their learning and day-to-day activities. Ontario, and particularly Toronto, became a focal point for alternative schools during the late 1960s and early 1970s, a development that would change Ontario's public schools profoundly.

The alternative schools of the 1960s were founded by groups of parents looking for a more creative education for their children, by Progressive teachers disillusioned by what they saw as the rigidity of the

H. Rothstein (✉)
University of British Columbia, Vancouver, Canada

© The Author(s) 2017
N. Bascia et al. (eds.), *Alternative Schooling and Student Engagement*,
DOI 10.1007/978-3-319-54259-1_6

public school system, and in a few cases by students themselves who were bored or alienated by high school. These were mostly private small-scale ventures characterized by teachers who worked for next to nothing, parents who were often involved and vocal, debates about educational philosophy that were long and contentious, and pedagogy that ranged from a moderately structured curriculum to almost complete freedom with no curriculum at all. Most proponents of alternative schools held some form of idealistic world view, were politically on the left, and wanted their children's schooling to be the expressions of the innovative ideas of the 1960s. The successes of these 1960s schools were often short-lived, and the majority did not survive, but they left a powerful legacy. The pioneering work of their founders was taken up by educational activists in the 1970s who implemented vibrant and lasting alternatives in the public school system in districts such as Toronto.

Alternative schools were part of a long tradition that can be traced back more than 200 years to the Romantic educational ideas of Jean-Jacques Rousseau and his publication of *Emile* in 1762. Rousseau believed in a naturalistic education that would leave children free to follow their desires, curiosity, and instincts with little adult direction. His ideas found an eager audience among eighteenth-century English Romantics, political radicals, intellectuals, poets, and educators, and Rousseau became a cult figure among his ardent followers. His ideas were further developed in nineteenth-century Europe by Johann Pestalozzi, Friedrich Froebel, and others.

A second great influence on alternative schools was the Progressive Education movement founded by the American philosopher John Dewey at the beginning of the twentieth century. Dewey emphasized the uniqueness of each learner, educating the "whole child," active rather than passive learning, a flexible curriculum appealing to each child's genuine interests, learning through experience, the value of the creative arts, and education for citizenship in a democratic society. Progressives advocated a broad, integrated, and child-centered curriculum, a stimulating classroom environment, co-operation rather than competition, an emphasis on critical inquiry and self-expression, and educational communities where children would be active participants in day-to-day school life. Progressivism reached its peak in the 1920s and 1930s with the establishment of dozens of private Progressive schools in northeastern United States. Hundreds of teachers were trained at Columbia Teachers' College by Dewey and his colleagues.

An offshoot of Progressivism was the pioneering work and writing of Maria Montessori and Rudolph Steiner, founders of what would become two worldwide educational movements, Montessori Schools and Waldorf Schools. Montessori's approach was to help children's understanding through concrete materials and activities, while Steiner emphasized the spiritual and artistic foundations of learning.

The Romantic and Progressive movements came together in twentieth-century Britain with the establishment of several well-known private schools in the 1920s. These included Dartington Hall, which was part of a self-sustaining intentional rural community, and Beacon Hill founded by philosopher Bertrand Russell and his wife Dora Russell. These schools pioneered ideas that later found their way into the alternative schools of the 1960s.

The most famous Romantic school was Summerhill, founded in 1924 by A.S. Neill, in a small town northeast of London. Throughout his long career, Neill developed several basic principles: that children would be allowed to pursue any activities that interested them, that they would not be compelled to attend classes, and that school rules would be set at weekly meetings of the school community where all teachers and students had one vote regardless of age. Neill's approach was based on Freudian psychoanalytic techniques as well as his own personal experience and intuition. Despite his success, with little theoretical framework, his methods were difficult to transfer to North American day schools.

Nevertheless, with the publication of Neill's *Summerhill* in 1960, Romantic ideas burst into the popular culture.[3] The widely read book was an inspiration to many dissatisfied parents and educators who initiated a wave of Romanticism that eventually became known as the free school movement. This resulted in an explosion in the number of alternative schools across North America, which by 1969 had reached several hundreds. Dozens of books about alternative schooling appeared between 1964 and 1972 by authors such as Paul Goodman, Sylvia Ashton-Warner, John Holt, Herbert Kohl, and Jonathan Kozol.

Much of this educational activity grew out of the political and cultural ferment of the 1960s. People were excited by the influential ideas generated by the American civil rights and peace movements, the counter-culture, and the Human Potential Movement. The goals of these movements were social justice, creative expression, and transformation, but above all an emphasis on personal freedom. A more humanistic and participatory education, for children and parents, was a natural extension of 1960s ideals.

ALTERNATIVE SCHOOLS IN CANADA

In Canada, American Progressivism, English Romanticism, and the American counter-culture combined with the rich Canadian traditions of social democracy and the social gospel movement[4] to produce a made-in-Canada approach to educational change. Child-centered educators and humanitarian reformers, as early as the 1890s, sought to eliminate the traditional nineteenth-century teaching methods that relied on memorization, rote learning, and a narrow curriculum. But unlike in the United States, few private Progressive schools were established with the exception of St. George's School in Montreal founded in 1930.[5] True to their social democratic roots, Canadian educational reformers of the 1920s and 1930s directed their efforts toward the public school system. Curriculum revisions in several provinces endorsed Progressive methods, such as in Alberta where the Department of Education implemented the locally developed "enterprise system" organized around broad themes.

But despite official endorsement by educational leaders, innovative methods rarely found their way into the average Canadian classroom. Historian Neil Sutherland vividly describes the traditional pedagogy that endured in Canadian schools well into the 1960s:

> It was a system that put its rigour into rote learning of the times tables, the spelling words, the capes and bays, a system that discouraged independent thought, a system that provided no opportunity to be creative, a system that blamed rather than praised, a system that made no direct or purposeful effort to build a sense of self-worth.[6]

It was this conservatism and inertia in the public education system that inspired the proponents of alternative schools.

Alternative schools appeared in British Columbia at the beginning of the 1960s. Inspired by a wave of American academics recruited to the University of British Columbia during the 1950s and early 1960s, these schools were established by parents and teachers in reaction against the government commissioned Chant report of 1960, which among other things, recommended that less emphasis be placed on the arts in B.C. schools.

The New School in Vancouver was founded by a group of UBC professors in 1962. The school adopted a Progressive curriculum where students followed their interests in an informal atmosphere emphasizing learning by doing, the project method, and the arts. The school was run by a parent co-operative that was involving but often contentious. In the mid-1960s, several other schools were established with a more radical philosophy of complete freedom for children. Some, including the barker free school, Knowplace, and the Saturna Island Free School, were funded by the Company of Young Canadians as were several Ontario free schools.[7] The CYC mandate was that their schools would have an educational component as well as a political or social one. However, the B.C. schools were far enough from CYC headquarters in Ottawa that they were able to carry on unsupervised with a minimal educational program.[8]

The alternative schools movement spread to other provinces in the late 1960s and early 1970s. The Greenhouse School in Regina and the Saturday School in Calgary were founded by parents dissatisfied with their neighborhood public schools.[9] The parents were heavily involved in school governance, typical in alternative schools, and there was frequent tension between those who wanted more freedom and others who wanted more structure.[10]

PRIVATE ALTERNATIVE SCHOOLS IN ONTARIO

The alternative school movement was so prolific that in 1973 a directory of Canadian alternative schools listed 41—over half of which were in Ontario.[11] Ontario, and particularly Toronto, offered fertile ground for alternative schools due to its diverse population, the presence of many young Americans escaping the Vietnam war, and a burgeoning counterculture. Alternative approaches to education were an integral part of the transformational aspirations of 1960s culture.[12]

Early 1960s Progressive schools in Toronto included the January School and the Toronto French School. The Toronto Montessori School began in 1961 with 12 students in a Don Mills basement and by the late 1960s had an enrollment of over 300 elementary aged students housed in a former public school building in Thornhill.[13] The Toronto Waldorf School opened a pre-school in 1965 expanding to an elementary school in 1968.[14]

Everdale Place

The alternative schools movement in Ontario began in earnest with the founding of Everdale Place, the province's first free school and the best known alternative school in Canada. Located on a farm near Hillsburgh

50 miles northwest of Toronto, Everdale was founded by Bob Davis and Alan Rimmer in 1966 and based roughly on the principles of Summerhill.

Bob Davis grew up in Quebec City and Halifax where his father was an Anglican minister. At Dalhousie University, influenced by philosopher George Grant, he was involved in activist organizations including the Combined Universities Campaign for Nuclear Disarmament (CUCND), the Student Union for Peace Action (SUPA), and the Student Christian Movement (SCM). "My political interests started in the sixties. So I was a New Leftie."[15] After 2 years studying at Cambridge in England, Mr. Davis taught high school in Toronto for 4 years. He objected to the mass size of the school, minimal input from students, the absence of choice, and lack of interest in the students' own views of the world.

Alan Rimmer was born in Manchester, England, and immigrated to Canada as a teenager. He was active in the New Democratic Party and involved in the Student Christian Movement, serving as national secretary for a year.[16] He spent several frustrating years teaching high school science in Newfoundland, British Columbia, and Toronto, resigning in 1965 having found mainstream schools too rigid in their teaching methods.

What would become the core of the Everdale community began in 1962 when Bob Davis and Alan Rimmer met and moved into a co-operative house in Toronto with a group of politically like-minded friends.[17] In 1965, at a meeting on educational change, some members of the household proposed the formation of a free school and a radical educational magazine to begin the following year. Mr. Davis resigned from his teaching job and worked as a staff member at Warrendale, a treatment center for disturbed teenagers, which developed his insight into the emotional lives of teenagers. Meanwhile, Mr. Rimmer and his wife, Eleanor, moved to Hillsburgh and bought a farm, on behalf of the school group.[18]

Everdale opened in September 1966 with five teachers and 16 high school students on the 100 acre farm. Other staff members were Jim Deacove, Ruth Deacove, Gail Ashby, and Eleanor Rimmer.[19] Most Everdale staff were Canadian, unlike in B.C. where most alternative school staff came from the United States. The school was advertised as a place "where children learn what they're ready for in an environment they help to create."[20] Most of the students came from Toronto middle-class families and had become alienated from mainstream schools. In 1967, the school expanded to 25 students and eight staff, as well as a nursery school for local children. By the beginning of its third year,

Everdale had grown to 11 staff and 37 students. The school added two new buildings to accommodate the increased enrollment and an elementary program.[21]

Everdale was based on the principle of student choice and, as at Summerhill, attendance at classes was voluntary. Although a full slate of courses was offered in English, Mathematics, History, Science, Geography, French, Music, Art, and Drama, only a few students showed sustained interest. Students could write government examinations and attempt to graduate but few did. The low attendance was enormously disappointing to some staff members who worked hard to prepare interesting classes. Despite this, occasional visitors reported observing students learning. "One 9 year old boy spent the day doing chemistry experiments, while a 15 year old was designing and building an intercom system for the school from old radio receivers," reported one.[22] Another visited a class in which three Grade 11 students were arguing about what was work and what was play in Plato's *Republic*.[23] Several staff taught classes which students recall as memorable, but most courses had small enrollments and were short-lived.[24] Music was a central activity, much of it generated by the students themselves.

There were only two compulsory activities at Everdale. Everyone had to participate in the weekly meetings, and everyone had to do chores.[25] The meetings were held to set school policy and discuss concerns, but increasingly an important function was interpersonal—mutual therapy, group dynamics, and simply letting off steam. Though sometimes tedious and time-consuming, the meetings were an important component of the Everdale experience. The goal in decision making was to achieve consensus and meetings could be frustrating, exasperating, soothing, hilarious, or at times deadly dull.[26] Technically, everyone was equal at meetings but the more charismatic staff members, along with one or two students, had more than their share of influence.

One unique aspect of school governance was that applications to attend the school were dealt with by a small committee of staff and students. Students constituted a majority of the committee's membership, an expression of Everdale's philosophy. Staff were chosen in a similar manner although staffing often depended simply on "who you have."[27]

The farm and rural environment were important aspects of day-to-day life at Everdale. Some students loved gardening or caring for the animals while others found their niche helping to prepare the large communal meals. The field trip program was also unique for that time and strongly political. Bob Davis regularly took groups of students to Toronto to observe trials at the courthouse. Some groups went farther afield to Quebec City and, in a much-publicized trip, to Milwaukee to witness the trial of several American anti-war dissidents.[28]

Most staff members at Everdale received minimal salaries of $150 to $180 per month from the Company of Young Canadians.[29] This allowed the school to keep fees relatively low from $1,000 annually in the first year to $1,350 in the third year.[30] However, in 1969, the CYC salaries ended and the school suffered financially. The school developed a cottage industry, the production of wooden toy trucks for children, under the supervision of teacher John Callender. The sale of these toys provided extra income and could have helped stave off bankruptcy had more students been committed to working in the shop.

As in many alternative schools, structure, or lack thereof, became a point of conflict at Everdale. Alan Rimmer became increasingly opposed to the unstructured nature of the school, and left in 1969. As the years progressed, less educational activity took place at Everdale. By 1971, financial instability, unwanted visitors, increased drug use, and exhaustion had taken its toll. Although the school continued to exist until 1973, it had largely become a rural commune. From the late 1990s to the present, the property has been run by a not-for-profit society operating an educational organic farm.[31]

Although a few Everdale students went on to university, most did not complete high school. Some pursued careers in art, film, and music. A number of students regret that their options were somewhat limited by the lack of a diploma, but suggest that they probably would have dropped out of school anyway and that Everdale provided a safer teenage environment than the streets of Yorkville.[32] Students recall Everdale as a place where they were recognized and expressed themselves as individuals, tried out new ideas, met a wide variety of people, learned to live as part of a community, and believed that if they wanted to do something they could.[33] As one former teacher said, the school provided "a greater sense of the reality of how people get along together."[34]

Although Everdale was the product of the combined efforts and ideas of a group of committed people, Bob Davis was ultimately its driving force. One student leader at the University of Waterloo, who had organized a presentation by Everdale staff and students, recalls: "I remember him being larger than life – a huge amount of energy and charisma."[35]

Superschool, Point Blank, and This Magazine

Superschool began with a series of meetings in Connie Mungall's Toronto living room in June, 1968.[36] In attendance were Ms. Mungall, her two children, several teenagers unhappy with the way they were being taught at their high schools, and some parents of younger children critical of the public school system. The meetings were led by the teenagers themselves.[37]

The result was Superschool, which opened that September with 28 students in a large old house in downtown Toronto.[38] Half of these were teenagers, some of whom had dropped out of public schools, while the others were elementary-age children. Among the teachers were Ms. Mungall, Gail Ashby who had taught for 2 years at Everdale, and John Ashby.[39] Eleven students stayed at the school while others commuted. Fees were low, $1000 per year for residential students and $400 for commuters, so that the school would be accessible to average families. But the low tuition fee also kept the school in financial difficulty, and by December, it was running a $5,000 deficit even though enrollment had grown to 35 students.

Superschool, like Everdale, was based on the Summerhillian principle that students were free to study what they liked at their own pace, or not to study at all. Like most urban alternative schools, Superschool made use of community resources visiting museums, the library, the docks, and the Planetarium. Decisions about school policy were made at weekly meetings at which both teachers and students had a vote. One student described the curriculum to a Toronto Star reporter:

> We're talking about Greek civilization. We don't just learn about the conquests of Alexander the Great. We talk about Greek culture and how it affects us today. I've also started writing—something I never enjoyed before—a story about the Warsaw Ghetto. At Superschool you are free to write when you want to write, read when you want to read, and do things in your own style.[40]

Point Blank School, another private alternative in downtown Toronto, was the creation of George Martell, a noted educational activist, writer, and sociology professor, and a group of teenagers he met while working at a local neighborhood house. He grew up in Halifax, came to Toronto as a CBC producer, and later became a Company of Young Canadians staff person. But he continued to volunteer and hang out with the teenagers from the neighborhood house. Most of these kids had dropped out of school and were part of a loose neighborhood gang. They had next to no education and could barely read and write. Inspired by Sylvia Ashton-Warner's approach to literacy described in her book *Teacher*,[41] Mr. Martell started an informal school in his basement with about seven kids. He recalls, "I often taught them to read and write by sitting across a typewriter from them and have them talk to me. I'd make it like a poem and then I'd hand it back to them and say, 'you can read that, can't you?' And they could because they just said it."[42] Some kids covered six grades of reading in a year.

Over the next 2 years, the school grew to about 15 regular teenage participants and moved to a small house in Toronto's Cabbagetown neighborhood. Most of the newcomers were local, but a few others came because their parents philosophically supported what the school was doing. Later a "little kids' school" for ages five to ten emerged when a larger house was purchased by Mr. Martell and his wife Satu Repo along with John and Carolyn Barber, all of whom played a large role in the school. The two families lived on the upper floors while the school occupied the ground floor and basement. By this time, Mr. Martell was teaching evening courses in sociology at York University, so he often taught the teens between 11:00 p.m. and 2:00 in the morning—"a good time," he says, "because the kids were awake then." In the meantime, the elementary school continued to attract children from the neighborhood. As with Everdale, Point Blank received support from the Company of Young Canadians in the form of staff salaries. The school continued to operate for several years until the young people were into their 20s.[43]

This Magazine Is About Schools was a quarterly journal devoted to radical education and politics edited by Bob Davis, Satu Repo, and George Martell, first published in 1966. Sarah Spinks, Gail Ashby, and others provided artwork, design, layout, and management. The magazine grew in parallel with Everdale, Superschool, and Point Blank as there were overlapping staff, philosophy, and friendships. The magazine therefore helped to raise the schools' profile. With a peak of over 10,000 subscriptions[44], the magazine's success wildly exceeded the expectations of its founders and was so popular that Random House published an anthology of its articles edited by Satu Repo in 1970.[45]

This Magazine was well-known and often cited across North America and helped make Toronto a vibrant center of the continent-wide alternative schools movement. The magazine functioned like a typical 1960s collective with passionate involvement, long discussions, and decisions by consensus. It dealt with far more than Toronto issues, addressing wider educational and political struggles. Partly because of the success of the magazine, Everdale organized an Alternative Schools Festival at the University of Toronto in May 1970 that attracted over 1000 participants from across North America. Speakers included John Holt, Edgar Friedenberg, and Everett Reimer, all well-known critics of the education system.[46]

Other Ontario Schools

The Ottawa New School was founded in 1969 by a group of professional and academic parents concerned about the rigidity of the public school system. The school opened with 18 elementary children and two teachers, one trained in Progressive methods in England and the other an American draft resister. Children chose their activities and, according to newspaper accounts, the children were busy and happy. The school was governed by parents, and tuition fees were low due to subsidies from two families. Like some other alternative schools, the New School split during its second year over how much freedom the children should have and how much structure the school should provide. Half of the parents left, and the school closed in 1972. Some hoped that the public school board would take the school in but, unlike in Toronto, there was not enough political support at the board level.[47] Two other Ontario alternative schools were Fairchild Free School started in 1970 where high school students were taught by volunteers on a farm near Paris, Ontario, and Cool School in Hamilton, founded in 1971 for bright students with drug problems.[48]

More Toronto private alternative schools appeared between 1969 and 1973 including Laneway, a parent-run school in a low-income neighborhood, Hawthorne Bilingual, a French-English bilingual school, and Inglenook, a community school where students spent 1 day per week out in the community. All experienced financial difficulty but instead of closing were taken in by the Toronto public school system.

POLITICAL AND EDUCATIONAL REFORM

The spirit of the 1960s sparked the ideas of change in Ontario society and in the provincial Ministry of Education.[49] The numerous critiques of the traditional school system written by educational reformers and the examples of experimental schools springing up in Ontario and across North America filled the air with new possibilities. The Education Ministry under the leadership of Minister Bill Davis embarked on an ambitious program of reform.

If there was any doubt that change was in the air, it was dispelled by the publication in 1968 of *Living and Learning: The Report of the Provincial Committee on Aims and Objectives of Education*. Authored by Justice Emmett Hall and Lloyd Dennis, an elementary school principal, the report shook the educational establishment by recommending massive changes to the traditional school system.

Living and Learning was essentially a Progressive document informed by the ideas and values of the 1960s. It advocated child-centered education and touched all Progressive bases including the needs and interests of the learner, a shift in emphasis from content to experience, the creative nature of the learning process through discovery, exploration, and inquiry, a more humane approach to discipline, and the elimination of lock-step systems of organizing students in favor of continuous progress and individualized learning.[50] Reaction was highly favorable among the public and in the press.[51] Lloyd Dennis received dozens of requests for speaking engagements, and *Living and Learning* sold over 60,000 copies within 4 months.[52]

The desire for educational reform also existed at the municipal level, inspired by 1960s political activists. In 1968, a group of parents from a public housing development, assisted by community organizers, presented a brief to the Toronto Board of Education. The group came to be known as the Trefann Court Mothers and their brief was entitled *Downtown Kids Aren't Dumb*. In it, they argued that the educational system was failing their children through unfairly streaming them into special needs and vocational classes that became an academic dead end. The parents wanted a curriculum that would engage and educate their children while recognizing their existing skills and knowledge.[53]

The timing was right. Just over a year later in 1969, a slate of reform trustees won the control of the Toronto Board of Education. Fiona Nelson, who later became chair of the Board in 1974, was active in reform issues over an extended career and was particularly supportive of Toronto's nascent alternative programs. Gordon Cressey was also elected in 1969 and became chair in 1975. Other reform trustees were George Martell of Point Blank School and *This Magazine*, Dan Leckie who became chair in 1977, Bob Spencer, and Doug Barr.[54]

The reformers' agenda included more support for inner city schools, a focus on equal opportunity to mitigate the effects of poverty on education, and an attempt to limit the power of school board administrators. Support for alternative schooling was a key component of the reformers' agenda to provide more choice to students who did not flourish in traditional school settings.[55] The development of alternative schools also fit with other reformist objectives including parent involvement and community building.

SEED

The creation of SEED, the first public alternative school in the Toronto School District, was a bold step toward what would become a vibrant offering of alternatives. The acronym stood for "Shared Experience, Exploration, and Discovery," and the program began in July 1968. It grew out of Fiona Nelson's concern that thousands of teenagers would be unemployed during the summer and aimlessly roaming the streets. The result was SEED, which was coordinated by teacher Murray Shukyn, administered by Les Birmingham, and run out of the school board's Education Centre building.[56] Mr. Shukyn relied on his experience as director of a lively summer camp and SEED offered a wide choice of activities, field trips, and informal discussions. The program attracted over 600 students.[57]

SEED was so successful that, at the request of many students, it continued in September as an after-school activity. Offered again as a summer program in 1969, it inspired a group of students, teachers, and volunteers to propose to the Board of Education that SEED be "established as an experimental alternative to the regular secondary school program."[58] It opened as a full-time alternative school in September 1970 with 100 students selected by lottery. The location, in the Young Men's Hebrew Association building at Bloor Street and Spadina Avenue, was ideal—central, on a major subway line, and close to the University of Toronto and the offices of many volunteers.[59]

Three core principles made SEED unique and successful. First, it was aimed at motivated students who had been bored in mainstream schools but were self-starters who could take responsibility for their education. Resource volunteers or "catalysts" from a variety of professions would provide the teaching, in a style consistent with Progressive ideas.[60] Students would "go out into the community, find a person who actually did what we wanted to study, and bring them into teach small groups."[61]

Second, the basic academic subjects were covered. SEED's founders wanted to avoid the pitfalls of 1960s free schools where too much freedom left students without a basic education.[62] The school district assigned four teachers to supervise instruction in English, Mathematics, Science, and languages, and collaborate with students in designing individual programs that would enable them to graduate.

Third, SEED utilized the resources of the urban community. In 1970-1971, over 60 non-credit courses were taught by volunteers including astrology, genetics, psychotherapy, Chinese, Sanskrit, pharmacology, science fiction, stereo amplifiers, graphology, computer construction and programming, yoga, and the occult.[63] One notable course in filmmaking, organized by a group of nine students, was so successful that their short film, *Life Times Nine*, was nominated for an Academy Award in 1973.[64] During a course on architecture, students became aware of the opposition to the proposed Spadina Expressway and met famed urban planner Jane Jacobs, a memorable experience.[65]

TORONTO PUBLIC ALTERNATIVE SCHOOLS

The success of SEED laid the groundwork for the rapid development in the early 1970s of alternative schools within the Toronto public school system, driven by parents, teachers, students, and the wider community. Although these schools were diverse, they shared certain characteristics including community input, Progressive pedagogy, and resourcefulness.[66]

In the fall of 1971, a group of parents submitted a brief to the Management Committee of the Toronto Board of Education proposing an alternative elementary school. Called ALPHA, the school would accommodate a variety of learning styles and promote community involvement in running the school. But for parents the involvement was challenging. They opposed traditional education, but when it came to hammering out policy on curriculum, teaching methods, and discipline there were strong disagreements.[67] This was typical of alternative schools as parents usually agreed on what they were against but not what they were for. ALPHA opened in September, 1972 and, after some initial volatility, enrollment stabilized at 65 students and two teachers.

Other schools were created at the instigation of teachers. In the spring of 1972, a group of secondary teachers led by Harry Smaller and OISE graduate students approached the Alternatives in Education Committee concerned about the increasing number of students leaving high school.[68] They thought that the practice of diverting potential dropouts into vocational programs was outdated and that some students might benefit from individually designed courses taught in small informal groups. CONTACT opened in September 1972 as a night school and became a full-time day school the next year. Students consisted of unemployed youth who had left school, as well as students identified by teachers and counselors as at risk of dropping out which was signaled by sporadic attendance. CONTACT was an immediate success with an enrollment of 100 students in 1973.

Subway Academy joined the family of Toronto alternative schools in 1973. Subway was unique in that, unlike SEED or ALPHA, the idea originated in the Board office. Administrators realized that due to the changing values and community expectations, the school district had to offer a wider range of program choice to retain public support. Subway opened in September 1973, emphasizing independent study, learning contracts, and shared decision making. Its use of community resources drew inspiration from John Bremer's pioneer Parkway Programme in Philadelphia. A requirement for the location of the school was proximity to a major subway line for access to urban activities, hence the school's name. Subway opened with 52 students and several teacher facilitators.

Laneway School began as a private alternative school in 1969 in the aftermath of the Trefann Court Mothers' brief to the Board. Enrollment was small, with 15 students and one teacher, and parents were closely involved. The school's primary objective was to teach basic skills of reading, writing, and arithmetic. Although Laneway was very unstructured in its first year, parents came to believe that a more structured but individualized program was preferable. Laneway became incorporated into the Toronto Board of Education in 1972 and, importantly, was the first private alternative school to do so.

The factors that gave rise to alternative schools in the Toronto School District also influenced other Toronto area school districts to develop alternatives in the early 1970s. These included Alternative and Independent Study Program (AISP) and Multi-Age Grouping Unit (MAGU) in North York, Alternative Scarborough Education (ASE) and Scarborough Village Bilingual in Scarborough, and School of Experiential Education (SEE) in Etobicoke.[69]

By 1973, there were five alternative schools in the Toronto education system. Each had a distinct genesis, but most were community initiated rather than created by administrators.[70] SEED was driven by students,[71]

ALPHA was developed by parents, CONTACT was conceived by teachers, Laneway was an existing private school adopted by the Board of Education, and Subway originated out of the Board office itself. This process was supervised by the Alternative and Community Programs Committee to which groups of parents, teachers, or students were welcome to make proposals. The Committee was chaired by senior administrator Dale Shuttleworth, who was a strong supporter of alternatives as providers of student and parental choice and as vehicles for community development.[72] Having an effective supporter inside the system was a big help to community activists advocating for change.

Conclusion

Much had changed between the mid-1960s and mid-1970s by which time the initial private experiments in alternative education had given way to the public alternative schools in the Toronto school district. During those few years, the Toronto experience with publicly run alternative schools was unique, and resulted in an impressive infrastructure of diverse schools permeating the city. Community activists wanted schools that encouraged parental involvement, that were centers for political change, and that celebrated Toronto's culturally diverse population and neighborhoods. Drawing on the Progressive educational tradition, they were committed to the principle of choice in education—for students, parents, and teachers. The Board leadership recognized the need to accommodate these expectations in the community, which grew out of the political ideals and optimism of the 1960s. The end result was a combination of the efforts of two groups. The Romantic visionaries who created the 1960s experimental schools brought the possibility of educational change to public awareness, and a few years later political activists realized those innovative ideas in the public realm.

Acknowledgements I would like to thank Helena Wehrstein and Wally Seccombe for providing me with access to the valuable Everdale archive containing enrollment and staff lists, school brochures, school newsletters, films, personal documents, and unpublished papers such as "How Everdale and Superschool began."

I would also like to thank Meredith MacFarquhar, long-time partner of the late Bob Davis, for generous access to documents and journals from her personal library, for her gracious hospitality in convening a memorable evening with former Everdale students, and for her encouragement.

I would also like to thank the following individuals who gave generously of their time and knowledge in personal interviews: Bob Davis, Alan Rimmer, George Martell, Satu Repo, Gail Ashby, Jim Deacove, Vera Williams, Brian Iler, Sarah Spinks, Diana Meredith, Patricia Berton, Rico Gerussi, Ruth Shamai, Heather Chetwynd, Naomi McCormack, Judith McCormack, Dale Shuttleworth, Murray Shukyn, Paul Shapiro, and Fiona Nelson. For bibliographic research assistance, thank you to Kathryn Pybus.

Finally, thank you to the editors of this collection, Esther Fine, Nina Bascia, and Malcolm Levin, for their professional expertise and years of commitment to this important subject.

NOTES

1. This is my term for the long-lived educational movement that began with the publication of J.J. Rousseau's *Emile* in 1762, surfacing periodically throughout the nineteenth and early twentieth centuries and re-surfacing in the 1960s with the publication of A.S. Neill *Summerhill* (1960), and the development of the Free School Movement.
2. Allen Graubard estimates that over 250 free schools were established in the United States between 1967 and 1970. Allen Graubard, *Free the Children* (New York: Random House, 1972), 41 (Graubard 1972).
3. A.S. Neill, *Summerhill: A Radical Approach to Child Rearing* (New York: Hart, 1960) (Neill 1960).
4. For an authoritative account of the Canadian social gospel movement see Richard Allen, *The Social Passion: Religion and Social Reform in Canada, 1914–28* (Toronto: University of Toronto Press, 1973) (Allen 1973).
5. The basic tenet of St. George's School was "Progressive not permissive." Sharon Kirsh, Roger Simon, and Malcolm Levin, eds., *Directory of Canadian Alternative and Innovative Education* (Toronto: Communitas Exchange, 1973) (Kirsh et al. 1973).
6. Neil Sutherland, "The Triumph of 'Formalism': Elementary Schooling in Vancouver from the 1920s to the 1960s," in *Vancouver Past: Essays in Social History, BC Studies*, ed. R. McDonald and Jean Barman, Number 69–70 (Spring/Summer 1986), 182–183 (Sutherland 1986).
7. Ian Hamilton, *The Children's Crusade* (Toronto: Peter Martin, 1970), Chap. 9 (Hamilton 1970).

8. For more on British Columbia alternative schools, see Harley Rothstein, "Alternative Schools in British Columbia: 1960–1975" (Ph.D. Dissertation, University of British Columbia, 1999). The dates of the B.C. schools were: The New School (1962–1977), Barker Free School (1965–1969), Knowplace (1967–1969), and Saturna Island Free School (1968–1971). Bob Davis, co-founder of Everdale, visited the Barker Free School on C.Y.C. business in the mid- to late 1960s (Rothstein 1999).

9. Robert Stamp, *The Saturday School: How It Began* (Calgary: Saturday School Society, 1973), and Robert Stamp, in discussion with the author, April 9, 1997. Robert Stamp also wrote an early definitive work on public alternative schools: Robert Stamp, *About Schools: What every Canadian parent should know* (Don Mills Ontario: new press, 1975). Saturday School became part of the Calgary public school system in 1975 (Stamp 1973, 1975).

10. Freedom versus structure was a common source of friction in alternative schools and was a major issue, as I show later in this chapter, at Everdale Place School.

11. Sharon Kirsh, Roger Simon, and Malcolm Levin, eds., *Directory of Canadian Alternative and Innovative Education* (Toronto: Communitas Exchange, 1973) (Kirsh et al. 1973).

12. Although most educational reform in the early 1960s occurred in private alternative schools, some incremental change was found in the public school system. See Kurt Clausen's article on an open area school in Willowdale, "Educational Reform in Ontario: The Importance of Pleasant Valley School, 1962–1975," *Historical Studies in Education* 26 no. 1 (Spring, 2014): 67 (Clausen 2014).

13. Jocelyn Dingman, "Would You Send Your Child to a New School?," *Chatelaine*, (August, 1968): 68 (Dingman 1968).

14. "New Schools in Canada," *This Magazine is about Schools* 2, no. 3 (Summer 1968).

15. Bob Davis, in discussion with the author, October 18, 1996.

16. Alan Rimmer, in discussion with the author, March 29, 2014.

17. Alan Rimmer, in discussion with the author, March 29, 2014.

18. The farm was referred to locally as "the Everdell place," after the early pioneer owners, which the school founders thought was a catchy name. But early on, someone misspelled it—and "Everdale Place" stuck. Brian Iler, in discussion with the author, April 1, 2014.

19. Other notable staff members were Sara Bezaire, Vera Williams, John Callender, Sandy Callender, Jeffrey Fritzlan, Jane Fritzlan, Phil Hazelton, Lee Hazelton, John Fassell, and Bill Goldfinch.

20. School Prospectus, "The Everdale Place: A School Community," *This Magazine is about Schools* 1, no. 2 (August 1966).

21. "How Everdale and Superschool Began," (unpublished paper, Everdale Place Archive, 1968).
22. David Copp, "The Everdale Place: A School Community," *Pro Tem* student weekly newspaper, York University, undated.
23. Jocelyn Dingman, "Would You Send Your Child to a New School?" *Chatelaine*, (August 1968): 66 (Dingman 1968).
24. Patricia Berton, Rico Gerussi, Naomi McCormack, Diana Meredith, Ruth Shamai, and Heather Chetwynd (former Everdale students) in discussion with the author, March 28, 2014. Judith McCormack, telephone interview by author, May 14, 2014.
25. Bob Davis, personal interview by author, October 18, 1996.
26. Patricia Berton, Rico Gerussi, Naomi McCormack, Diana Meredith, Ruth Shamai, and Heather Chetwynd (former Everdale students) in discussion with the author, March 28, 2014. Judith McCormack, telephone interview by author May 14, 2014.
27. Bob Davis, in discussion with the author, October 18, 1996.
28. Bob Davis, "Where's the School? Everdale at the Milwaukee War Trial," in *What Our High Schools Could Be … A Teacher's Reflections From the 60s to the 90s* 1990, ed. Bob Davis (James Lorimer& Company, July, 1990) (Davis 1990).
29. Jocelyn Dingman, "Would You Send Your Child to a New School?," *Chatelaine*, (August 1968): 66; Del Bell, "Scratch a quiet farm, find a rebel school" *The London Free Press*, (March 11, 1967); "Those no-rule schools are staggering to success," *The Toronto Daily Star*, (April 7, 1969): 7; Timothy Plumptre, "In the company of Young Canadians," *The Globe and Mail*, (January 12, 1967): 7. For more on the CYC, see Ian Hamilton, *The Children's Crusade: The Story of the Company of Young Canadians* (Toronto: Peter Martin Associates, 1970) (Dingman 1968; Bel 1967, 1969; Plumptre 1967; Hamilton 1970).
30. "What Can You Do to Change Schools?" Everdale School Brochure, *This Magazine is about Schools* 3, no. 2 (Spring 1969).
31. Everdale Organic Farm and Environmental Learning Centre in Hillsburgh was founded by Gavin Dandy, Karen Campbell, Wally Seccombe, and Lynn Bishop in 1997 and is governed by an incorporated not-for-profit society. Between 1973 and 1997, several ventures were attempted on the property, but none came to fruition. http://everdale.org/history/.
32. Stuart Henderson documents a degeneration of the Yorkville hippie community by 1968 into drug addiction, disease, sexual predation, violence, and criminal activity, in *Making the Scene: Yorkville and Hip Toronto in the 1960s*, Toronto: University of Toronto Press, 2011.
33. Patricia Berton, Rico Gerussi, Naomi McCormack, Diana Meredith, Ruth Shamai, and Heather Chetwynd (former Everdale students) in discussion

with the author, March 28, 2014. Judith McCormack, telephone interview by author May 14, 2014. Beth Savin, "School Prospectus, 1966/67", School Archive. Patricia Berton, "A Choice in Schools—Free or Traditional?" *Miss Chatelaine*, (August 14, 1969) (Berton 1969).

34. Vera Williams, telephone interview by author, August 13, 2014.

35. Brian Iler, in discussion with the author, April 1, 2014.

36. Constance Mungall, "Superschool: Disgruntled Teens in Search of Something Better," *Toronto Daily Star* (August 17 1968): 10.

37. "What Can You Do to Change Schools?" Everdale School Brochure, *This Magazine is about Schools* 3, no. 2 (Spring 1969).

38. By the following year, enrolment had increased to thirty-three. "Those no-rule schools are staggering to success," *Toronto Daily Star* (April 7, 1969): 7.

39. Gail Ashby, in discussion with author, March 29, 2014. John McGravey also taught at the school reported in "28 students off to Superschool," *The Globe and Mail*, (September 3, 1968): 5.

40. Terry Edwards, "I came to Superschool because I was fed up," *Toronto Daily Star*, (April 7, 1969): 7 (Edwards 1969).

41. Sylvia Ashton-Warner, *Teacher* (New York: Simon and Schuster, 1963) (Ashton-Warner 1963).

42. George Martell, telephone interview by author, April 14, 1997.

43. George Martell, telephone interview by author, April 14, 1997.

44. Satu Repo, in discussion with author, March 25, 2014.

45. Satu Repo, ed., *This Book is About Schools* (New York: Random House, 1970) (Repo 1970).

46. William Johnson, "Festival of Alternatives in Education: 1,000 youths 'bury' the contemporary school system," *The Globe and Mail* (May 9 1970): 5 (Johnson 1970).

47. Deborah Gorham, "The Ottawa New School and Educational Dissent in Ontario in the Hall-Dennis Era," *Historical Studies in Education* 21, no. 2 (Fall, 2009). Another school with more structure was formed by some of the remaining parents (Gorham 2009).

48. James Anderson and Ted Ridley, *Cool School: An Alternative Secondary School Experience* (Toronto: Ontario Ministry of Education, 1977). Original funding for Cool School came from a local hospital and an Opportunities for Youth grant in 1971. For Fairchild School, see Kirsh, Simon, and Levin, *Directory of Canadian Alternative and Innovative Education*, op. cit. (Anderson and Ridley 1977).

49. Malcolm Levin and Olga Dimitri refer to the "spirit of the sixties" as a motivating force in the establishment of alternative schools in Levin and Dimitri, "SEED Alumni Survey," 1980 (Levin and Dimitri 1980).

50. Robert Stamp, *The Schools of Ontario* (Toronto: University of Toronto Press, 1982), 217–218 (Stamp 1982).
51. Some educators opposed the government's reform initiatives believing that the Hall–Dennis Report went too far. There were also critiques on the left. For example, *This Magazine* argued that the report's Progressivism ignored the social class and racial discrimination of the schools reflected in the Trefann Mother's brief. The magazine was also critical of the Davis plan to centralize the school system. George Martell, e-mail message to author, March 16, 2016.
52. Robert Stamp, *The Schools of Ontario* (Toronto: University of Toronto Press, 1982): 219 (Stamp 1982).
53. Jane Gaskell and Ben Levin, *Making A Difference in Urban Schools: Ideas, Politics, and Pedagogy* (Toronto: University of Toronto Press, 2012): 74 (Gaskell and Levin 2012).
54. Ibid., 74–75. Other reform trustees were Doc Yip, Sheila Meagher, Penny Moss, and Pat Case. Reform trustees in the North York school district included Mel Shipman and Mae Waese.
55. Fiona Nelson made an eloquent case for alternative and community schools in her article, "Community Schools in Toronto: A Sign of Hope," *Canadian Forum* (October/November 1972): 52–57 (Nelson 1972).
56. Dale Shuttleworth, *Schooling for Life: Community Education and Social Enterprise* (Toronto: University of Toronto Press, 2010): 152 (Shuttleworth 2010).
57. Murray Shukyn, personal interview by author, March 26, 2014.
58. Dale Shuttleworth, *Schooling for Life: Community Education and Social Enterprise* (Toronto: University of Toronto Press, 2010): 152 (Shuttleworth 2010).
59. See note 58 above.
60. Among the volunteer catalysts during the first year were university professors, other professionals, and social activists such as June Callwood.
61. Paul Shapiro (former student) personal interview by author, May 14, 2014.
62. Murray Shukyn, "Shared Experience, Exploration, and Discovery," *NASSP Bulletin* 55, 355 (May 1971): 151 (Shukyn 1971).
63. Douglas Yip, *SEED: A Preliminary Report* (Toronto: Board of Education, Research Department, 1971), 8 (Yip 1971).
64. Loren Ruth Lerner, *Canadian Film and Video: A Bibliography and Guide to the Literature* (Toronto: University of Toronto Press, 1997). And Paul Shapiro (former student) personal interview by author, May 14, 2014 (Lerner 1997).

65. Paul Shapiro (former student) personal interview by author, May 14, 2014. The route for the proposed Spadina Expressway went directly past the school.
66. Malcolm Levin, "What's Alternative About Toronto's Alternative Schools?" (September, 1984) (Levin 1984).
67. Dale Shuttleworth, personal interview by author, March 31, 2014 (Shuttleworth 2014).
68. Dale Shuttleworth, *Schooling for Life: Community Education and Social Enterprise* (Toronto: University of Toronto Press, 2010): 157 (Shuttleworth 2010).
69. AISP and SEE were founded in 1971, and ASE in 1974. For more on these Metro Toronto schools, see Elizabeth Durno and Lesley Mang, *Public Alternative Schools in Metro Toronto* (Toronto: Learnxs Press, undated) (Durno and Mang 1978).
70. Dale Shuttleworth, *Schooling for Life: Community Education and Social Enterprise* (Toronto: University of Toronto Press, 2010): 168 (Shuttleworth 2010).
71. According to Fiona Nelson, the major motivating force behind SEED as an ongoing program was the students themselves. Fiona Nelson, personal interview by author, April 1, 2014.
72. Mr. Shuttleworth has written widely about alternative schools and his experience as a school administrator in Toronto (see bibliography) and has contributed a chapter to this collection.

REFERENCES

Allen, Richard. 1973. *The Social Passion: Religion and Social Reform in Canada, 1914–28*. Toronto: University of Toronto Press.

Anderson, James E., and Ted Ridley. 1977. *Cool School: An Alternative Secondary School Experience*. Ontario Ministry of Education.

Ashton-Warner, Sylvia. 1963. *Teacher*. New York: Simon and Schuster.

Bell, Del. 1967. Scratch a Quiet Farm, Find a Rebel School. *The London Free Press*, March 11.

Bell, Del. 1969. Those No-rule Schools are Staggering to Success. *The Toronto Daily Star*, April 7, 7.

Berton, Patricia. 1969, August 14. A Choice in Schools—Free or Traditional? *Miss Chatelaine* 6 (3): 37.

Clausen, Kurt. 2014. Educational Reform in Ontario: The Importance of Pleasant Valley School, 1962–1975. *Historical Studies in Education* 26 (1): 67–88.

Davis, Bob. 1990. *What Our High Schools Could Be…A Teacher's Reflections From the 60s to the 90s*. Toronto: Our Schools/Our Selves.

Dingman, Jocelyn. 1968. Would You Send Your Child to a 'New' School? *Chatelaine*, Aug, 15.

Durno, Elizabeth, and Lesley Mang. 1978. *Public Alternative Schools in Metro Toronto*. Toronto: Learnxs Press.

Edwards, Terry. 1969. I Came to Superschool Because I Was Fed Up. *Toronto Daily Star*, April 7: 7.

Gaskell, Jane, and Ben Levin. 2012. *Making A Difference in Urban Schools: Ideas, Politics, and Pedagogy*, 74. Toronto: University of Toronto Press.

Gorham, Deborah. 2009. The Ottawa New School and Educational Dissent in Ontario in the Hall-Dennis Era. *Historical Studies in Education* 21 (2): 104–122.

Graubard, Allen. 1972. *Free the Children: Radical Reform and the Free School Movement*. New York: Pantheon Books (Random House).

Hamilton, Ian. 1970. *The Children's Crusade: The Story of the Company of Young Canadians*. Toronto: Peter Martin Associates.

Johnson, William. 1970. Festival of Alternatives in Education: 1,000 Youths 'bury' the Contemporary School System. *The Globe and Mail*, May 9: 5.

Kirsh, Sharon, Roger Simon, and Malcolm Levin. 1973. *Directory of Canadian Alternative and Innovative Education*. Toronto: Communitas Exchange.

Levin, Malcolm. 1984. And Now for Something Completely Different: What's 'Alternative' About Toronto's Alternative Schools? *Mudpie* 5 (7).

Levin, Malcolm, and Olga Dimitri. 1980. SEED Alumni Survey. Alternative Schools Follow-Up Project.

Lerner, Loren Ruth. 1997. *Canadian Film and Video: A Bibliography and Guide to the Literature*. Toronto: University of Toronto Press.

A.S. Neill. 1960. *Summerhill: A Radical Approach to Child Rearing*. New York: Hart Publishing.

Nelson, Fiona. 1972. Community Schools in Toronto: A Sign of Hope. *Canadian Forum*, October/November.

Plumptre, Timothy. 1967. In the Company of Young Canadians. *The Globe and Mail*, January 12, 7.

Repo, Satu (ed.). 1970. *This Book Is About Schools*. New York: Random House.

Rothstein, Harley. 1999. Alternative Schools in British Columbia: 1960–1975. Ph.D. Dissertation, University of British Columbia.

Shukyn, Murray. 1971. Shared Experience, Exploration, and Discovery. *NASSP Bulletin* 55 (355): 150–153.

Shuttleworth, Dale E. 2010. *Schooling for Life*. Toronto: University of Toronto Press.

Shuttleworth, Dale E. 2014. Flemington Road—Ontario's Original 'Hub School'. *Journal of Unschooling and Alternative Learning* 8 (16): 13–17.

Stamp, Robert. 1973. *The Saturday School: How It Began*. Calgary: Saturday School Society.

Stamp, Robert. 1975. *About Schools: What every Canadian parent should know*. Toronto: New Press.

Stamp, Robert. 1982. *The Schools of Ontario, 1876–1976*. Toronto: University of Toronto Press.

Sutherland, Neil. 1986. The Triumph of 'Formalism:' Elementary Schooling in Vancouver from the 1920s to the 1960s. In *Vancouver Past: Essays in Social History 1986*, ed. Robert AJ. McDonald and Jean Barman, 69–70 (Spring/Summer). Vancouver: UBC Press.

Yip, Douglas. 1971. *SEED: A Preliminary Report*. Toronto: Research Department, Board of Education for the City of Toronto.

AUTHOR BIOGRAPHY

Harley Rothstein holds a Ph.D. in Educational History from the University of British Columbia, and has done extensive research on alternative schools. His Ph.D. dissertation, *Alternative Schools in British Columbia: 1960–1975*, documents the rise of independent alternative schools during that period and their eventual appearance within the public school system. A former public school teacher, he has also taught and supervised in the U.B.C. Education Faculty. Currently an independent scholar, he has also co-written a book on effective university teaching.

CHAPTER 7

Looking Backward and Forward: Fifty Years of Alternative Schools

Myra Novogrodsky

THE DAYS OF INTOXICATION

In the summer of 1968, my husband and I graduated from an East Coast American university and decided to come to Canada. The Vietnam War was raging and thousands of U.S. resisters had either burned their draft cards or mailed them to Ho Chi Minh in Hanoi. Martin Luther King and Bobby Kennedy had been assassinated, and U.S. cities were burning. I was only 21 and had always dreamed of going west. I told my husband Charles, "I will go with you to Toronto but before we go I want to see the Rocky Mountains. Who knows when we will get the chance again?" Somewhere between Colorado and Utah, Charles decided to try his hand at fishing in an ice-cold stream. The only thing he caught that day was strep throat. We waited out the illness in a small hotel in Salt Lake City, and in that most unlikely of all places, I bought a used copy of A. S. Neill's **Summerhill**. That yellowed, underlined tome still sits on my bookshelf.

M. Novogrodsky (✉)
Toronto, Canada

© The Author(s) 2017   95
N. Bascia et al. (eds.), *Alternative Schooling and Student Engagement*,
DOI 10.1007/978-3-319-54259-1_7

Having received a very good traditional education, I was gob-smacked by **Summerhill**. Imagine a school governed by a general meeting in which each adult and student had a single vote. It was refreshing to think about a school without bells ringing, tension-filled exams, or hours of mind-numbing rote learning. Could there be a school in which play was exalted and fear of adults non-existent? What about a school in which books were less important than tools, sports, clay, theater, and freedom?

A year later, on a cross-country train from Toronto to Vancouver, I read every back issue of **Our Schools, Ourselves**, the groundbreaking education journal edited by Sarah Spinks, George Martell, Satu Repo, and Bob Davis, who was one of the founders of Everdale Place, an independent school outside of Toronto that was heavily influenced by Neill and other progressive educators. How exciting to be living in a city where there was an active group of parents, students, and educators who were opening new independent schools and challenging a lethargic public education system.

That September, I entered the Ontario College of Education, a one-year program to obtain my elementary and secondary school teacher certification. On the first day of class, one of the professors looked around the room of an elementary education class and saw five men and 20 women. His first words were, "I am delighted to see so many men in an elementary education course. You guys play your cards right and you will be vice principals in five years." I raised my hand and pointed to the 20 women in the class and asked, "What about us?" to which he replied, "Sorry girls, that's just the way it is."

And that is just the way it was. Schools were rigid, hierarchical, and controlled by male administrators even though the majority of teachers were women. But the winds of change were blowing across the continent and found many Ontarians ready for significant educational changes. The Hall–Dennis Report of 1968 officially known as **"Living and Learning," the Report of the Provincial Committee on the Aims and Objectives of Education in the Schools of Ontario,** was igniting serious debate about the structure of public education. Influenced by the **U.N. Declaration of the Rights of the Child**, the report called for putting students at the center of learning and called into question the lock step structures of the past. Publications such as **This Magazine** and **Community Schools** (1971–1974) encouraged lively debate about educational issues at a national and local level.

In 1974, I was ecstatic to be hired at SEED, a publicly funded alternative secondary school within the Toronto Board of Education. In many ways, SEED was an urban, non-residential version of Summerhill, but teachers were Board of Education employees and members of their teacher unions. SEED students were called Seedlings, and the school philosophy maintained that learning happened everywhere so it did not matter much whether students were in the physical space of the school or not. When students did come to school, many spent most of their time playing bridge with staff members or merely relaxing in the student lounge. Those who actually did attend classes called those who didn't "lounge lizards."

Given many opportunities for learning but no coercion, some students failed to earn a single high school credit in an academic year at a time when 27 credits plus 6 Grade 13 credits were required for graduation. At that rate, SEED students could theoretically have a 33-year high school trajectory and still not have enough credits for graduation. One of the questions constantly debated at SEED was what, if anything, should be required of students and staff at an alternative school. By the end of my first year, some staff and students wanted it to be a more purposeful school in which academic learning would be valued and encouraged. Some others wanted the school to be more therapeutic, a setting in which students from an overly monolithic and demanding public schools could recover and, without a designated time frame, set their own directions.

Trouble in Paradise

The fissures within the SEED community exploded with the 1975-1976 strike of the Ontario Secondary School Teacher's Federation against the Toronto Board of Education. This fractious nine-week strike in the dead of winter for better wages and working conditions exposed enormous philosophical differences among the members of the community. Of the eight members of the SEED staff, two were completely fed up with both traditional schools and unions. They regarded the federation as an organization that acted solely in the interest of teachers without regard for the needs of students. One of these staff members had himself graduated from a private school and Ivy League university and loathed anything that smacked of class or labor politics. The other was one of the two coordinators of the school who wielded a lot of personal power as he challenged students to defy the strike. These two staff members crossed the picket line daily and encouraged students to come into the school as well. A third staff member did not teach or cross the picket line but refused to participate in the strike. She basically sat it out. The other five staff identified with the union and were sympathetic to teachers' poor working conditions and relatively low wages. The student population was left to either support the teachers who crossed the line, show solidarity with other teachers freezing during a long strike that stretched from November through January, or to be neutral.

As staff, we wore two hats. We were part of the public education system and teacher federation that negotiated our collective agreement. We were also teachers in a non-traditional school and had loyalty to our school community.

The questions generated by the strike included:

1. How can teachers in publicly funded alternative schools serve their school communities and also advocate for system-wide changes to benefit all students, teachers, and staff?
2. How can progressive teachers reconcile the individual-focused philosophy of some alternative schools with the organizational needs of a large public school system?

New Beginnings

The bitterness generated by the strike was palpable, especially in the first year. A low-level ideological war had broken out between the laissez-faire anti-union staff and the pro-union, more actively political staff. Some students tended to align with one faction or the other while others ignored the differences among the adults and focused on themselves.

As the schism widened, some of the SEED staff started to chat about forming a different alternative school. At the same time, a group of parents had started to meet in late 1979. Their children had gone to Spectrum, a successful Grades 7–8 alternative school, and were now feeling restrained and unchallenged in some of the most prestigious secondary schools in the city. These parents were interested in starting a high school for their own children would have both high academic standards and be a small, safe, caring community. Parents were also interested in hiring a young, well-educated and energetic group of teachers.

Three other staff members from SEED were also interested in a new beginning and joined me and the parent community in putting together a framework for a new alternative secondary school.

The five aims of the school as stated in the letter of Intent to the Toronto Board of Education of 13 March 1980 were:

1. To maximize the individuals' achievement in academics, creative arts, and physical fitness.
2. To respect the dignity of the individual.
3. To share a high commitment to integrity and social justice.
4. To experience the importance of community in one's life, and in the life of others.
5. To create a small school community with an atmosphere of openness and security.

It is no. 3 on the above-mentioned list, the commitment to social justice, that most clearly distinguished City School from SEED. Feminism had been openly mocked by some at SEED, including one of the coordinators, who thought the use of the term Ms. was misguided and hilarious and would pronounce the word MSSSSS. At City School, that was a social justice issue.

The lightning speed at which City School was created indicates the enormous support given to alternative schools by the left-leaning Toronto Board of Education. The March 13th proposal was approved by the Board on March 27, a mere two weeks after submission, and the school opened on September 2 with 85 students, five teachers, and a half-time secretary. Many students were children of the founding group of parents, while others came from SEED following four of their teachers.

The summer was a mad rush to find a suitable space for the school. The community was offered space in a west-end elementary school whose population had declined. The location of the school was less than ideal as it was located near the meat-packing district of the city and it was not on the subway line. However, it had a lot of vacant space and City School was given five classrooms in one area of the building. The principal of the elementary school had a big job on his plate as his staff, students, and parents felt they had been invaded by a gaggle of hippies from downtown. There was also a fear that placing a high school in the middle of a senior public school would create issues. Outside of some City students needing repeated warning about not smoking on school property, the fears were unwarranted. Still, sharing space with the host school was tricky, especially since City School required gym and swimming pool time. Negotiations between the school communities often depended on the skill of school administrators. In the first year, I was assigned a classroom that a teacher from the "host" school had taught in for many years and had refused to vacate. With days to go before the opening of school, I had to move his old books aside and tear down out-of-date articles on his "Current Events" bulletin board.

City was considered a *school* from the outset, not a therapeutic community. Since many of the founding parents were professionals or academics, there was no question that City was primarily an academic school but lacked the authoritarian governance and procedures of traditional schools. All staff members were addressed by their first names in an effort to reduce the social distance between adults and students. In fact, I once received a telephone call from my physician who asked for "Mrs. Novogrodsky." A student, answering the phone at lunch hour, did not know who that was and had to ask for the first name. Students were required to do a minimum of 6 credits per year but many did more. All incoming students had interviews where the mandate of the school was explained to them. They were required to sign a contract not only to do a full-time academic program, but also "to attend meetings and participate in the governance of the school by accepting their share of the responsibility."

Similar to Summerhill and SEED, the weekly General Meeting where all issues outside of things mandated in the Education Act or by Toronto Board policy were discussed and debated was a wonderful opportunity for students to learn how to operate in a democratic forum. City was strict about meeting attendance requirements, but that eventually became a sticking point as not all students were interested in long debates about destinations of field trips and things they considered unimportant. Still, this forum, common to many alternative schools, gave students a chance to participate in decision-making. Additionally, City School actively trained students in meeting protocol and there was an expectation that at least once in their time at City School, each student would chair a meeting.

Another idea borrowed from SEED was tapping people with high levels of expertise who were willing to give "catalyst" courses to students in fields where the staff either did not have expertise or were too busy with required courses. Some of the courses were for credit if they met

Ministry guidelines, while others were more experiential. In the first years, a retired Latin teacher taught Latin, a University of Toronto parent and physicist taught physics, and a parent taught economics at 7:30 a.m. before going to his job at a community college. There were courses in ceramics, photography, typing (taught by the secretary), women's self-defense, genetics, computer science, psychology, music, science fiction, and alternative energy sources taught by a staff member of Energy Probe. These courses not only expanded the roster of available offerings, they also provided the opportunities for dozens of members of the outside community to work with eager students and pass on their personal passion for their disciplines and art forms.

A unique feature of City School in the early years was a commitment to offer one course a year that was interdisciplinary. This was extra work for staff, as they often had to spend a lot of time in the summer designing brand new curriculum, but it was an opportunity to model life-long learning. Early disciplinary courses were The Life Cycle, Utopia and Dystopia, The Holocaust, and The Sixties.

The Life Cycle course was particularly poignant, as one of the students had a progressive neurological disorder that was rapidly robbing him of his ability to use his muscles or even to breathe. A beloved member of the community, he was always included in their student lunchtime outings. Fellow students made sure he could get to their neighborhood destinations in his motorized wheelchair. In January, shortly after we had visited a funeral home to talk to the director about modern burial practices and cremation, this student contracted influenza and died. Not only were the students more prepared for death than they otherwise might have been, they took over the organization of the funeral, sang, played their guitars, and prepared a memorial booklet for the family. Almost all of the students participated in the funeral and in the mourning afterward.

In 1982, the City School staff won an Innovative Development grant from the Alternative and Community Programs Committee of the Toronto Board of Education to spend a week in Brookline, Massachusetts, studying a new methodology for teaching about the Holocaust developed by small group of American educators. Facing History and Ourselves, an organization founded in 1976, used the case study of the Holocaust to raise issues about tolerance, obedience, and civic responsibility. All seven City School staff spent a week of their summer vacation at an intensive seminar in order to prepare the interdisciplinary course for the 1982-1983 school year. City School teachers were very impressed with Facing History and Ourselves and the summer seminar, and the following year other Toronto teachers from both an alternative and a mainstream school also took the course. In this way, a project started at an alternative school became an incubator for bringing new educational ideas into mainstream schools. So successful was this ongoing relationship that Facing History now has a Toronto office with four staff and is working in hundreds of Canadian schools.

Field trips were an important part of the learning at City School. In the first year, four staff and about 40 students pedaled to Niagara on the Lake, a distance of about 75 miles, over two days. A senior student with a driver's license drove the support vehicle with tents, food, and cooking and eating utensils. Fortunately, we had good weather and not only saw several plays at the Shaw Festival (which we had all studied) but also cycled through the verdant and fertile areas below the Niagara Escarpment. We had received training in distance cycling from the Ontario Cycle Association, but that did not prevent me from nearly collapsing on the first day. A student with more experience in long-distance cycling gave me water and a granola bar and, reversing the traditional student–teacher role, cheered me on for the last stretch. We also boned up on the rich history of the Niagara peninsula, both its loyalist and its abolitionist traditions. Community was forged at City School both inside and outside the school building—in Quebec speaking French, in Cuba studying the revolution, at outdoor education centers learning orienteering, on hiking, rock climbing, horseback, and ski trips.

By the end of the first year, the strong reputation of the school had made the rounds in student circles. A decision was made to expand the school so that we could also hire teachers with expertise in art, music, and physical education. In September 1981, the number of enrollment was 130 and there was a lengthy waiting list. While we were staffed for 120 students, we accepted an extra 10 students, knowing that some students would not be a good fit with the school despite admission procedures, which included interviews with prospective students. That way, if we lost 10 students at the end of the first semester, our staffing would correspond to the agreed-upon student–teacher ratio negotiated by the union with the Board of Education.

Expanding the enrollment also decreased the intimacy of the school, but that seemed a small price to pay for our initial success. In the first heady years of the school, the wind was at our back and the program was working for most of the adults and students.

When staff vacancies occurred, there were often many applicants for the positions and a hiring committee was established with representation from Board administration, parents, staff, and students. There were times when surplus staff from other schools were "bumped" into City. A few did not buy into the philosophy of the school. Most of these teachers transferred after a year, but while they were there, they caused others to have extra heavy loads.

Not only did City School students and teachers travel through the city to films, museums, archives, and other destinations, we also invited the outside world into City School with the establishment of the Speaker's Lunch on Wednesdays. One of the invited guests was the Associate Director of Education Don Rutledge, who had a passion for poetry. We wanted his continued support for the school and invited him to this voluntary hour, and the small crowd was wowed by his love of poetry and his incredible memory for poems he loved and recited. One City School student who was having social difficulties sat under her desk instead of at her desk eating her lunch. She often took to the floor when she was uncomfortable, and everyone let her be. About halfway through his presentation, this student started to recite poetry along with the Associate Director. The two loved and had learned many of the same poems. Afterward, he commented that in traditional schools she would have been in the principal's office. Here, she recited poetry. How happy he was to be an administrator in a system that recognized and appreciated difference.

One day, this same student was on the floor in my history class when a prospective student came in with his mother. The two visitors were surveying schools for the next year. About 15 min into the class, the mother could not stand it, and blurted out, "One of your students is sitting on the floor." "Yes," I replied. "She is comfortable there and is learning. Is there a problem?" The mother couldn't take it, and she pulled her son out of the room and the school. Clearly, City School was not for everyone. But it was a wonderful place for the girl on the floor who later went on to win honorable mention in the Grand Theatre's Young Playwrights Competition and became a professional journalist.

One dilemma City School encountered was the lack of racial and ethnocultural diversity within the school community. Students returned from a four-day residential race relations camp with increased awareness of the low percentage of visible minority students at the school compared to the high percentage living in the city. Strategies to increase the number of immigrant and visible minority students, including advertising the school in particular geographic communities, were only partially successful. Most visible minority students who did come were the children of successful professionals who believed in the philosophy of the school. Many immigrant parents did not think that a less authoritarian methodology would produce good academic results. Perhaps the huge sign over the front door of the school which said CITY SCHOOL— NUCLEAR WEAPONS FREE ZONE was a turnoff for some. Since we had no English as a Second Language (ESL) capacity at the school, our ability was diminished to attract many recent immigrant students. Others wanted to go to larger schools with their sports teams, bands, orchestras, and other enticements which small schools could not offer. However, there was one newcomer community attracted to the school. For several years, City had a high number of the children of Chilean refugees who came to Canada to escape the murderous regime of Augusto Pinochet. A City staff member originally from Chile increased their comfort level in the school.

After the euphoria of City School's first few years, adjustments had to be made. Not everyone shared the founders' passion for the school. Some came because semestering worked for them. Others heard about the fine reputation of the staff but did not care about the decision-making process. Some students wanted parents out of their hair and resented their involvement in the school community. Some of the original staff were burnt out working in such an intense community and left to attend graduate school or to teach in other schools. Replacing staff became a crucial challenge. Faculties of education at the time rarely placed student-teachers in alternative schools and did not offer courses on alternative education. Placing the "wrong person" in an alternative school which has a small staff can be disastrous. One teacher was placed at City School for a year after a minor case of misallocating funds at his home school, a year of purgatory where he was very uncomfortable being called by his first name.

As I left City School for a position coordinating Women's and Labor Studies programs for the Toronto Board of Education, I had these questions:

1. How can founding teachers transmit to newer teachers, who were not part of the creation of the school their passion for the community?
2. How can alternative schools work in concert with other schools sharing the same building to create a safe space for all?

3. How does parent involvement in alternative schools differ depending on the age of the students? What is an effective level of participation of parents of secondary school students?
4. How can alternative schools appeal to a broader range of students and parents?
5. How can alternative school teachers find opportunities to work with other teachers in their discipline in order to stay current with resources and practices?

GOING FORWARD

Writing this chapter brings me back to the days of SEED in the late 1970s and the question posed earlier about the relationship between the excessively individual-focused philosophy of some alternative schools and the collective well-being of the public. Recently, several alternative elementary schools in Toronto received negative media attention because of the low rate of students, in one case less than 50 percent, who were vaccinated. Public health officials sounded an alarm bell, warning that at least 95 percent of the population needs to be inoculated to prevent the resurgence of diseases such as measles. Although the question of compulsory vaccination is complicated, it is not entirely surprising that a large percentage of unvaccinated children are students at alternative schools given the libertarian philosophies of some of the schools. Going forward, supporters of alternative schools need to revisit the question of where to draw the line between individual preference and collective good. As always, there will be as many answers to this question as there are alternative schools.

I was blessed to have had the opportunity to work in two Toronto alternative high schools for 12 years and to help found one of them. One of my sons attended a grades 7–8 alternative school where he learned to think outside the box. Now, I look at my five grandchildren and wonder which of them might benefit from this experience.

With the amalgamation of six school districts into one mega-district in 1998, and with fewer supportive elected trustees, alternative schools had to struggle to protect these small gems. With organization and hard work, not only did most of the existing schools survive, but a few more were created. Notwithstanding philosophical differences among schools, what is unique about Toronto is the number of people who believe students are entitled to a broad menu of learning options. The oldest alternative schools in Toronto will soon be celebrating their 50th birthdays. Their legacy is worth celebrating.

Author Biography

Myra Novogrodsky B.A., B.Ed., M.Ed., was a teacher for 12 years in two alternative schools and a founder of City School in Toronto. She served as Assistant Coordinator of Social Studies and as Coordinator of the Equity Studies Center, Toronto Board of Education. She worked as a course director at the York University Faculty of Education. After her retirement, she volunteers time to non-profit organizations with an education and social justice focus such as Facing History and Ourselves and Amistad Canada.

CHAPTER 8

From the Release of the Hall–Dennis Report to the Founding of Alpha II Alternative School—My Personal Journey

Carol Nash

Alpha II Alternative is a grades 7–12 Toronto District School Board alternative school. Founded over the 2006–2007 school year by nine ALPHA Alternative School parents, learning is self-directed in a community based on consensus, where every person participates in making school-wide decisions. There are no grades, no marks, and no report cards. Application for post-secondary education is based on a student portfolio. In any year, there are approximately 75 students, and 1.5 elementary and 3 secondary teachers. Parents and others act as additional mentors to students in their areas of interest. The school, conveniently located in Bloor Collegiate across from the Dufferin subway station, serves young people throughout southern Ontario. This chapter focuses on my own educational experiences, starting from the 1968 release of the Government of Ontario's *Living and* Learning report (commonly called the Hall–Dennis Report), which initiated alternative

C. Nash (✉)
University of Toronto, Toronto, Canada

© The Author(s) 2017
N. Bascia et al. (eds.), *Alternative Schooling and Student Engagement*,
DOI 10.1007/978-3-319-54259-1_8

education in Ontario, and reveals the ways that my personal journey led me to co-found Alpha II.

RELEASE OF THE HALL–DENNIS REPORT

The Hall–Dennis Report was released when I was in grade 5. The report recommended that education be directed to the full development of the human personality in moving toward the twenty first century. At my school, this meant that students were permitted a new freedom to choose. Our report cards were non-graded and evaluated work developed by small groups of students rather than teacher-directed lessons. Yet, as a child who valued teacher input, my initial reaction to the changes was that substance was lacking in my learning. This was reinforced when a small cadre of students organized a student walkout to demonstrate to teachers the power of students acting together. The students' message to their peers was that freedom would only happen if students neglected individual interests and took control as a group refusing to attend class.

As an elementary student, I was glad for the physical freedoms brought by the Hall–Dennis Report but felt the influence of student leaders limited my intellectual freedom.

JUNIOR HIGH

When I entered junior high in September 1969, the teachers either embraced the Hall–Dennis Report or retained a traditional classroom. Some teachers believed that supporting Hall–Dennis was equivalent to advocating for free student experimentation and that mentorship was unnecessary. Teachers who ignored the Hall–Dennis Report, on the other hand, made a point of designing practices that reinforced the belief that boys were superior to girls. In these classes, girls were ignored or belittled.

Over the 3 years I was in junior high, the ideas of the Hall–Dennis Report were increasingly brought into the classroom. I learned that freedom was something that could be interpreted in more than one way, ranging from teacher neglect to something some teachers believed only boys deserved. I did not feel safe with this range of pedagogies entering high school. In co-founding Alpha II, I advocated for the importance of the mentor relationship between students and teachers, and simultaneously that all members of Alpha II were to be considered equal.

HIGH SCHOOL

By September 1972, I was at the local collegiate secondary school. Although I had not liked how self-directed learning had been interpreted by my junior high teachers, I was now eager to self-direct my learning, because the secondary teachers I encountered were interested in their chosen subject matter as well as in the students. I spent time with teachers in their offices, looking through their books and educational equipment and asking them questions about what engaged them in their subject. I experienced mentorships with artists and entrepreneurs outside the school system. The learning I gained from these experiences was the basis for further research I would undertake, either in the library or elsewhere. I negotiated the evaluation of all my work with my teachers. While students got report cards, the marks I received were ones my teachers and I had agreed on.

In high school, once I had experienced the variety of opportunities that could be created through self-direction, I felt that students who still chose the traditional route were missing something important. So, it was with much surprise that when our teachers went out on strike in November 1975, they cited one of the reasons as no longer wanting to deliver the learning model envisioned by the Hall–Dennis Report. The teachers were out until February 1976, when the government agreed that public education would go "back to basics."

My experience in high school taught me the importance of real mentorship to learning, where the mentor and mentee work together in focusing on common interests and evaluation relates to an agreement on the criteria demonstrating excellence. But the teacher's strike of 1975/1976 taught me that the interests of public school teachers include more than their area of expertise. Mentorship was also foundational for Alpha II.

UNDERGRADUATE EDUCATION

Like other high school graduates in the greater Toronto area, I had missed three months of school because of the teacher strike. But this did not hamper my admission to the University of Toronto nor my receiving an Ontario Scholarship, giving me a reason to question the need for regular school attendance when founding Alpha II.

Significant changes were happening at the University. After years of increased funding by the Ontario Government, in 1976 there were major cuts to university funding. Officials seemingly took their frustrations out on new students, keeping them waiting in lines for hours to register and then refusing to answer their questions. Professors also displayed disdain for students, constantly reminding us how much better things used to be and how incompetent we were compared with previous generations. Disturbed by this reception from faculty, I was also perturbed to find out that my classmates purchased exams from other years rather than learning material out of interest. It appeared that most of them had not benefitted from self-directed education. The formal parts of my undergraduate years were depressing. It was participating in extracurricular activities—becoming a writer (then jazz editor) on the Varsity newspaper, an elected student representative, and a newscaster with a weekly news show on two campus radio stations—that allowed me to regain the excitement I had had in high school. This experience reinforced to me that when students are focused on getting high marks, they lose sight of why they are pursuing an education. As well, when they do what they love, students gain the energy and interest to experiment with enriching their learning. Both these points were important to the core values we later developed in founding Alpha II.

FACULTY OF EDUCATION

During the time I was completing my undergraduate degree, my six younger siblings were making their way through the public education system. What I heard from them was that each year secondary education became increasingly controlling, and the freedoms we had been given when I was in high school were no longer available. It made me feel angry enough to decide to go into teaching. My intention was to graduate, get a teaching position, and try to convince teachers I worked with to bring back self-direction in the classroom.

I started at University of Toronto Faculty of Education in September 1980. The education I received there was as if the Hall–Dennis Report had never existed. We were taught that the most important things in teaching were classroom control and well-crafted lesson plans.

Luckily, one professor, Laurence Stott, still embraced a semblance of the self-directed learning I had come to hope for. In his philosophy class, I heard of the thinkers behind the self-directed learning I valued, most specifically Dewey, Neill, and Buber. Rather than lecture, this professor told us stories, describing what an education system would look like under the guidance of each of the theories we studied. It was this class that clarified my commitment to self-directed learning, to the study of philosophy of education, and to learning through storytelling.

This experience showed me how important it was to study the philosophical foundations of self-directed learning in order to gain support for reestablishing its tenets, providing me with a discourse that would prove useful later in convincing board representatives to found Alpha II.

EAST YORK BOARD OF EDUCATION

Being self-directed gave me the confidence, upon graduation, to go to the then East York Board of Education, a month after I was married, and assert that I had looked at all the Boards in Toronto and determined that East York was the best. The person interviewing me was impressed with my initiative and hired me to be a secondary teacher. I quickly set about trying to convince other teachers at my school to reintroduce self-directed learning into the classroom. They let me know the last thing they wanted was to give students control. This lack of success with teachers convinced me that I needed to gain more education, so I could be more persuasive about the importance of self-directed learning. The many years I then devoted to my graduate education gave me the patience to wait for the right moment to co-found Alpha II.

GRADUATE EDUCATION

After recognizing that my colleagues were unwilling to reestablish self-directed principles in education, I decided I would only teach night school and summer school so that I could pursue an MA in philosophy of education full-time at the Ontario Institute for Studies in Education (OISE).

What I had loved about my previous philosophy course at the Faculty of Education had been its focus on the foundations of self-directed learning and the use of narrative in teaching. At OISE, Professor Malcolm Levin supported self-directed learning in Ontario education.

Looking for a way to stop the erosion of self-directed learning, I turned to the most important development in Ontario education during the 1980s—Bill 82, the *Education Amendment Act, 1980*. Bill 82 meant that, for the first time in Ontario, all children with special academic needs had access to publically funded special education. Now, gifted students were entitled by law to receive special programming, permitting self-directed learning for at least this group of learners.

I was supervised during my graduate education by philosopher of education Ian Winchester. My master's thesis looked to understand intelligence by investigating those usually identified by educators as the most intelligent—scientists, in particular, especially physicists. I noted that although the most acclaimed scientists were self-directed, science education had become increasingly other-directed. My doctoral thesis argued that what a society identifies as intelligence is a construct of what is valued by that society. I concluded that it requires democracy for intelligence to be self-directed. In hierarchical systems, intelligence is necessarily other-directed. If those who are most acclaimed in science are self-directed, I became increasingly convinced that public education in Toronto needed democratic practices to support self-direction.

What I gained in pursuing my graduate education when forming Alpha II was the understanding that the school needed two foundational pillars—self-directed learning and democratic decision-making.

THE GRADUATE STUDENTS' UNION

Once I understood the value of democracy to self-direction, what encouraged my commitment to completing a PhD was delving deeply into OISE politics. The most important issue at OISE during that time was the Ontario government's surprise announcement that OISE would no longer be a self-governing body; the granter of its graduate degrees, the University of Toronto, would now govern it. Although intellectually, OISE faculty and students may have liked the idea of a closer connection with U of T, the price to be paid was OISE's ability to self-direct. As someone who primarily valued self-direction in education, I was eager to help stop the transfer of OISE's governing structure. Our lobbying efforts were successful in permitting OISE to retain its governing structure for ten more years.

Working with a diverse group of graduate students, I began to realize that self-direction in a democracy was not possible in a broader sense without community decisions being made by consensus, where consensus depends on ensuring that each person's views are taken into consideration rather than adopting the view of the majority. What this meant was that, politically, I saw my role as one of listening to everyone's ideas and devising practices to include diverse points of view in meaningful ways.

I believe it was because of my concern for listening to many points of view that, in 1987, I was acclaimed President of the University of Toronto Graduate Students' Union, the political body representing over 10,000 graduate students. As President, my aim was not agreement; it was requiring that everyone's point of view be included in each decision. This method of decision-making made for long, involved, and intense meetings, yet it invited each voice to be taken into consideration.

Being President of the GSU demonstrated to me that democracy in a self-directed environment depends on a special type of consensus of adding together all points of view. This experience of mine was the basis for my maintaining that the second pillar of consensus at Alpha II required adding together all points of view.

EMPLOYMENT AT THE UNIVERSITY OF TORONTO

My efforts to listen carefully to others while President of the GSU had made me well known to the fellow members of the School of Graduate Studies Council. Once my presidency was over in 1988 (but before I completed my PhD), I was appointed Director of Graduate Alumni Affairs. In this position, I experienced the increasing complexities of contacting alumni in the ever more centralized University and reported these difficulties to the SGS Council.

One member of SGS Council was particularly interested in my insider's point of view on the School of Graduate Studies—Dr. Aubie Angel, Director of the Institute of Medical Science. In February 1989, at the SGS meeting just following the successful defense of my doctoral thesis, Dr. Angel asked me to take on the organization and administration of a joint University of Toronto and University of Costa Rica program in cardiovascular risk factors and diabetes mellitus. At the same time, a third position became available to me when Professor David Rowe, the Associate Dean of the Physical Sciences and a Professor of Physics, hired me to create a way for physics students to achieve more self-direction in their learning. Because this mirrored the work I wanted to do, I gladly accepted the additional responsibility.

What was important to me about each of these positions was that I was hired to develop self-directed university-level programs. Even though it meant I had to work very long hours, the work was exciting and stimulating. As well, it produced improved opportunities for democratic self-directed learning at U of T, which was my goal. I was very grateful for the open-mindedness of the faculty members supporting my efforts.

Once I began creating programs within the already-established departments at the University, I was eager to design an entire graduate program to focus on self-directed learning, in a community where each person's point of view was included in developing that learning community. I had the opportunity at the end of 1989 when the U of T Director of the newly created Centre for Bioethics, Dr. Fred Lowy, hired me to be Program Coordinator based on my work at SGS.

As Program Coordinator, I helped organize how the Centre would be structured in relation to the University in order to give the Centre the best chance of maintaining its ability to self-direct as an institution. Researchers from various disciplines could come together and include each other's points of view in developing policy related to the issues in bioethics without direct administration by SGS.

One final employment opportunity was offered to me in 1995, concurrent with most of my other positions at U of T: work with Professor Boris Stoicheff, a laser physicist, to develop a program for students in the humanities and social sciences that focused on understanding light. We offered this interdisciplinary program for two academic sessions before I left paid employment at U of T to become a mother.

The years of employment at the University of Toronto taught me that it was not classroom instruction that gave me the ability to excel at work, it was my interest and dedication to trying to make a difference. Because of personal motivation, I was able to gain the experience of starting programs in a complicated public education institution—something that was very useful to successfully following TDSB guidelines for creating an alternative school and meeting the deadlines the Board presented to us in founding Alpha II.

MOTHER

Our son was born in 1996, the day I left all employment at the University—almost 15 years after I was married. It soon became clear that he was both highly intelligent and displayed the signs of Asperger Syndrome. Two years later, our daughter was born. She quickly demonstrated the behaviors associated with Attention-Deficit Hyperactivity

Disorder (ADHD). For the next few years, I visited doctors and took my children to various types of therapy. My purpose in going to therapy was not to make my children fit into the norm. As a mother who supported self-directed learning, I accessed therapy to help my children develop skills to enable them to engage in their areas of interest.

When it came time for my son to go to school, we went to the community school just down the street. I expected a kind, friendly environment. However, despite the good intentions of the teachers, what I found was a place that primarily tried to control children rather than permitting self-direction—an atmosphere in conflict with my philosophy of education.

Thinking of how I could help my son to have a better school experience, I had him tested for giftedness in grade one. His score permitted him to join the city's primary gifted program. With just eight children in the special gifted class, my son was able to experience the self-directed learning that I had hoped for.

However, when it came time for my daughter to attend school, she was unable to concentrate on activities she did not initiate herself. This made her highly unsuitable for the regimentation and intellectual control school required. She would sit at her desk in grade one, put her head on the table, and silently cry. She was miserable, yet she was so capable of doing things on her own when she was not controlled. Feeling her pain, I looked for a solution.

It had been many years since I had been a student at OISE, but I started to think about what Malcolm Levin had introduced to me all those years ago—alternative education in Toronto. I wondered whether there was an alternative school in Toronto that still adhered to the principals of the Hall–Dennis Report. I checked the information available on the Internet for the Toronto District School Board and there I found it—ALPHA Alternative School.

During these early years in my children's lives, what I had learned at graduate school was of great value in helping me negotiate what was publically available to my children with respect to their education. What I learned was that many of the children diagnosed with both Autistic Spectrum Disorder and ADHD are those who flourish with self-directed learning. Some of the most self-directed and personally successful students at Alpha II have been those diagnosed with either one or both of these disorders.

ALPHA

It took until grade three for my daughter to be admitted to ALPHA. ALPHA stands for A Lot of People Hoping for an Alternative. Although at this point in ALPHA's history there were classes to attend and, therefore, it was not as self-directed as I would have hoped, ALPHA was a democratic school that made school-wide decisions by consensus. A year later my son joined my daughter at ALPHA because the focus of his larger junior gifted program had become intense competition instead of self-directed learning. What I learned from the experience of ALPHA in founding Alpha II was that although maintaining the core values of the school is imperative, what is most important is for parents and students to feel they can continue to support those core values and that their support is reaffirmed and reestablished on a regular basis.

But all of this would come after the first day I walked into ALPHA with my daughter and I met Norma-Lee Weiss, a mother of a student at ALPHA, who introduced herself and said, "We are thinking of forming an Alpha II, would you like to join us?" I jumped at the chance.

I was one of nine ALPHA parents, in collaboration with Board representatives, who worked intently from October 2006 to April 18, 2007, the day it was approved by the Toronto District School Board, to create Alpha II. Founded on self-direction and a democracy of consensus including each person's voice, Alpha II's creation was the fulfillment of my dream to bring back the promise of the Hall–Dennis Report to students in Toronto. Alpha II depends on an understanding of self-direction and democracy for freedom to happen. Both of my children attended Alpha II throughout their grades 7–12 school years and are now successfully engaged in their chosen career paths.

WHAT I LEARNED

What I learned on this journey was that the Hall–Dennis Report confused and concerned many parents, teachers, and students. As a result, the Report, intended to serve Ontario until the twenty first century, was set aside by most educators after only 7 years. However, if we are to support the type of intelligence democracy requires in our province, public education must take up the aims of the Hall–Dennis Report again, permitting young people to self-direct their learning in a community based on consensus. Unfortunately, few people in today's Ontario recognize the necessity of self-directed learning to maintaining democracy in fostering the type of intelligence on which our society depends. For those who do, Alpha II Alternative is a committed and continuing choice in Toronto public education, and I am grateful that my own educational experiences encouraged and permitted me to be one of its co-founders.

AUTHOR BIOGRAPHY

Carol Nash PhD, is a Scholar in Residence in the History of Medicine Program of the Department of Psychiatry at the University of Toronto. She is a co-founder of Alpha II Alternative School in the Toronto District School Board.

CHAPTER 9

An Administrator's Perspective on the Politics of Alternative Schooling in Toronto

Dale E. Shuttleworth

School system administration has always been an intensely political process. As a staff consultant and administrator advocating for alternatives and community involvement in the school system, I always felt like a man in the middle of a complex process of change. An institutional schooling regime devoted to system maintenance can be a very challenging environment for a school administrator committed to institutional change.

Learning how to work both sides of the street as a line administrator and a change agent within a school board is not a subject taught at faculties of education. During my 30 years as an administrator with three school boards in Metropolitan Toronto, I often found myself struggling to mediate between progressive community representatives demanding change and school system administrators supporting the status quo. In this chapter, I will try to convey the dynamics of this struggle in examples drawn from my experiences with each of the three boards that employed me.

D.E. Shuttleworth (✉)
Toronto, Canada

© The Author(s) 2017
N. Bascia et al. (eds.), *Alternative Schooling and Student Engagement*,
DOI 10.1007/978-3-319-54259-1_9

NORTH YORK BOARD OF EDUCATION

In 1965, after 5 years as a classroom teacher in Windsor, Ontario, I began my career as a community educator in North York at the Flemington Road Public School, serving families who lived in Lawrence Heights, Canada's first suburban social housing project for low-income families. The project was fenced off from the middle-income single-family homes surrounding it. Those living in the surrounding neighborhood often referred to Lawrence Heights as "the jungle," a label that contributed to the project of 5000 residents' feelings of inferiority and alienation.

My mandate was to help make Flemington Road Public School an extension of the community it served, employing the community school concept envisioned by John Dewey and Edward Olsen. In carrying out this mandate, I was fortunate enough to work with a very supportive principal, Whit Morris, who had participated in a Ford Foundation sponsored study group that had visited low-income "inner-city" neighborhoods in the USA to learn about schooling there.

We organized a Community School Advisory Council to provide a forum for discussing issues and concerns and to guide the development of the program. Membership included resident parents and representatives of agencies serving the community. The Council brought many resources together in a coordinated effort to improve the quality of life in the school community.

Flemington Road pioneered an extended day program led by parents, teachers, and service providers. The program offered a full range of educational, social, and recreational activities for all ages. These included child care, a hot lunch program catered by students at the nearby Yorkdale Vocational School, a drop-in center providing employment and upgrading for school leavers, a grocery cooperative, a health services center, legal assistance, and a variety of adult-focused programs.

However, my days of working with a supportive school principal came to end when Whit Morris was promoted to School Inspector and was replaced by an "old school" principal who saw the community school concept and the Council as a threat to traditional school culture. Without my knowledge, he contacted the local newspaper—the North York Mirror—to complain that the extended day program was damaging the school. In response to the reporter's accusations, I defended the program vigorously. The next thing I knew, the Mirror published my picture along with that of the new principal on its front page below a headline that read "Educators Clash." The new principal and I soon found ourselves "on the carpet" in the Director of Education's office.

It was only the intervention of local school trustee Saul Cowan and the support of the Director, Fred Minkler, that saved the community school and my job. I was promoted to the newly created position of Social Services Consultant with a mandate to extend the community school concept to other schools serving public housing projects. The principal took early retirement the following June.

TORONTO BOARD OF EDUCATION

Starting in 1969, a new group of school trustees committed to educational reform and closer school-community relations was elected to the Toronto Board of Education and organized themselves as a "reform caucus." The Administration responded by creating a Special Task Force on Inner City Education chaired by school inspector Bill Quinn, who recruited me from the North York Board as a "principal-on-special-assignment" to be Vice-Chair of the Task Force. The Principals' Association opposed my appointment on the grounds that I was an outsider who had not come up through the administrative ranks in the Toronto Board. Ron Jones, the Director of Education, held firm on the appointment even though some senior administrators and even reform trustees supported the Principals' Association's position.

The Task Force was given a broad mandate, including pre-school programs, school/community relations, community use of schools, multiculturalism, and alternative programs. When it delivered its final report in 1972, I was retained as a special assistant to the Director and later appointed Coordinator of Alternative and Community Programs with a mandate to implement the report's recommendations. As I was still seen as an "outsider" by many within the Board, this was a very challenging assignment.

Getting proposals for new alternative schools approved was often a political struggle as some administrators, teachers, and trustees saw the concept as an implicit criticism of what they were accustomed to doing. They were also quite wary of the community school concept. The Task Force's promotion of more community involvement in the schools drew criticism and opposition from teachers, school administrators, and even some community activists. It was only through behind-the-scenes political bargaining that approvals were achieved.

My first challenge as Coordinator was to create an orderly administrative process for vetting and approving proposals for new alternative schools. I drafted a General Policy for Alternative School Programs that became the blueprint for proposals at all levels, from kindergarten through adult education programs. The General Policy outlined what needed to be addressed in each proposal and how, if approved, a proposal would be implemented. Among the issues to be addressed in a proposal would be the proposed school's philosophy and purpose, staffing and space needs, and projected enrollment.

The first alternative established for high school students, SEED, which began as a summer enrichment program in 1968, was approved and opened in the Fall of 1970. It was housed in rented space in the downtown YMHA building located on the subway line, near the University of Toronto campus. It was initially staffed by four teachers, augmented by several volunteer instructors, called "catalysts," who were recruited by the students themselves. SEED's program coordinator was Murray Shukyn, the teacher who had helped initiate the project. (See Chap. 6 by Rothstein and Chap. 7 by Novogrodsky for a more complete description of SEED.)

The Toronto Board of Education's first elementary alternative school—ALPHA—opened in 1972 on the third floor of a YMCA building located in the middle-income Riverdale area just east of the Don Valley. The proposal was submitted by an activist parent group under the banner of "A Lot of People Hoping for an Alternative." The proposal called for a learning environment where children, parents, teachers, and adult volunteers would share their knowledge, skills, and life experiences in an egalitarian school community. The Board approved the proposal with the proviso that it would require an initial enrollment of at least 100 children, considerably more than the initial parent group had envisioned. I was designated as "acting principal" and worked with the parents in a desperate recruitment drive to achieve their enrollment target.

ALPHA reached its enrollment target, but this resulted in a collection of parents who had only one thing in common—they all hated traditional schooling. At weekly planning meetings, the parents discussed and disagreed about curriculum, teaching methods, appropriate learning materials, and discipline. As acting principal, I often had to intervene in these disputes to explain and defend the existing administrative policies.

For example, the parents wanted to interview and hire the four teachers for the school. This was against Board policy and practice but we worked out a compromise where parents could provide advisory input to the administration concerning teacher hiring.

Differences over discipline, teaching methods, and curriculum were not so easily resolved. By Christmas, nearly one-third of the parents and their children left ALPHA and there was even talk of forming a BETA (Better Education than ALPHA) alternative school. Fortunately, enough new parents and children were recruited to replace those who had left. (See Chap. 2 by O'Rourke and Chap. 6 by Rothstein for a more complete description of ALPHA.)

Wandering Spirit Survival

In 1976, two Native Canadian families chose to withdraw their children from the public schools owing to perceived racism experienced by their children. Led by Vern and Pauline Harper, they first established a private volunteer school operating out of the Native Canadian Centre on Spadina Road. When the school proved not to be financially viable, they went to the Ministry of Education, which did not provide direct funding to schools. They were directed to the Toronto Board of Education due to its alternatives in education policy.

The sight of Vern and Pauline marching in full Native regalia caused quite a stir at Toronto's Education Centre. The Harpers demanded full funding for a Native Way school that stressed the heritage, spiritual, and cultural aspects of aboriginal life. I was responsible for working with the Harpers to develop a proposal for presentation to the Alternatives in Education Committee. The alternative elementary school was to be named after Wandering Spirit, the famous Cree war chief who was instrumental in the efforts of the Riel Rebellion to protect his peoples' way of life. However, the real controversy over the proposal centered on the spiritual belief that all objects in nature should be venerated as the work of the Creator. The school was to be governed by a Native Council. Native elders and a shaman were to actively promote spiritual and cultural values. This focus was opposed by many, including the Toronto Star, as religious teaching.

After much debate and political maneuvering, the Wandering Spirit Survival School was approved by the Board in February 1977, to be located in the basement of the Winchester Public School Annex. The administration of Wandering Spirit was indeed a challenge, but today the first Native Way urban school in Ontario (if not Canada) still operates as the First Nations Alternative School in the Dundas East and Gerrard Street Area. (See Chap. 15 by Berg for a more complete description of Wandering Spirit.)

CONTACT was the next alternative secondary school. CONTACT was proposed by a group of teachers led by Harry Smaller and graduate students from the recently created (1965) Ontario Institute for Studies in Education. CONTACT proposed to serve the needs of a growing number of dropouts from mainstream high schools with a more structured curriculum taught in an informal egalitarian environment. The CONTACT proposal was approved in principle in the Spring of 1972 and began as a part-time summer and evening program before opening as a full-blown alternative secondary school in the Fall of 1973, housed initially on the third floor of the Duke of York Public School near the Regent Park social housing area. (See Chap. 6 by Rothstein and Chap. 13 by Smaller and Wells for a detailed history of CONTACT).

One of the outcomes of the Toronto Board's Special Task Force in 1972 was a group of trustees, administrative staff, and representatives of the Ontario Ministries of Education and Labor, the Metro Toronto Labor Council, and local business and industry who met to explore the feasibility of work-study programs in secondary schools. The deliberations of this group resulted in two proposals. One was to establish LEARNXS a Learning Resources Exchange & Information Sharing and Retrieval Systems, and the other was to create another alternative secondary school called Subway Academy.

Subway Academy opened in September 1973, with three teachers and 60 students housed in portable classrooms at Toronto's Eastern High School of Commerce. Instead of attending regular classes, students negotiated independent study learning contracts with individual teachers in schools along the Subway line. The Director of Education designated the principal of Eastern Commerce, Aubrey Ramey, as Subway's principal of record. Rhamey was also president of the Toronto Secondary School Headmasters Association, a position that assured support for Subway from other secondary school principals. His inclusionary style of leadership, involving students, teachers, and members of the community, was an essential component of Subway's success. A second alternative, Subway Academy II, was soon established further west along the Bloor-Danforth subway line.

SPECTRUM

Toronto's first grade 7/8 intermediate alternative school was launched in 1978 by three teachers at Deer Park Senior Public School located in an affluent neighborhood in North Toronto. The teachers, David Clyne, Ellen Dorfman, and Brian Taylor, with a group of supportive parents, presented their proposal to the Board's Alternatives in Education Sub-Committee but were opposed by the local area superintendent. The parents then mounted a political campaign in support of their proposal. When the proposal reached the Board's Program Committee, they packed the room. A Canadian Broadcasting Corporation (CBC) videographer also attended the meeting, ostensibly to record the discussion and decision. The committee members seemed visibly flustered by this media attention and approved the proposal over the objections of the area superintendent. When I approached the cameraman later to ask when the coverage would be aired, he replied, "What coverage? There was no tape in the camera."

Spectrum tended to attract highly motivated students who wanted the opportunity to set their own goals and work independently and in small groups in an informal, supportive environment. Media studies, music, visual arts, social studies, and fitness were key elements of the program along with the language and math "basics." It attracted more students and parents than could be accommodated in the north Toronto public school where it was housed. Two of the teachers—Clyne and Taylor— eventually left to launch a similar grade 7/8 alternative school called Horizon in midtown Kensington Community School. Other teacher/ parent-initiated grade 7/8 alternatives—Delta and Quest—were started up as well in the 1980s. All still operate today.

In following the community education and development model, Toronto's approach to establishing alternatives has been unique in North America. Through its Alternative and Community Programs Department and its General Policy for Alternative School Programs, the Toronto Board of Education helped groups and individuals' identity their needs and meet them using both Board and community resources.

CITY OF YORK BOARD OF EDUCATION

In 1980, I was appointed Assistant Superintendent Community Services for the City of York Board of Education. In 1982, the Board approved a new alternative in education policy similar to that of the Toronto Board and a number of alternative schools were subsequently established.

In 1981, the Community Services Office received a letter from parents proposing a community alternative elementary school in the affluent Cedarvale/Humewood neighborhood. The Board directed its Community Services Office to work with parents, subject to its new criteria for alternative programs. The parents wanted the school to be a natural extension of the home with parents taking an active role in helping to enrich their children's learning opportunities. They wanted multi-aged classes with an activity-centered program that encouraged self-direction, self-discipline, and extensive use of community resources. The new school, called Cherrywood Alternative, opened in September 1982, occupying vacant space at Humewood Community School. However, enrollments at Cherrywood soon outpaced those at Humewood, and a political struggle ensued. When a new Director of Education was appointed in 1990, senior officials and area trustees decided to close the program. Cherrywood Alterative ceased operation in 1994.

In 1983, an intermediate alternative Program for Academic and Creative Education (PACE) was launched in Arlington Senior Public School, which had declining enrollment and vacant space. To encourage their responsibility for their own learning, students attending PACE were required to negotiate individual learning contracts with their teachers. Starting with two teachers and 55 students, PACE's enrolment grew to 180 with six teachers by 1986.

The rapid growth and success of PACE indicated a need for more arts-oriented secondary school programs, especially for students in the performing arts who were taking private lessons in music, drama, and athletics. These students required a more flexible school schedule than available in a regular secondary school. In 1985, a proposal was presented to the Board for a flex-time program that would allow students already pursuing professional careers in the performing arts and athletics to maintain their high school studies along with their professional career demands. The program, called INTERACT, was approved and housed at Vaughan Road Collegiate under the direction of Elaine Vine, former dramatic arts teacher at PACE.

INTERACT students have performed in Canadian and American TV shows and films, danced with professional ballet companies, and participated in national and international athletic competitions.

In 1986, a joint committee from the York Board and Humber College proposed the establishment of an alternative program in integrated machine technologies to be known as MacTECH. The program was jointly sponsored by the York Board, Humber College, and three local business corporations—Standard Modern Technologies; Weston Machine and Tool; and Magna International. It was housed at George Harvey Collegiate and Standard Modern Technologies. After earning a secondary school diploma, students went on to gain a Humber College machine technologies certificate. I represented the York Board and Marina Heidman represented Humber.

Also in 1986, the Community Services Office was approached by a group of parents led by Jackie Wilson who proposed the establishment of an Afro-Caribbean alternative secondary school program for early school leavers (dropouts) whose families were from the West Indies. The proposal called for Black teachers and an Afro-centric curriculum. Some senior officials and trustees saw this as a form of racial segregation and opposed the proposal. After much debate and political infighting, the proposal was approved and the school opened with 45 students in three vacant classrooms at the D.B. Hood Community School. However, the ongoing controversy among some trustees and senior officials led to the relocation of the program and its incorporation into the George Harvey Collegiate Re-entry Program, open to all school leavers. The Afro-Caribbean program soon ceased to exist.

In the 1978 census, The City of York was singled out as having the highest rate of functional illiteracy in Metropolitan Toronto. Forty percent of families spoke a language other than English at home. Community service agencies and concerned citizens petitioned the Board of Education to respond to the educational needs of adult York residents. In response, the Board established the Adult Day School at York Humber High School to provide adult basic education, English as a second language and education in the workplace. By the end of the decade, enrolment reached 2,400, with students meeting in 23 different locations across the city. Initially, the Adult Day School program was opposed by some trustees and senior administrators and the Secondary School Teachers Federation. But the influx of more new full-time students and teaching positions and the support of Director of Education, John Phillips, helped keep the program alive.

Finally, the Learning Enrichment Foundation, modeled on Toronto's LearnX Foundation, was established by the York Board and school-community parent councils in 1978, with the capability of partnering with federal, provincial, and municipal governments and the York

Association of Industry to develop childcare, training for school leavers, and the new Adult Day School. It was due to the leadership of Director Phillips and key progressive trustees such as Steve Mould and Harriet Wolman that resistance to these new initiatives was overcome.

Concluding Reflections

During my 30 years as a change-agent school system administrator, I learned that institutional schooling has always been politicized and resistant to change. However, alternative school programs have made a valuable contribution by being anticipators of, rather than reactors to, social and economic change. If the future of education is "process" rather than just "content," alternative schools will continue to play a leading role in public education, particularly in relation to minority interests. In this age of consumer accountability and budget restraint, public education must be more communicative, responsive, and effective in its use of scarce resources. These are the basic principles upon which alternative programs were established.

Author Biography

Dr. Dale E. Shuttleworth's professional career as a community educator has included experience as a teacher, school-community worker, consultant, principal, coordinator, school superintendent, university course director, and executive director. From 1965 to 1995, he was employed by the North York, Toronto, and City of York boards of education. He also has been a course director for the Ontario Ministry of Education, York University, University of Toronto, Ontario Institute of Studies in Education, Antioch University, and Central Michigan University.

He is the author of more than 120 published articles in journals and periodicals and 10 books including: *Enterprise Learning in Action (Routledge); School Management in Transition (Routledge); Schooling for Life (University of Toronto Press)*. He is currently Executive Director of the Training Renewal Foundation and Expert/Consultant to the Organization for Economic Cooperation and Development (OECD) in Paris.

PART III

Teaching

CHAPTER 10

Learning to Teach and Becoming a Science Teacher at City School

Katherine Bellomo

INTRODUCTION

From 1981 to 1987, I worked at City School, a public alternative school in Toronto that was based on principles of democracy, community, and social justice. As a novice teacher in my second year of teaching, I came to the job full of hope and enthusiasm and energy, and I learned. I learned to question, explore, and weave together the issues of social justice with science education. I learned from everyone—from the interaction with students, colleagues, parents, and the community. I learned to create curriculum that met the needs of my students. I learned from the students as they learned from me. The force of these ideas propelled me into a future that culminated in a doctoral dissertation about science, social justice, and curriculum development for a diverse student population. I was fortunate, indeed, to land at City School so early in my career, and to have had the structures around me (some imposed, some sought after) that encouraged me to learn and grow.

K. Bellomo (✉)
Toronto, Canada

© The Author(s) 2017
N. Bascia et al. (eds.), *Alternative Schooling and Student Engagement*,
DOI 10.1007/978-3-319-54259-1_10

During my fourth-year teaching at City School, two students, Ben and Tom (all names are pseudonyms), who had graduated and were headed for university, contacted me and another teacher (Jim) to lobby for a course for the following year—a course they would not be taking, yet a course they felt so passionate about that they offered to help us "run" it. City School had a tradition of offering, each year, one inter-disciplinary course on a theme or comprehensive topic—other offerings had been "The Holocaust" and "The Decade of the 60s." Ben and Tom were lobbying for a course about the United Nations (which would have included the components of role-play and debate during a model assembly) and which had been considered earlier but then eliminated as a choice. The staff had felt that the course presented too many obstacles around structure, course content, and planning and implementation issues. The boys (and they really were still boys) took Jim and me out for coffee and in short order convinced us to offer the U.N. course the next year. It is odd how still today I can recall exactly how and when I realized that they were right—we should offer the course.

After Jim and I voiced all of our prudent concerns (such as how would we assess role-play activities and how students would be assigned to represent specific countries), and after the boys had countered with all of their exuberant and enthusiastic reassurances, I can still remember thinking: how charming that they are so young and fearless and enthusiastic. After the pair had assured us that they would come to the school and help with course implementation—which we all agreed should, hypothetically, include a mock U.N. assembly, and while I still remained concerned about the issues of course structure and assessment, Tom said: "Being worried that the course will fail is not a good enough reason to not do it." That was it. The penny, as they say, dropped. I realized he was right. This young man, so wise, had yet again taught me how to be a better teacher. I should not have been surprised. Ben and Tom were students that I taught for four years at City School. For them it was grades 10–13. They were thoughtful and understated in their feedback to me. They were joyful learners, hard-working students, and honorable people. Additionally, I learned a great deal from the other teachers at City School. They were all more experienced than I and several had worked in other alternative school settings. I have referred to Jim above, and need to add that all of the teachers were supportive and nurturing of me as a novice teacher. They were also respectful of my teaching space and of decisions I made, and trusting that I would use good judgment.

While they never offered unsolicited advice, they were all open to talking through any situation for which I sought guidance. I will always be thankful for the help and wisdom that I gleaned from the teachers and students at City School.

CITY SCHOOL AND SOCIAL JUSTICE AND PEDAGOGY

City School, as I understood it, was formed when some parents wanted a school environment that was academic in focus and that had an overarching social justice consciousness and demonstration. Social justice is generally or broadly understood to refer to "the right treatment of others and the fair distribution of resources or opportunities" (Reiss 2003: 160). Social justice involves the removal of behavioral and institutional barriers, including prejudice and discrimination, which preclude the equality of opportunity, freedom, and responsibility to choose and realize individual capabilities (Sen 2009). It often is referred to in terms of a movement to address justice issues such as inequalities, oppression, issues of marginalization, and unequal distribution of wealth. Social justice issues often include the inequalities due to race, class, gender, and sexual orientation or are linked to matters of poverty, disease, and environmental degradation. It is a set of principles (or a lens) through which we question and critique issues that can be applied to individuals, groups, or institutions.

I am not at all sure when I began to consider how science and social justice were intertwined and how my pedagogy would reflect this, but teaching in this alternative school environment, I developed my own brand of pedagogical knowledge (or knowledge about teaching as a practice). Learning to teach at City School and learning to position science teaching and learning within this particular school framework forced me to consider ways of approaching content within a context and helped me to develop my pedagogical *content* knowledge (or knowledge about the best way to teach particular content). For example, we might design a debate to explore a controversial issue but perform a demonstration to confirm a scientific law such as conservation of mass.

While some of the students were interested in science, others had no interest in taking science beyond the required compulsory courses. Glen Aikenhead (1996) describes science students as falling into one of several categories from "potential scientists" who experience no barriers to learning science to "outsiders" who do not care about and who have no interest in science. Aikenhead describes how some students can easily border cross into the sub-culture of school science, while for others this border crossing is virtually impossible. And so, years before I had ever considered Aikenhead's (1996) work on types of science students and science student identity, I was considering the ways to engage students, to motivate them to learn science, and to help them border cross. They had enacted a type of border crossing by rejecting the regular school and coming to an alternative one, and many needed further border crossing help to be able to successfully enter and navigate the science sub-culture.

Finally, I learned to integrate the contemporary justice issues with which my students were absorbed into my thinking and my teaching. And so, years before I had read Calabrese Barton (2003), I was beginning to formulate a teaching philosophy around the place of social justice issues in science education. Justice issues were in the air and in the water, so to speak. They were a part of what we did daily, and so I also began to develop my political knowledge in this area, including the idea that science education and scientific literacy is a civic right in a democratic society (see Calabrese Barton and Upadhyay 2010).

As my social justice lens began to develop, during my curriculum development and in my teaching, it seems to me now that I saw through such a lens more and more as a result of school community meetings, events, and conversations, and that slowly over time I began to wear my justice "glasses" more and more and eventually never took them off. The lens had become fixed. How it happened is not entirely clear to me, but it happened, in part I think, through the alternative school enculturation environment specific to City School, some of which happened at the meetings.

MEETINGS

At City School, we had a love affair with meetings. We had "General Meetings" once per week, each Wednesday at 11:00 a.m. that were chaired by students and had an agenda that was set previously at the "General Meetings Planning Committee" meeting. All manner of things were discussed among the 120 students and 7 teachers, from global issues of nuclear weapons, to community events and bowling excursions, to the sharing of space, to garbage in the student lounge—literally from the sublime to the mundane—we discussed it all.

Once per month, we had a Parent Council Meeting that included teachers, students, and parents to discuss the ideas about the running of the school, as well as long-term plans and vision (or mission) matters. Weekly, we had staff meetings. Every Tuesday, the faculty met to discuss everything—individual student achievement; needs of the school; issues of space, equipment, and supplies; and administrative items such as timetable and staffing, and one teacher was fond of saying: "we even have meetings about how many paper clips to buy."

While we were a small alternative school, we did have administrative and support staff in the form of a secretary, a principal, and a superintendent who oversaw some of the school operations; on a day-to-day basis, two of the teachers acted as "co-coordinators" and even though I was a novice teacher, I took my turn. I did it for two years with two different partners, and I must say it was challenging. I would sleep with a notebook by the bed so that if I awoke fretful about some looming deadline or issue, I could jot down my notes and get back to sleep. As co-coordinators, we met regularly, and we also had weekly meetings with the principal.

I learned a great deal about meetings—their structure, the importance of an agenda, the importance of a good note-taker and minutes, and that a disciplined chair is essential. I recall a special meeting where a facilitator guided us through a workshop on the topic of planning and implementing productive meetings. I grew to like all the meetings. They helped me feel part of a vibrant, dynamic community of teaching and learning. From the meetings, I also learned about power and control—who had it and who vied for it in this school context. While I have only on one other occasion worked with a group of teachers as talented and dedicated as the City School faculty, we did have raucous discussions, the occasional disagreement, and the rare but jarring explosive bout. It was all a bit grueling really—so many things to deal with and all the while trying to learn to teach science with no science colleagues who could share the responsibility of the biology and chemistry course planning. During my tenure at City, we did hire a wonderful physics teacher. Even with all these meetings, I often felt isolated.

SCHOOL BOARD CONNECTIONS

It was amidst all of this work and movement and buzz and chaos that I began to attend what were then called Heads Meetings. Biology department heads from other schools met about once per month, to talk about such things as curriculum, "labs" or practical work, equipment, Ministry

of Education[1] and school board initiatives, and assessment and evaluation. We shared resources and exams, and we discussed how to best teach
difficult concepts in biology. I had joined a professional learning community, and years before I could fully grasp the concept, I was developing
my pedagogical knowledge as well as my pedagogical content knowledge.
After a year, I became the recording secretary, taking meeting notes for
the group (yes, more work), but I loved it all. Had I been working in
a larger secondary school, there would have been a department head. I
would never have thought to go to these board wide heads' meetings,
and I would never have had this unique learning and enrichment experience. And so, here, too, I grew as a teacher! Interestingly, the isolation
of being the only biology teacher, the one thing that I did not like about
teaching at City, actually propelled me to seek a community of science
folks, which informed my practice at City immeasurably and also helped
to inform many of my career decisions in the years to come.

THE STUDENTS

When I began teaching at City, the school was in its second year, and
there was a critical mass of students (and their parents) who were committed, involved, dedicated, and powerful. The students were interested
in ideas. They exhibited a spirit of sharing and openness, and the feedback they gave me was subtle, gentle even, yet powerful. I was lucky to
have begun my career in this place with these students. It was at City
that I learned to create a sense of community and family within each
of my classes. It was at City that I developed a sense of teacher identity
as I navigated what could be negotiated (such as deadlines, assignment
choices, and content examples) and what could not (such as homework,
assessment, and evaluation).

The students were in many ways typical teenagers, and they exhibited
typical high school teen behavior such as coming late to class, skipping
classes, not handing in assignments, and challenging teachers. I was in my
early 20s and so could identify with them in many ways; however, as a
group, they were very different from me. In general, the students in those
early years of City School were children of middle-class families whose
parents had post-secondary educations. These were the youth whose
dinner table conversations were about politics and philosophy. Many of
our parents were university professors, school teachers, community activists, and artists. Most of our students were white and had been raised in

tony neighborhoods. I had been raised in a working-class neighborhood, my father was a tradesman, and I was just beginning to understand how being a teacher was channeling me into a middle-class lifestyle.

Getting to know these students and their families added much to my emerging understanding of what it meant to be political. In my family, we talked about my grandmother who was arrested in Italy for trying to start a union in a textile mill and how my mother had to bring her dinner to the jail. In the City school families, you would have been more likely to find parents who were academics who studied the politics and history of labor movements. It is possible that many of my students would have had grandparents who were more like my own parents in terms of background and culture.

While I had attended a large suburban secondary school in North York, many of my friends had attended a North York school board[2] alternative school named Alternative and Independent Study Program (or AISP), and so I felt I understood some of the reasons students choose alternatives and what they are rejecting about what we called "regular" schools. I had considered transferring with my friends to AISP, but did not, in part because I did not know what it would mean for me. I could not "risk" my education and so, while at times I found my high school to be difficult and oppressive, I stayed, and graduated and went off to university. In many ways, I admired my City School students for their self-assurance, confidence, and ability to take risks.

I need to add here that at City School there were several students who clearly wanted to study science in their future, who had chosen to like me and work with me, and who had constructed their learning environment (including our classes) as co-operative and interesting. They were supportive of me. They deftly helped me to become a self-examining teacher as they questioned the status quo and voiced their needs for a safe and supportive learning environment. Reflecting back, I wonder how I might have developed my understanding of teaching as political if I had started my career in another school.

MY CHALLENGES AS A NOVICE TEACHER

The freedom and autonomy of the alternative school setting was at times liberating and at times frustrating. I (in some ways like the teenagers I taught) was learning to understand the limits and the scope of what I could do. Without ever having read about Schwab's (1973) four commonplaces (the subject discipline, the learner, the teacher, and the milieu) that inform curriculum development, I was immersed in a learning experience where I was constructing the importance of each of these commonplaces as well as their interdependence. In those early years of my career, I was trying to make my science classes relevant and inspiring for all the students while covering the mandated content (i.e., teaching the subject matter content knowledge and concepts). Then, I was trying to be balanced and fair and perhaps neutral in my teaching. Today, I would say that science, often seen as neutral, objective, and about pure and unsullied facts, is also seen by contemporary educators and researchers as socially constructed, culturally determined, and political. Science as a practice and as a discipline has many traditions in social justice issues and perspectives. It was these tensions that I had begun to explore, understand, and navigate while at City School.

In small increments, as I developed courses of study and from a great deal of reading, I began to consider what science is as a discipline, what it means to be a science teacher, and how science fit into our City School ethos. I tried to include a balanced approach to topics such as nuclear power, genetically modified foods, and medical research. Sometimes, I was not sure about what balance even meant. At one Parent Council Meeting, a parent said, "Teachers cannot be neutral, so I would just prefer that teachers state their bias, so that it's clear to my kid what their perspective is." This was indeed a tension for me. And another parent said: "I find it odd when we talk of presenting 'both' sides of an issue since it implies that there are just two sides that are equal, but sometimes there are lots of sides and one side is just wrong!" These parents made me stop and think: Can teachers be balanced and neutral? What does it mean to include multiple perspectives in one's teaching? What is the place of these themes in a science course such as senior chemistry? These ideas, that I continue to struggle with today, were seeded and began to germinate years ago during my time at City School.

TEACHING SCIENCE AND SCIENCE LITERACY IN AN ALTERNATIVE SCHOOL SETTING

Teaching science at City School was not without its day-to-day challenges. We had a less-than-adequate laboratory facility, limited equipment and materials, and no real library. I learned to create many of my own resources, borrow materials and supplies from colleagues whom I had met at head's meetings, and ask the school board science consultants for additional support. I think that the lack of resources actually inspired me to be creative and to approach the challenges of course design and content together with the students.

It would be a long while before I would be reading the works of Derek Hodson (1993, 1998, 2010), Michael Young (1998), and Michael Apple (1999, 2004a, b). I recall that when I did begin to study in a graduate program, the works of these education theorists and others resonated for me. I had developed a sort of intellectual clothesline upon which to hang the ideas. I still remember quite vividly sitting in one of Derek Hodson's classes at the Ontario Institute for Studies in Education (OISE), four years after transferring from City. In that class, we were discussing pitfalls of practical work (lab work) that does not at all achieve the purpose we intend. Hodson asserted that during labs we spend too much time asking students to collect data, often with confusing multi-step protocols that require complex equipment use, skills, and not enough time analyzing the data (see Hodson 1996).

While at City, I often attended a nearby secondary school to audit a senior chemistry class and participate in their labs. I would bring the data they had collected back to City, where I would describe the lab protocol to my class and give them the task of analyzing the results. Hodson said that what I had been sheepishly doing was actually his preferred pedagogy! My instincts had been right; data analysis is even more important than data collection procedures in a lab.

So much of what he considered key in science programming at the secondary school level (such as learning about science, and learning about how science is done) I had developed as curriculum pieces while at City. To teach about animal behavior, I encouraged students to carry out a behavior experiment. Some students watched the pigeons in Queen's Park, while others went to the zoo to observe and analyze the behavior of gorillas and sloths. I encouraged my students to consider multiple perspectives; I assigned research papers on the topics that included the history and sociology of science as a practice and as a constructed body of knowledge.

Science also had a place in the City School interdisciplinary curriculum. As mentioned earlier in this chapter, each year City School mounted one "Interdisciplinary" course, which was team-taught and in which a large proportion of the students enrolled. I was part of the teaching team for three of these courses and was responsible for some of the science that was integrated into the course. For example, in "The Decade of the 60s," I taught the section of the course concerned with the Green Revolution and the "race for space" which culminated in the moon landing. For the "Model U.N." course, I was responsible for the resolutions that dealt with the environment, specifically desertification, deforestation, and ocean pollution. These courses were unique as team teaching interdisciplinary experiences. It was at City that I first explored the possibilities of teaching science with a Science, Technology, Society, and the Environment (STSE) focus. Today, this approach is contained in Ontario's Ministry of Education science policy documents.

THE RIPPLE EFFECT OF GOOD EARLY YEARS

After six years at City School, I became restless for new and different experiences, and so I moved through a number of school and non-school settings as I continued to develop as a science educator. I worked at two mainstream secondary schools, became a department head, worked as an instructor at a science museum (the Ontario Science Centre), and became a school board science consultant. In all these positions, I continued to learn and grow, and I became more and more interested in combining social justice issues with science education.

Eventually, I worked at three different universities teaching science methods and pedagogy courses and completed my doctoral work in the area of integrating science curriculum and social justice issues within the STSE portions of science courses. City School experiences and the school's underlying ethos of meeting individual student needs and integrating social justice issues were still guiding me. In many ways, the spirit of the alternative school students, along with the wisdom of the teachers and parents, has stayed with me.

From my early years as a novice teacher at City School, I have maintained and nurtured an interest in social justice and sociopolitical issues within the high school science curriculum and in the politicization of teachers. Science as a practice is embedded in a society and is affected by the politics, economics, and values of that society (Gould 1981). City School helped me understand how these aspects of science fit within an inclusive curriculum.

NOTES

1. In Ontario, school matters and policies are governed by a Ministry of Education.
2. North York was one of the six boroughs that made up the city of Toronto, Ontario. Until recently, each of the six boroughs operated a school board. Currently, the six boroughs have been amalgamated into the Toronto District School Board or TDSB.

REFERENCES

Aikenhead, Glen S. 1996. Science Education: Border Crossings into the Subculture of Science. *Studies in Science Education* 27 (1): 1–52.

Apple, Michael W. 1999. *Power, Meaning, and Identity.* New York: Peter Lang.

Apple, Michael W. 2004a. Creating Difference: Neo-Liberalism, Neo-Conservatism and the Politics of Educational Reform. *Educational Policy* 18 (1): 12–44.

Apple, Michael W. 2004b. *Ideology and Curriculum,* 3rd ed. New York: Routledge Falmer.

Barton, Angela Calabrese. 2003. *Teaching Science for Social Justice.* New York: Teachers College Press.

Barton, Angela Calabrese, and Bhaskar Upadhyay. 2010. Teaching and Learning Science for Social Justice: Introduction to the Special Issue. *Equity & Excellence in Education* 43 (1): 1–5.

Gould, Stephen Jay. 1981. *The Mismeasure of Man.* New York: W.W. Norton & Company.

Hodson, Derek. 1993. In Search of a Rationale for Multicultural Science Education. *Science Education* 77 (6): 685–711.

Hodson, Derek. 1996. Laboratory Work as Scientific Method: Three Decades of Confusion and Distortion. *Journal of Curriculum Studies* 28 (2): 115–135.

Hodson, Derek. 1998. *Teaching and Learning Science: Towards a Personalized Approach.* Philadelphia: Open University Press.

Hodson, Derek. 2010. Science Education as a Call to Action. *Canadian Journal of Science, Mathematics and Technology Education* 10 (3): 197–206.

Reiss, Michael J. 2003. Science Education for Social Justice. In *Social Justice, Education and Identity 2003,* ed. Carol Vincent, 153–165. London: Rutledge Falmer.

Schwab, Joseph J. 1973. The Practical 3: Translation into Curriculum. *The School Review* 81 (4): 501–522.

Sen, Amartya. 2009. *The Idea of Justice.* Cambridge, MA: Harvard University Press.

Young, Michael F.D. 1998. *The Curriculum of the Future.* Philadelphia: Falmer Press.

AUTHOR BIOGRAPHY

Katherine Bellomo has been a science educator for over 30 years; has taught a variety of high school level biology, chemistry, and physics courses; has been an elementary school mathematics, science, and technology consultant; and has taught at the Ontario Science Centre Science School. More recently, she has been an instructor for science pedagogy courses at Mount Saint Vincent University (Halifax), York University (Toronto), and the Ontario Institute for Studies in Education (OISE) at the University of Toronto, and has been part of a team to implement a teacher development initiative in Guyana. Her doctorate is in the area of curriculum development to support social justice in Biology and she has several publications (journal articles and books) in science education. She has been involved in research in the areas of inquiry-based science instruction, environmental education, and action research and has presented at a number of international conferences.

CHAPTER 11

New Beginnings

K. Omar

I feel as though I have been teaching my whole life, but I am a relatively new educator in the Toronto District School Board. In 2009, I got the opportunity to do my teaching practicum at an alternative school, and it positively changed the course of my career, and the course of my life. My identity as a teacher is marked by constant reflection, reinvention, and passion. When I tell people I teach at an alternative school with a social justice focus, I sense that they do not understand what this means. So in taking part in this project and in our public alternative schools, I believe it is of some value to look through the lens of personal experience.

As a teacher and a co-chair of the Alternative Schools Advisory Committee (ASAC), I have a unique perspective on the workings of alternative schools. To try to explain, I will describe my experience as a learner and as a beginning teacher. Then, I will discuss my learning curve as a teacher with six years of experience. My overall aim is to share my experiences in ways that enable readers to understand.

Jean-Paul Sartre put it best when he said we are the sum total of our experiences. My learning experiences framed my entry into alternative teaching in ways that my standard university degrees could not. I grew

K. Omar (✉)
Toronto, Canada

N. Bascia et al. (eds.), *Alternative Schooling and Student Engagement*,
DOI 10.1007/978-3-319-54259-1_11

up halfway across the world, and my schooling spanned three continents. This influences my career choices and the way I approach teaching.

As a young person in the 1980s, I attended Somali language-based schools in the heart of Mogadishu. At that particular school and at that particular time and place, a typical classroom consisted of more than 30 students, far more on some days. As an elementary student, I enjoyed studying different subjects in Somali, a recently adopted Latin alphabet-based language. My elementary curriculum did not include a second language; the option for basic English or Italian came later, in secondary school. As a young learner, what was important to me rarely paralleled with what was important to my parents, who were both educators at the time. They wanted a second language to be introduced much earlier, and the guinea pig was my brother, who was sent to an Arabic private school. In addition, we attended a religious after school program, which was also in Arabic. The predominantly Somali-language environment stood in stark contrast to the Arabic-based teachings, but this was not unusual in Mogadishu. The Arabic schooling in contrast to the Somali made me realize that veering away from public education was an option. I did not realize at the time what this would mean for the life that I would eventually lead.

In Somalia, the concept of alternative was not differentiated from private education, but some teachers and parents did talk about learning styles and new approaches. One would hear about classmates being pulled out for private or home schooling in lieu of the government-run programs. Others would opt for community schooling, which was essentially a larger adaptation of home schooling.

Some conditions limited students' choices in terms of curriculum and curriculum delivery. It did not matter that students could attend Arabic, Italian, or English based schools or after school programs. Ultimately, what mattered was that those wanting or needing more options had to seek education elsewhere.

Although there were other wonderful educational opportunities in Mogadishu, my parents' search for an alternative turned up a traditional western school in Geneva. There was less rote and repetition and more immersion through activities and play than in my schooling in Mogadishu. Activities differed across the four seasons; each season was associated with specific sports or leisure activities. We also learned through role-play, something I had rarely experienced previously. I came to understand that there were some things in place in Geneva that allowed for these approaches to take place. For one, the class size was smaller, roughly about 20 to 25 students, but more important, there was no fluctuation in the number of students throughout the year. Second, discipline was drastically different. Teachers used less harsh methods in managing students. In fact, without the corporal punishment I had witnessed previously, the power differential between teacher and student seemed minimal. Third was the presence of human and technological resources. I had daily one-on-one instruction that supported both the technical and emotional aspects of learning. The encouragement of support in individual or small group tutoring was drastically different.

Access to technology, after school programs, sports, and curriculum content, including French and German, were incredible to us. I enjoyed turning on the computer or listening to cassettes during and after school because it allowed me to set my own pace. Public education in this new community met my family's needs on learning other languages.

Toronto, where I spent my high school years, is where I first heard the term alternative education in the form that I understand it today. I remember my best friend explaining that her elementary studies were at a Montessori school. In grade 10, friends whispered about SEED and Inglenook. By grade 11, some had switched to these seemingly mysterious schools. At first, I understood them to be a type of private school, because my prior experiences were of choices between public and private. However, paying closer attention to what teachers and other students said about this new term, I learned that it was another type of public education.

When I was in high school, students who chose to leave the mainstream schools were labeled misfits. According to classmates and teachers, schools such as City School and SEED were established to address the needs of "problem" students who did not fit the regular schools. No one asked whether the system itself might be the problem, a question that would later become a crucial part of my own education as a teacher.

I chose to study and teach in the public housing area of Regent Park in Toronto. I was familiar with the area, having been a student in a nearby high school. This was a natural progression for me, to contribute in some form to the community that had welcomed me as an immigrant 15 years earlier.

Early on as a student in York University's teacher education program (Regent Park Site), I was expected to articulate a personal teaching philosophy. I tried; I had taught in many settings—office trainings, one-on-one with patients—but none of these experiences had to do with children. After spending a couple of weeks in a school in Regent Park, I had some ideas. Before I could finish, though, a strike put my teaching into a holding pattern for months. Strike directives interrupted our practicum opportunities. I made the best of this situation and spent my time observing teachers, administrators, and parents in action. The strike gave me enough time to form questions, gain perspective, and think more about my teaching philosophy. The time I spent watching and better understanding the school was the best learning experience I could have had at that time.

By the time the strike was settled, I had plenty of ideas about the way I would approach instruction. I made lists defining expectations, professionalism, standards, what it meant to have positive learning environments, a variety of management styles, teaching methods, and notes on government mandates. From behaviorism to Gardner's Multiple Intelligences, I systematically reviewed relevant learning theories and packaged them into a neatly organized set of values. These lists and notes were organized into two giant binders. However, I sensed that something was lacking, and I looked forward to having my next placement at an alternative school. That changed my life.

Cue into my first aha moment: the realization that the alternative program I saw closely matched the teaching philosophy that I was developing. In my new placement, continual reflection, focus on arts, creativity, environmental impact, and social justice would now make up the foundation of my practice. I found myself thinking a lot about diverse methods of teaching, alternative models, inclusivity, and safe space. The breadth and depth of the curriculum in the alternative school was beyond what I had ever experienced as a student, but clearly craved. I knew then that I wanted to work in a school exactly like that one. I applied for a teaching position with the Toronto District School Board (TDSB).

In my gray suit, I roamed the Board hallways for about thirty minutes before I sat down in a hard chair for my interview. The time had come. I was facing a panel of board members, cue cards in hand, and I thought, If I don't get this job, what will I do? My heart was racing, maybe from fear, but also from excitement. Just for a second, I wondered what had brought me to that boardroom. But, that did not distract me from the bigger picture—I had to teach in a public alternative school.

Then I had my second *aha* moment—I was almost a teacher! I was thinking about how far I had come since the year before. I had crammed so much more than a year's worth into that time, yet the next six years in an alternative school have proved to be even more enlightening. And despite warnings about how difficult the first few years of teaching would be, I am happy to have this opportunity to write about the challenging times and positive experiences I have had there.

MORE THOUGHTS ABOUT MY ALTERNATIVE SCHOOL PLACEMENT

When I showed up at my alternative placement, I got a little surprise: Students called teachers by their first names. I came to understand that, although this social contract was different from my previous experiences, it had its purpose. What's in a name at an alternative school? Using the first name in teaching played a role in balancing the authority one exerted so that respect went both ways, and I found that it was also rooted in the rapport one created with students. It enabled me to create a trust and bond with students. In dropping the formal titles, a social dynamic was created, one that recognized everyone involved as people, and people who would also continue to earn each other's respect beyond the job title. Was I worried that they would refer to me as "yo" or "eh"? Yes, I was. Did that happen? No, it did not. Schools are inherently hierarchical and to some degree that hierarchy sustains, regardless of the school system one is in. What did I take away from dropping my last name? I gained a better understanding of the power in given names, ones that were painstakingly chosen by family and friends. Using the first name that was given to me by my grandmother just felt right.

I realized early on that the principles guiding my alternative placement were successful as long as student engagement was taken into consideration. Students need to be active in their own learning. This was obvious from how the school had created an educational environment focused on an intersection of academic development, creativity, and independence. Learning is not always easy, and students were expected to demonstrate responsibility for being present and participating.

The program assumed that all students were creative and could benefit from learning through the arts. While many schools were reeling from budget cuts in the 1990s, this school managed to maintain its arts focus by integrating the arts throughout the subject areas. The integration of the arts allowed students to explore all the issues in an organic manner. Art became an avenue for students' self-discovery, rather than a separate subject. This required collaboration among teachers who were willing to take up the challenges involved.

Fostering critical thinking skills through social justice and citizenship required the curriculum content to be meaningful in a way that I had not seen before. Nurturing a sense of citizenship in middle schoolers was easier than one might think, especially when the approach was to explore the issues of race, gender, class, sexual orientation, and globalization with an arts focus. Engagement is necessary for parents and community, as well as for students and teachers.

A SOURCE OF POWER

One thing that surprised me was the presence of parents in the school. When I think back to my own experience, my parents were only allowed to come to school for meetings. I believe that in most school parents need invitation because they look at schools as the territory of students and teachers. I was once told by a parent that the home is ours, the school is theirs.

Seeing parents in a school helping out with projects or putting student work up on walls has its wonderful benefits too. I agree with the belief that student success in school is correlated with parental involvement. The high degree of parental involvement at my new school was reassuring and encouraging. Not only had the school been founded in 1996 by a group of parents, over the years parents continue to be involved. At first, I thought it would be a fun and exciting way of incorporating family and allowing students to take ownership of their learning, but I became cognizant of the fact that it was also a necessity.

As all small school communities know, teachers need a lot of support in providing the kinds of extra-curricular activities that traditional schools enjoy. In this school, parents are essential and parent involvement is one of the school mandates. I also learned that it is important to establish formal interactions between students and community leaders, businesses, and organizations. Parental and community participation that consistently supported the regular function of the school reminded me of the African proverb, "it takes a village to raise a child." If I've learned anything from my short time in the alternative system, it is how true this is. The school community sustains itself through collaboration. It was not until my teaching studies that I witnessed that power, for this I am grateful.

CHALLENGES

Though my teaching experience at an alternative school was extremely fulfilling in more ways than I can count, I would not be providing an honest picture without discussing some of the challenges of teaching in an alternative school. Being in a "social justice and arts" focused environment has its benefits, but one major disadvantage I had not anticipated was the small staff size. At one point, we had a group of four teachers to cover all subject areas and activities. The probability of cutting certain extra-curricular activities would have been higher had we not had parent volunteers. Even with parents' help it was a challenge to offer a full range of experiences.

I also saw the need for a cohesive team of teachers. It is imperative that working with such a small number of people day in and day out requires sharing a philosophical approach. There are all sorts of positives in having a small staff, and one I particularly enjoy is the inherent responsibility and accountability of sharing leadership. This means that we are all in a position to have a huge impact, not only in the decision-making, but in the culture of the school as a whole. I have participated in defining school goals, establishing traditions, and creating an environment that is as much a part of me as I am a part of it. It is easier for a staff member to have a voice and be heard in a small school. On the flip side, the risk of making mistakes and the ripple effect they can have are also heard, out in the open and visible.

PART OF SOMETHING BIGGER

In considering this chapter, I thought about how I currently help define the alternative school culture in the Board, and I feel as if I am part of something bigger than my teaching position. I looked for alternative ways of working with the community, and so I got involved in the Alternative Schools Advisory Council (ASAC). This committee was established to allow parental and community input in board policies in an advisory capacity and to support and improve the communication among alternative school staff, parents, students, and community. I first joined ASAC as a representative of my own school. I found that through ASAC meetings, all parties were provided with opportunities to advocate for students and programs. I enjoyed my participation, and took the opportunity to co-chair the committee, with the goal of learning more about the matters that concerned the other alternative schools in the Board. The role of co-chair also allowed me to take on a more supportive stance as a facilitator.

In co-chair, I have become more aware of the varied issues alternative schools face. These concerns often revolve around the misalignment of administrative regulations and school philosophy. Nearly 7 percent of TDSB schools are in the alternative stream, and almost all of them are housed in a building where regular programs also run. When that is coupled with the fact that administrators are not always knowledgeable about the "alternativeness" of the schools they inherit, issues of control and politics can arise. In some of the extreme cases I have dealt with, alternative schools were managed as if they were regular programs. When the principal requires an alternative school to function in the same way as the regular program in the same building, the purposes of the alternative school are threatened.

The small size of alternative schools also seems to be a major problem when it comes to funding and staffing. As an ASAC member, I have had the opportunity to ask questions and have meaningful discussions about such issues. For me, understanding the way the system works is important in the process of coming up with solutions. This understanding is a source of power, because the more I know about the TDSB alternative schools, the more I can contribute. I am part of a team of educators, parents, students, and administrators who work toward articulating people's collective concerns to the Board or to the provincial Ministry of Education. Alternative schools survive because there is a collective will to keep them alive. Parents, community, and staff struggle passionately, and brilliantly.

Two years into my teaching, I found myself in a heated dinner table conversation about how school reforms of the 1960s intersected with the racial and feminist reforms of the time. We eventually came to some form of understanding that perhaps the term "alternative schools" should not even exist. Schools and education approaches should be diversified, and if it was the case, there would not be a need for the designated alternative schools. I have been thinking about this for a few years now, because I believe there's some truth in it, but I am not yet ready to expand upon that. My experience has been unique; it has fostered inclusivity and embodied hope. So, I continue to work through the challenges, grateful that our leaders in education have paved the way for Toronto's public system to include so many wonderful and diverse alternative schools.

AUTHOR BIOGRAPHY

K. Omar is a teacher with the Toronto District School Board. She has worked both in the regular and alternative programs within the school board. She currently enjoys and hopes to continue discovering more within the alternative system in her board.

CHAPTER 12

Notes on Big Ideas and Incremental Change

Liam Rodrigues

My initial attraction to teaching was tempered by trepidation. If I had been excited and engaged in school as a child, I was often isolated and ashamed. By high school, these confused feelings had been replaced by disdain, and I was not alone. Many of my peers were similarly scornful, sharing in the perception that schooling had nothing at all to do with us and that we learned despite school. If anything has persisted from that time in my life, it is the impression that school should and could be different.

Most of my teaching career has been spent in alternative schools and the rest at infiltrating traditional ones with a touch of the progressive. Currently, I am at SEED, North America's oldest public alternative school. My first encounter with SEED was when I had the opportunity to join a team starting an alternative school in Toronto's East End.[1] Seeking shape and direction from the existing models, we visited as many alternatives as we could. SEED came late in our itinerary and left an indelible mark. Its spirit is everywhere in the notes that follow.

As it is with an education, it is in the nature of notes to be sketchy, fragmentary, and invariably incomplete. Often, they drift from big ideas to seemingly small events recorded for posterity—because, of a moment,

L. Rodrigues (✉)
Ontario College of Teachers, Toronto, Canada

© The Author(s) 2017
N. Bascia et al. (eds.), *Alternative Schooling and Student Engagement*,
DOI 10.1007/978-3-319-54259-1_12

one imagines that in some not-too-distant future, a detail might fill a gap, reveal a pattern, and birth a big idea—or stand as evidence for something as yet not fully formed. The following is of this order, but is note-like in another sense, too. It asks the reader to fill in unsounded space, to hear music hanging in the silent intervals between improvised chords, to find in a core sample a coherent tale of forces, conditions, opportunities, and incremental change.

FORCES: RETHINKING A MANIFESTO

At a meeting of the American Educational Research Association in New York City, Ivan Illich spoke at some length to a set of problems he identified with modern education. He labeled them "irrational consistencies."[2] These, he explained, troubled schools, endemically, if not fatally, were "the contradictions inherent in the very idea of school," (*Deschooling* 67). Among them were the emphasis on "valuable learning" (*Deschooling* 39)—what we might now call the measurable, on the obligatory curriculum, on the corporatization, commodification, and industrialization of education. In *Deschooling Society*, published soon after, he calls for the "disestablishment of the monopoly of the school and thereby of a system which legally combines prejudice with discrimination" (*Deschooling* 11), for the dismantling of school, wherein "the pupil is … 'schooled' to confuse teaching with learning, grade advancement with education, a diploma with competence, and fluency with the ability to say something new" (*Deschooling* 1). In its place, he would have a diverse program with an infrastructure of wise, compassionate and practical educators, phenomenal and interactive learning experiences, collaborative peer-to-peer interest models, immersion in professional workplaces, paid school-aged employment, authentic skills training, mentoring, and a healthy dose of socio-economic reform.

Nearly half a century on, the project of universal public education perseveres while Illich, Paulo Freire, Valentine Borremans, Everett Reimer, and Ernst von Glasersfeld evoke the revolution in education that never came. Few systems saw or even cared to embrace the kind of movement that would breach the fortifications of traditional state schooling. As one of my colleagues keenly observed,

> The perception is that institutionalized education is just too big. Look at Waldorf and Montessori; they have capitalized on this and rightly so.

They are emblems of how progressive education cannot exist as part of public schooling. Insofar, as people are even aware of alternative or non-traditional education ... the understanding is that private has the freedom to think-tank progressive and public does not. Public has neither the inclination nor the infrastructure ... is always behind the curve. This is the perception. Why? Because historically this has been the case ... anywhere it's not is the exception ... places in Europe seem to have worked it out, but not over here. Here "it is easier to take it than it is to create it." In North America, at least, progressive models of education have always been the domain of private schools.

True, but only half true. Charter and private schools in some contexts move the aspects of the education project forward, but pose a fundamental problem that cannot be resolved or addressed comprehensively in a short chapter. A gloss, however, is possible and relevant. Private and charter schools largely stand outside of public education, because they are not encompassed by any genuine definition of a public enterprise. Whereas what Illich and other progressive educational theorists call for is a comprehensive overhaul of the institutionalized state schooling apparatus. Private and charter schools stand abutted to or against the project of public education and are ultimately apart. By-standers to the public project, they are conceptually and by design exclusive and privileged. They embody—intentionally or otherwise—prejudice and discrimination, reinforcing the "schooled" society. They set certain groups outside of access and fortify the social order that fails those who would most benefit from reform and universal gains, from a relevant and enabling system of public education. The very existence of charter and private educational enterprise is irrational and inconsistent with the project of a truly public education. If this sounds socialist, that is because it is. The very notion of public anything, of universal anything, is. It is in the service of the entire society and is entirely unqualifiable. To provide any economic barrier or categorical proviso against equal access to a state institution is to negate the Western project of the last three centuries. It is duplicitous to organize societies around systems of rights, such as the right to "medical care" (as in Article 25 of the Universal Declaration of Human Rights) and then limit access to the infrastructure that services these rights. It is no less so as it pertains to Article 26 of the Universal Declaration concerning education. Choice is emphasized, but nowhere is there mention of a corresponding fee. So it is with the Canadian Education Act, where education is a universally required and acknowledged state responsibility, regionally administrated. Access to charter and private schools is neither universally accessible, nor free. *Ipso facto*, they are not a solution to a public problem. It is symptomatic of the problem, perhaps, but no answer to public education's irrational and inconsistent adherence to compulsory or common curricula, to the subject/discipline model, to the teacher-centered classroom, and to the universal application of arbitrary standards.

So what happened to the revolutions? Books have been written on this, so do not expect a comprehensive discussion to follow. Instead, I offer two extremes. They are the bitter pill of skepticism (not unwarranted, considering a progressive public engagement's track record in the face of state power) and the conviction born of a phenomenal experience of what is possible in public alternative schools—a case study, in effect.

The easy answer to the question of why we have made so little progress in our schools is the same as our answer to the question of why we have seen so little movement in the progress of our social institutions in general. What happened is what happens to all revolutions. They get co-opted, their leaders subdued, discredited, or imprisoned. Like Freire and Critical Pedagogy, they are splattered with the Socialist or Marxist brush. Subject to feeble concessions and local splintering, revolutions have been absorbed into the ritual and myth[3] of the Right. Many people were satisfied or pacified with promises and imbibed the staid course. After all, are we not supposed to be uncomfortable with change?

A more nuanced response lies in further reflection on Illich's own critique and the issue of power and governance. Modern societies are built on schools. For all their faults and failings, they are the stone and mortar of Western Civilization. Illich admits as much, but the problem is not with educating or schools per se, but rather with the institutions they have become. Their own internal contradictions have evolved to make them untenable and a threat to the social fabric. "Not only education but social reality itself has become schooled," claims Illich, and deschooling society would mean replacing the manipulative institution with a system that extends the safety and security of childhood, instills democracy, inclusion, and convivial-sustainable living, and provides for autonomy and skills.[4] The schooled society's addiction to exploitive and self-perpetuating forms of power is at once doctrinaire and imperialist. It demands a responsible and accountable citizenry, masquerades as the principles born of democracy and benevolence, but is first and foremost preoccupied with the maintenance of institutions that preserve the sites of power, including knowledge and governance. Where power is concentrated in the hands of a few people, institutions or corporations, individuals seek it out. When it comes to power, everyone needs some, and no one wants to give theirs up. If you do not have any, then one of your few points of access is to challenge the right of others to have it over you. When one is powerless, like a child, power means something very different than it does to those with it. It is something one relies on others to wield on one's behalf, or not. It is bound up with trust in those who presumably have one's best interests at heart, or not. When not, there are inevitable abuses and a certain distrust. Consequently, it is not to be traded recklessly or brandished irresponsibly, because the innocent and vulnerable are subject to it. The powerless do not take power lightly, and its place in the schooled society does not escape Illich. In its various guises, it permeates *Deschooling*. Throughout, he writes of economic, social, political, and institutional power; of semantic and syntactic power, the power to make chaos, deplete, destroy, demand, and to deal death; the power to hold power, the power of money-makers, of privilege, of industry, bureaucracy, the workforce, of schools, universities, churches, and of teachers. Power is what he is challenging in *Deschooling*. It is what he would return to local communities, learners, and their parents, what he would see democratized in service to all.

Illich's revolution was never realized. Institutions do not just surrender power. His prescription and course of treatment was not taken up. *Deschooling* was universally well received as a critique of education. The institutions did not all come tumbling down. Was *Deschooling*'s call for a revolution in education simply naïve? Untenable? Too idealistic?

Illich hurled himself at the megalith with the understanding that it might not move, but he knew that it would have to one day. That is why *Deschooling* is a manifesto rather than a manual. He must have known that power was not about to willingly legislate away its hold on education. He may have wished power to be responsible and benevolent, but he understood that powerful institutions are most often indifferent or ruthless in their efforts to maintain themselves. In acknowledging this, however, I am not planting the second pole on our vector beside the first.

Big changes in education are currently upon us, perhaps even as radical as those envisioned by Illich, but the terrain has shifted. Traditionally, visible forms of power called upon authority and lay claim to the right to exercise it, but globally these mechanisms are being scrutinized. People without power and those willing to share it have developed a more critical relationship with power. As part of the hangover left by the coup delivered upon critical human endeavor by post-structural thinking and practice—of which Illich played no small part as it pertained to education—more discerning relationships with agency, authority, identity, choice, and equity have emerged as have the tools to challenge hegemony. Together with the democratizing impact of the internet, digital technologies and social media—through which children and youth have acquired remarkable political, social, and economic currency—the critiques of power and authority are altering the landscape of education.

Addressing the expressions of power in schools—its abuses and constructive uses alike—is our subject going forward. The will and theory are in place to produce more effective schooling and we are advancing—however glacially—to move public education in the direction of public need and pupil learning. It might be argued that we have moved in that direction since the publication of *Deschooling Education*—but public schooling still clings vehemently to the troublesome ideas, failing practices, and misguided values that underpin it. Each of us needs and has a right to education. In this respect, schooling should be universally devoted to the ends of the user, but as Illich and others before and since have reminded us that this has not been the case. Schools should be as much the domain of the student as they are the jurisdiction of the institutional administrations maintaining and supporting them, but this is not how institutional power has traditionally operated. Reclaiming the power of schools to provide for the realization of socially and culturally relevant learning, to foster meaningful, individuated critical and practical skills does not lie in frontal assault. Rather, it lies in the acts of subterfuge, both incremental and virulent. Progress in education toward learning does not reside in some perfect system but with an evolving and responsive one, subject to dialectical forces and policies that embrace change. Children and youth who participate in progressive learning contexts, including alternative schools that provide for participatory democracy, individuated and self-directed learning, and non-traditional pedagogies and practices, will have the opportunities to reshape public education. Learning as distinct from education is the agency of students, presenting opportunities to exercise agency through the construction of socially, politically, and academically valuable experiences. Perhaps revolutions actually take hold by a thousand little opportunities to resist or insist, to empower through curiosity, exploration, and investigation.

As Gil Scott-Heron suggested in 1970, "the revolution will not be televised. The revolution will be lived." It may come quietly and unevenly and sometimes at a snail's pace, but as the need is real, it will be realized. It is the story of young people in schools, specifically a small alternative school named SEED. It is the story of young women finding voice and of students taking over a school to talk about learning, power, and visions of education for the future, about how they would change it if they could and, how they did, if only for themselves for a brief period of time.

CONDITIONS: A CLIMATE OF CHOICE

Toronto is home to the largest holding of public alternative schools in any one school district in North America, if not the world. It is unlike many other experiments in alternative education that were little more than knee-jerk reactions to disengagement, criminality, and willful ignorance about mental health and addiction. From the outset, Toronto's emerging alternative system was sufficiently diverse as to preempt many of the challenges that gave rise to the problems of delinquency that troubled traditional schools. They did not set out to be solutions in this respect, but in conception and practice, they avoided many of the institutional failings that contribute to such concerns in the first place. Several simple factors contributed directly to this quality. First, they were not products of civil engineering. With rare exceptions, Toronto's public alternative schools emerged one by one as local and organic. At various times, parents, teachers, and even students knocked on the door of the education establishment and asked for the roadmap to a new approach to schooling. Over and over again, the district validated these public alternative experiments by approving proposals that had made their way through the process. They were schools of choice. Students did not have to go to these schools. They (or their parents) heard about them, researched them, and chose them. These new learning options were a restart of the enlightenment project with a progressive twist. The call was not so much for down with schools as it was for up with learning, emphasizing the egalitarianism and individualism of Rousseau's *Emile*, while providing systems of access. Often, they were fueled by elitist principles, but at heart they constituted (knowingly or not) a movement toward Illich's ideas.

The progressive paradigm was different. Progressive education came to emphasize the learner, rather than the system. State curriculum was a thing to be toppled in favor of interests and collective well-being. Democratic needs of the group displaced the tyranny of the classroom teacher, who by the very nature of the role actuated state indoctrination and oppression.

OPPORTUNITIES: IN ALTERNATIVES

When I first became aware of SEED, I had already been teaching for six years. I had had a short stint instructing at St. Lawrence College in Kingston. I had spent a semester with a small private school that was imploding in one of Toronto's affluent neighborhoods, and the next semester, I taught in the school that had absorbed the students displaced from the first. Two nights a week, I taught academic courses at a yeshiva in Richmond Hill. On the other two nights, I tutored.

When an opportunity to teach in the East York Board of Education presented itself, I took it. The school had a self-contained Special Education class with a few teachable electives thrown in for good measure. This was in one of the city's few remaining junior high schools. The school was populated with some of the loveliest people I have ever known, many of whom I count among my dearest friends to this day. But without fully understanding why, I did not seem to belong. Somehow, I was routinely troublesome. When young people wanted to do something, I saw a learning opportunity. I could not see why not. I was young, but there were even younger teachers on staff who were not as inclined to advocate on behalf of troubled students, who did not, for example, want to book the library for the entire afternoon to reconstruct the Paris Commune. After five years, the guidance counselor asked whether I might be interested in an alternative school. I said, "Why not. What are they?" I applied. I was late for the interview and ill-prepared. I had not done my homework. I was sure it would be a bust, but apparently I made a positive impression on someone, because I got the job. It was then, in an East York alternative school, that my education in education started.

Throughout my fourteen years there, I never stopped looking at what other alternative schools were doing, the established and the new. My eye was always on the pedagogy. The more the student-centered, the more impressive the learning and the more integrated the development of transferable critical skills. Many schools had intrigued me along the way, but none endured with the excitement I associated with SEED. So, when the opportunity came to work there, I took it.

I first visited SEED when it was in an office building on College Street in Toronto's downtown. It was awkwardly partitioned and cluttered. The bathtub that had inspired the title of Murray Shukyn's book was gone,[5] in a closet, or buried under pillows. My first thought was, this is the most organic learning space I have ever stepped into. People of every age filtered through the rooms; the studio was a hive of activity and everywhere were clustered together small groups hotly debating, madly scribbling, or intently focused on projects. It may have been an off day, but I could not tell the teachers from the students, or the catalysts from the researchers. Something was going on in there and it felt right. It did not feel like school as I knew it, but people were learning and challenging one another openly and respectfully. The conversation was sophisticated, thoughtful, and often loud. I thought to myself, I wish I had had the opportunity to go to a school like this. Strangely enough, even now, this is the most common remark I hear from parents when they come to visit SEED for the first time.

INCREMENTAL CHANGE: A CASE OF SEED

On a weekend in November 2012, several hundred people gathered for an important event in Toronto's education history. Co-sponsored by the Social Sciences and Humanities Research Council of Canada (SSHRC), York University's Faculty of Education, and the Toronto's two public boards: the Toronto Catholic District School Board (TCDSB) and Toronto District School Board (TDSB), the conference was the first of its kind. Held at Ryerson University and at the Ontario Institute for Studies in Education of the University of Toronto, the event represented the scope, depth, and reach of public alternative schools in southern Ontario.

The conference drew elementary; secondary; and post-secondary students; parents; teachers; administrators; and a curious public, including half a dozen students from SEED. The SEEDlings ranged in age from 15 to 20 and, for such a small group, reflected a remarkable cultural and ethnic diversity. These Somali, Malay, South and East Asian, Franco-, and African-Canadian students reflected the nation's visage and the new face of alternative schools. Only two of them had ever attended a conference before. During the second day's conversation, the number dwindled, but not the engagement. The students had a great deal to say about all they had heard and seen, but I had no idea what they would do with the experience.

When I arrived at work on the following day, they had already drafted a full-page proposal calling for a student-led conference on alternative education. Overnight, they had secured more than fifty signatures through social media. By day's end, there were one hundred assurances of outside support and commitment. As a staff, we were certain that the movement would lose steam. Instead, it intensified. A girl's group formed, wanting space and occasion to talk about the issues young women were facing in Toronto's schools. They wanted to speak frankly to each other, name the issues, and talk about strategies. Moreover, they wanted a place at the conference planning table. They were welcome, but what conference? Then I got our first phone call from the administrator of a Catholic School, half the city away, "What's this about a conference at SEED? I have a group of students here clamoring about coming. Is it okay if we come? I need more information...I need to assign a teacher to this. What are the dates?" Dates? Web site? There had not even been a call. There were no workshops. There were a thousand legal considerations. Did these young people have any idea what they had started? Did they have any idea what still had to get done?

The call went out early in December, later than we would have liked. The Web site went live two days later. Students from all over the city came together to plan. They were not just from alternative schools, but also from remote and far flung traditional schools, including public Catholic schools. The students were not aping what had happened at the 2012 conference. This was going to be different. Certainly, they solicited the aid and guidance of the adults around them, but as momentum built it became more and more clear that this was uncompromisingly about their choices.

The first Re-Imagining Education Conference took place at SEED in May 2013 on a Friday. Our keynote was a former Olympian. She stood before a crowd of eighty to one-hundred. By noon, the number in our small space had nearly doubled. Attendees had registered in advance for four sessions. By the end of the day, we estimated that more than two hundred students had flowed through the space. They came from all over Toronto and from as far away as Simcoe and Peterborough. Most of the young people were of high school age, but nine-year-olds presented workshops, as did twelve, seventeen, and twenty-year-olds. The Bonerkill (an intergenerational feminist art collective) session ran double length, in a large room swelling to bursting. There were academics presenting on unschooling, teams of students presented on entrepreneurship, stewardship, and alternative pedagogies; youth presenters from the Oasis Skateboard Factory, sessions on youth violence, discrimination, and equity. More than half the presenters were under the age of twenty-one. They were tireless. The adults stood about gobsmacked. They were exhausted. Everyone had learned something; we all had been treated to a renewed sense of what is possible in schools.

The next year's Student Conference brought a different crop drawn by stories of the first. They started the process all over again in their own image. It was becoming something that SEED does; the second year was bigger and better; the third was smaller and more focused on activism and local change. In becoming a tradition, it birthed offshoots: student projects with the Shaw Festival, in collaborations with theater groups and conferences. And Bonerkill? Well, they had outgrown us and the conference even before it was over, but, occasionally they still send representation from some sub-committee, if they are not too busy. One former SEEDling, Braxton Wignall, a stalwart, returns to support in the planning every year since. Last spring, he asked me whether I had ever heard of Ivan Illich. He had come up in some class he had taken at university. No. Tell me about him, I said.

I first read *Deschooling* when I was seventeen or eighteen years of age. I was stuck at a friend's cottage, up on the Shield, north of Haliburton. It was raining. Everyone else had gone into town. *Deschooling* was the only book on the shelf that kept catching my eye. Over the next couple of days, I picked through it. Some of it, I did not care for or did not get. Other parts I read over a couple times. It was a little dog eared even before I had started. My friend's parents were public school teachers. So far as I could tell, they were nice people; a little conservative, perhaps, but nice. Why did they have this book? They did not look the type. I asked. Ms. D. was a recent convert to Buddhism, so when she answered with something aphoristic I was not surprised. It had become her thing. "We all need revolutionaries," she said (or something close), "to point out what needs to change, and we need you kids to make sure change happens." I must have looked perplexed, because she gave me the book. I still have it. That is how big ideas work, through small uncontainable processes, the stuff of changes, at once great and infinitesimal.

Notes

1. For this opportunity and ongoing guidance, I am forever indebted to Ron Gray.
2. Although Illych never defines the term explicitly, he "evokes" its logic in the postmodern vision of Jorge Luis Borges' "passage from an imaginary Chinese encyclopedia" and with allusion to the institutional nightmares of Franz Kafka and Arthur Koestler.
3. See *Deschooling Education*, p. 10 and 37 (Illich 1971).
4. I use Illich and the *Deschooling* argument broadly, here, to invoke the similar values incorporated in more recent educational discourse.
5. See Beverley and Murray Shukyn's book, *You Can't Take a Bathtub on the Subway: A Personal History of SEED*. It is arguably the best book on the early days of an alternative school, excepting maybe A.S. Neill's *Summerhill* (Beverley and Shukyn 1973).

References

Illich, Ivan. 1971. *Deschooling Society*. London: Marion Boyars Publishers.
Shukyn, Beverley, and Murray Shukyn. 1973. *You Can't Take a Bathtub on the Subway: A Personal History of SEED*. Toronto: Holt, Rinehart, & Winston.

Author Biography

Dr. Liam Rodrigues is a founding teacher of East York Alternative; co-writer of the Ontario College of Teachers' Guidelines for Alternative Education, writer and instructor of York University's AQ Course in Alternative Education, and he has been affiliated with alternative schools for a quarter century. In 2014, he worked with alternative school students, Ontario's Shaw Festival and ORION research and education network, to develop the first student-sourced curriculum material for the season's production of *Arms and the Man*. The same year, he mentored students in the development of Re-imagining Education, now an annual, student-led conference for students. He is the Secondary Co-chair of Toronto's Alternative Schools Advisory Committee and Curriculum Leader at SEED, the continent's oldest public alternative school. Rodrigues has written and presented internationally on Life Writing in Jazz and Education, on literature and drama. His doctorate examines the connection between music and language in the life writing of black, jazz musicians.

PART IV

School Stories

CHAPTER 13

Contact—An Alternative School for Working-Class and Racialized Students

Harry Smaller and Margaret Wells

CONTACT SCHOOL: THE BEGINNING

Contact School grew out of the experiences, knowledge, opinions, and feelings of a number of teacher activists and educators working in inner-city[1] Toronto—during a time when the downtown area of Toronto alone officially reported over 5000 dropouts annually.[2] Mainstream theories on why students living in poverty did not do well in school blamed genetics (these children simply did not inherit higher intelligence as one Toronto school board trustee maintained)[3] or the "material and culturally deprived" environments in which these students were raised (an opinion expressed by at least one Toronto director of education[4]). Based on our first-hand understandings of the experiences and outcomes of inner-city students in traditional and highly streamed schools within Toronto, we knew that something else must be tried. We were motivated as well by the fact that the Toronto Board of Education had already agreed to establish

H. Smaller (✉) · M. Wells
Toronto, Canada

© The Author(s) 2017   167
N. Bascia et al. (eds.), *Alternative Schooling and Student Engagement*,
DOI 10.1007/978-3-319-54259-1_13

and fund its first two alternative schools—ones that (whether or not intentionally) enrolled mainly students from White middle-class families. As members of a small "study group," we met frequently during an entire school year (1971–1972), reflecting on contemporary writing of the time (e.g., Kozol, Neill, and Reimer), pondering what kinds of alternative school structures, curriculum, and pedagogy might achieve more success for inner-city students.

Certainly, our beliefs about the learning capacities of working class and minority students lay in direct opposition to those espousing cultural (not to mention, racial) deficiencies. Teachers in the group that set up Contact believed that curriculum change, in the full sense of curriculum as all that happens for a young person within the school, would lead to different results. We wanted a curriculum that was more relevant to students' lives but maintained high academic standards together with a supportive environment in which their abilities were recognized. Our aims for the school, as later enshrined in a school constitution, were the following:

1. To enhance the self-worth of each individual within Contact.
2. To encourage the attitudes and skills which aid in positive interactions among people at Contact and in the community at large.
3. To help each individual develop the attitudes, knowledge, and skills necessary to assume the power and content that each person should have over his/her life within a truly democratic society.

By the Spring of 1972, a detailed proposal had been drawn up requesting that Contact be established with a first-year complement of 50 inner-city students and four teachers. While the curriculum would follow official high school credit courses, the pedagogy would be much more student-centered. Affective as well as cognitive development would be stressed—emphasizing the enhancement of self-worth and social skills through a focus on co-operation rather than competition and achievement levels based on individual interests, needs, and abilities rather than group norms. As far as possible, the school would be democratically run, with regular town hall meetings to promote student input.

After considerable lobbying of sympathetic school board trustees, a formal motion directing schooling officials to establish, fund, and staff

Contact, passed successfully through the requisite Board committee. It was at this point, however, that we met our first real opposition, and we began to understand the ways in which a traditional school board structure worked to divert or undermine the challenges to its dominant modus operandi. Even though our motion passed at the next full Board meeting, it was amended to allow administration to effectively prevent the school from opening in the fall.

Rather than letting the whole plan die, the group decided on an interim strategy—to establish Contact as a part-time night school providing high school credit courses for inner-city youth, whether or not they were still enrolled in day programs. Over the following school year, the "Contact Night School" operated quite successfully. It was located in a house owned by the Board of Education in the downtown Regent Park[5] neighborhood and offered a variety of high school credit and upgrading courses taught by a number of teachers who took on this responsibility in addition to their full-time employment in Toronto schools.

By the end of that school year, another petition was made to the Board to establish a full-time day school. Given our commitment to an inner-city alternative, and our persistence, this time we met with success. In September 1973, Contact Alternative Secondary School began its first full-time program with four teachers and an administrative assistant housed on the third floor of an operating elementary school near Regent Park. Given the numbers of working class, recent immigrant and racialized teenagers who had dropped (or been pushed) out of school, unwilling or unable to find work, we had no difficulty in quickly enrolling our quota of 50 students.

Contact School Program

The curriculum for the school was governed by the existing Ministry of Education standards for secondary schools. The proposal to the board in the spring of 1973 outlined a curriculum that would focus on the development of skills in language and mathematics, community studies and optional topics such as art, music, and physical and health education.

Mornings began with a group meeting of each teacher with a small number of students for whom the teacher acted as a mentor/guidance counselor. What was then called "affective education," and what today would be referred to as social and emotional learning, was infused into the group meeting sessions. The rest of the morning consisted of two instructional periods in which students focused on English and Mathematics. These classes involved both full-group and individualized instruction, given the wide range of achievement levels. Students were free to choose their classes and their teachers.

The afternoon program consisted of a range of courses that ran for just three weeks and provided the opportunities to use the community as an important part of students' learning, either through field trips or by bringing in community representatives. Teachers hoped that this style of focused, problem-based learning would be engaging and rewarding for students who had generally experienced little success in school.

Credits were granted only at the general and advanced level. No basic level credits were provided, because we as teachers knew from experience that a diploma based on such credits was a dead end that would not allow students to pursue apprenticeships, college, or university programs.

Also included in the program was a weekly speakers' hour for the whole school community. This involved presentations and question periods with a diverse range of people. Some examples included George Hislop, an early gay rights activist; Ms. Setsuko Thurlow, a survivor of Hiroshima who worked as a Board social worker; local school Board trustees and city council members; representatives from community organizations such as Women's Press (a feminist publishing company); Oxfam; Greenpeace; young members of the National Ballet corps; and former Contact students who were attending the University of Toronto's Transitional Year Program.

Additionally, each week there was a whole school meeting where decisions were made about the operation of the school. Teachers saw these meetings as opportunities for students to develop group decision-making skills. Many students became much more aware of the routines of a meeting and grew more self-confident about expressing themselves. Most discipline issues were addressed through a "Judiciary Committee," which included both staff and student representatives. At the end of the first year, when the school was able to expand, the staff and student representatives were involved in the hiring of new teaching staff.

The Contact teachers tried to create a relaxed environment in addition to a varied, intellectually interesting, and challenging curriculum. Students were asked to address us by our first names. Teachers chose to "dress down," in clothes similar to what the students wore. This was at a time when female teachers were expected to wear dresses or skirts and blouses rather than pants, and typically male teachers wore ties. The first Halloween at Contact, the teachers decided to dress up as mainstream teachers. The students loved it; they laughed, they addressed us as Ms. and Sir that day, and thoroughly understood the point we were making.

In the first year of the school, teachers provided guidance and support to a group of students who wanted to create a smoking lounge in the school. Again, it is important to remember the context at this time. Teachers, like most workers, were allowed to smoke on school property usually in staff rooms. Students were not allowed to smoke on school property; the Contact students felt that those over sixteen should have the same right to smoke as people working in the building. Despite the fact that the teachers were all non-smokers, we knew that this issue was important to the students, and we saw it as a way for them to develop political skills. The students developed a proposal to present to the appropriate Board committee, and they learned how to speak to this proposal and to lobby school trustees who would be voting on the proposal. The proposal was approved. Interestingly, the only serious opposition came from some concerned parents. Students, having participated in a democratic process that allowed for the creation of the smoking lounge, felt an ownership of it, and the teachers were rarely involved in monitoring it.

One of our former students told us recently that two important messages she received in those early years of Contact were that students' views were important and that they could make a difference in the world. Creation of a smoking lounge would probably not have been the issue that teachers would have chosen for an experiential lesson on developing political skills, but this was a significant issue for most of the students, and they learned that they could make a difference through strategic collective action.

The various stereotypes and stigmas that were attached to working class and poor students were very well known to Contact teachers, and we saw how they operated in several instances. When we decided to take the students for a week-long program to an outdoor education center run by the Board, we encountered these stereotypes in full force from the students and staff from other schools. Our students were seen as the "problematic students" regardless of what they did. Similarly, when a few teachers took a group of students to a film adaptation of a novel that was studied in several schools across the Board, other teachers attributed the noisy response to some scenes in the film and the at times disruptive behavior to *our* students. It soon became clear that it was students from mainstream schools, in fact from some mainstream schools in affluent neighborhoods, who were using the cover of darkness in the theater to act out. The only "acting out" from the Contact cohort came from one male who stood up at one point and not so politely asked those who were talking and spoiling the opportunity for everyone to hear the film to be quiet.

However, these stereotypes had already been internalized by many, if not most, of our students, which of course happens with any marginalized group. The concept of "stereotype threat"[6] is now well-documented and acknowledged within academic educational literature.

On one occasion in the first year of the program, a teacher took an afternoon class to the University of Toronto campus. In terms of spatial distance, the campus was not far from the school, but we soon learned how distant it was from the students' lives. The accompanying teacher realized that the students did not seem to be their boisterous usual selves and asked what was wrong; the response from several students was, "We don't belong here." The campus of a publicly funded university seemed totally out of reach, not just as a destination for them as students but even as a site to visit.

On another occasion, the teachers kept hearing about "the brain," the brother of a friend of several students attending the school. Finally, one of the teachers asked who was this "brain." It turns out that the young man was completing grade 13 at Central Technical School. It was clear that this level of academic achievement was seen as beyond the norm for these young people. All the stereotypes about their academic capabilities that the students were very well aware of and had, in many cases, internalized, affected their learning, even in a supportive environment such as Contact. This existed alongside the reality of their intellectual skills, as evidenced by a student who was a profoundly gifted chess player, a student who did complex mathematical calculations in his head, and others.

CONTACT SCHOOL: GROWTH AND DEVELOPMENT

Over the ensuing years, Contact grew considerably in numbers of both students and staff. From its initial full-time occupancy of the third floor of the elementary school, Contact moved in the spring of 1977 to a former supermarket building on a main street directly across from

Regent Park. This space was outfitted as a general open-plan area with pods for individual classes, a general meeting area, and office space, all separated from each other by filing cabinets, book shelves, and moveable room dividers.

In January 1976, Contact opened an outreach center staffed by one Contact teacher and two staff paid through the Local Initiatives Program (LIP), a federally funded community initiative. We saw this outreach center, located in a storefront on a street near the school, as a place that would attract young people in the community whose anxiety and/or antipathy around school were so strong that they could not enter the regular Contact program. In addition, in September 1977, we set up a non-credit program for those students whose skills were so far below grade level that they could not engage fully in the work required to earn general and/or advanced level credits. Neither the outreach center nor the program for students who needed more support to improve their basic skills were departures from our central belief that all students, given sufficient support, were capable of earning credits at the general and/or advanced levels and that these credits were the ones that were most likely to open post-secondary doors for our students.

In October of 1979, the Research Department of the Toronto Board of Education released a report, *Contact: An Alternative School: How It Meets the Needs of Dropout Students*. The researchers found that the majority of the students indicated that they felt relaxed, safe, and respected at Contact and appreciated a new kind of relationship with teachers. Students commented:

"They [teachers] talk like your friends."

"We have mutual respect and the same rights."

"Teachers are nice and fair."

"We talk and express ideas freely."[7]

Some students suggested a need for more discipline, more structure, and less freedom. However, most students indicated that the freedom they experienced at Contact was the most important aspect of the school for them.

A majority of the students also felt that their self-confidence and ability to get along with others had improved. The research report found that most students became more knowledgeable about citizens' rights, social issues, and the community. The researchers found that most students improved their reading and writing skills. The researchers attributed this to the fact that there was considerable student time spent on reading and writing, what educators refer to as "time on task." However, this increase in skill level was not as obvious in the attainment of mathematical skills.

CONTACT SCHOOL: THE NATURE OF TEACHERS' WORK

From the very outset, Contact operated as a staff collective. Faculty meetings were held weekly and everything to do with the school—curriculum, students, policies, events, and so on—was discussed and determined at these sessions. Responsibilities for all of the tasks required to make the school a success were shared among the staff. Contact teachers themselves, along with student representatives, undertook the selection of new teachers (although this was a responsibility which was eventually usurped by the board). While Contact had a school coordinator responsible for overseeing the general organization of school routines and liaising with parents and Toronto Board officials, this person was selected by, and remained responsible to, the staff. It was a position without any official authority beyond that held by every other teacher in the school and did not include extra salary or other material advantage. As a result of this totally collegial structure, every teacher felt responsible for the overall success of the school—there was no other person, on or off site, who could be held responsible for any of the internal problems that occurred over the course of the week or year—there was no one to whom the "buck" could be passed. It was up to the staff themselves to come to grips with solving each and every problem. The fact is that the school ran as a collective, and the considerable control this gave staff over the development of curriculum, school activities, and selecting new staff members were very attractive features of the school for teachers, in spite of the heavy responsibility involved. In truth, Contact, and we assume most of the alternative schools, was an alternative for teachers as well as for students.

Teaching at Contact stood in marked contrast to our experiences as teachers in "mainstream" schools. The hierarchical nature of schools went largely unchallenged, and while students were at the bottom of that hierarchy, teachers were just above them and below the layers of administration from department heads through to the director of education. This lack of teacher autonomy existed despite the fact that the Ministry of Education guidelines at the time were far less restrictive than those introduced in later years. When as a teacher, one had a supportive department head, broader guidelines could mean that you would be able to be more innovative in the classroom, for example by bringing popular culture into the mix of what was studied. However, in many cases, teachers experienced a school system in which they were expected to "keep up" with their subject colleagues in the curriculum, while students of all teachers wrote a common exam in each subject at a specific grade for which the teachers were expected to prepare their students.

While we were more than willing to take full advantage of the autonomy, this also brought a considerable responsibility. Staff met frequently after school, and at times even on weekends, to discuss issues or make plans for curricular and extracurricular activities. Some of the activities required staff to persuade parents/caregivers of the usefulness of these activities and assure them that their children would be safe. For example, when we wanted to take the entire student body to the Board-owned outdoor education center, we spent many evenings and weekends visiting the students' families to discuss the trip, answer questions, and address any concerns.

Several staff members financed the purchase of an old school bus. With this, we were able to take students on trips around the city and beyond, on a weekend trip to the Quebec Winter Carnival, a March Break trip to New Orleans, and a Christmas-break trip to Key West. Of course, we enjoyed all of these activities with students but, as with any school-based field trip, we were responsible "24/7" for our students.

We spent many hours during the school year, especially when planning for the next year, analyzing *our* successes and failures in great detail, and considering ways to create conditions that would improve the students' academic success. In saying this, we do not suggest that many teachers in mainstream schools do not work hard to support their students both in curricular and extracurricular activities. However, because we had created the school, we took an extraordinary amount of responsibility for the fact that the school was not working for some of our students. As a result, we spent many hours discussing, analyzing, and one might even say agonizing over whether our pedagogy, the structure of the program, and the types of courses offered could be improved to better meet all students' needs.

CONTACT SCHOOL: THE PRESENT

With the promise in 1995 of the construction on site of a new school building in conjunction with a provincially-funded medium-rise social housing complex, Contact moved to "temporary" interim quarters on two floors of a nearby low rise office building. However, before construction could begin, a conservative provincial government was elected, and plans for the new construction were summarily abolished. Contact was left to search for a new permanent location. After many temporary locations, a permanent site was finally identified— a former government office building in the center of the city, which the school board acquired and eventually renovated. For the past dozen years, Contact has shared this building with a child care center and some school board administrative offices. Presently, Contact has approximately 200 students registered; its staff includes fifteen teachers (two of whom hold the position of "Curriculum Leaders"), two youth workers, and an office administrator. The school continues to enroll the students who are not well served by mainstream schools. The teachers remain committed to the success of these students who have often been written off as not being capable of academic work. There remains also an emphasis on the need for the school to address the whole student. For example, a community lunch prepared by a teacher and a small group of students is held every day. The program has evolved over the years not just in response to the changing needs of students but also in response to general changes in the educational bureaucracy.

For example, as compared to its original non-hierarchical structure, Contact now has a principal and two vice-principals who are responsible for a total of nine alternative schools across the city. The office for these administrators is in the same building that houses Contact School. All Contact teachers are now selected centrally, which has been the case for some time in all Toronto alternative schools. The "Curriculum Leader" positions are also filled through an outside process. School staffing committees mandated by the Board and headed by the principal determine courses and teaching assignments each semester. Whatever the source, it is clear that the days of a collaborative, classroom teacher and student directed school are over, for Contact at least.

CONCLUSION

During the 1960s, the Toronto Board of Education built and opened up eight basic-level secondary schools serving working-class, immigrant, and racialized young people (two of which the authors taught at before Contact). With one exception, they all closed, long ago, in a period of low enrolments. Students voted with their feet as they realized that their work in these schools would likely not lead to future success. However, despite many vicissitudes and location changes, forty-three years after its inception, Contact Alternative School is thriving and continues to serve the needs of marginalized students. Just as the students in the first year at Contact have told us that they were made to feel welcome and they were supported in their academic growth and their personal development, so the students of today's Contact report that the school offers a similar welcoming and nurturing environment.

NOTES

1. The term "inner-city" was used (and continues to be used by the Toronto District School Board) to refer to the areas of the city in which residents live in poverty. The following report indicates the growth of these so-called "inner- city" neighborhoods in suburban areas and the increasing disparity in income across the amalgamated city of Toronto. Hulchanski, J. David (2007). The Three Cities Within Toronto: Income Polarization Among Toronto's Neighborhoods, 1970–2005. The Centre for Urban and Community Studies (now Cities Centre), *Research Bulletin 41*, University of Toronto (Hulchanski 2007).
2. Social Planning Council of Toronto (1971). *A Report on School Drop-Outs.* Toronto (Social Planning Council of Toronto 1971).
3. Golden, Mark (1971). "Downtown children dumb??!" *Community Schools,* Toronto, *10.* The exact quotation from Maurice Lister, school trustee from Ward 10, is: "Children of high-income families enter academic streams more easily than poor families simply because they stand to inherit higher intelligences from their parents" (Golden 1971).
4. Novogrodsky, Myra (1972). "The Board Goes to Park school (Well... some of them)." *Community Schools, 14.* The exact quotation from Ronald Jones, director of the Toronto Board of Education at the time is: "They (poor children) don't know as many words; they don't have as many ideas and logical thoughts; they don't speak in sentences to the same degree as more affluent children" (Novogrodsky 1972).

5. Regent Park was a public housing development in the east end of the city of Toronto built in the late 1940s.
6. See for example, Steele, Claude M. (2010). *Whistling Vivaldi: How Stereotypes Affect Us and What We Can Do*. New York: W.W. Norton & Company (Steele 2010).
7. Larter, Sylvia & Janis Gershman. (1979). *Contact: An Alternative School: How It Meets the Needs of Dropout Students*. Research Department of the Board of Education for the City of Toronto, 134 (Larter and Gershman 1979).

REFERENCES

Golden, Mark. 1971. *Downtown Children Dumb??!*, 10. Toronto: Community Schools.

Hulchanski, J. David. 2007. The Three Cities Within Toronto: Income Polarization Among Toronto's Neighborhoods, 1970–2005. In *Research Bulletin 41*, The Centre for Urban and Community Studies (now Cities Centre), University of Toronto.

Larter, Sylvia, and Janis Gershman. 1979. *CONTACT: An Alternative School: How It Meets the Needs of Dropout Students*. Toronto: Toronto Board of Education.

Novogrodsky, Myra. 1972. The Board Goes to Park School (Well…some of them). *Community Schools, 14*.

Social Planning Council of Toronto. 1971. *A Report on School Drop-Outs*. Toronto: CommunitySchools.

Steele, Claude M. 2010. *Whistling Vivaldi: How Stereotypes Affect Us and What We Can Do*. New York: W.W. Norton & Company.

AUTHORS' BIOGRAPHY

Harry Smaller is a former teacher and university faculty member. His research interests include teachers' unions, schooling structures and streaming, and global education.

Margaret Wells was a secondary school teacher and a curriculum consultant and co-coordinator focusing on equity in the Toronto Board of Education. She also has taught in the Initial Teacher Education Program at the Faculty of Education at York University and later at the Ontario Institute for Studies in Education. She has volunteered for many years with various social justice organizations in Toronto. Currently as a volunteer, she is teaching a course based on the work of Facing History and Ourselves on the history of Indian residential schools and the process of reconciliation at the LIFE Institute, Ryerson University.

CHAPTER 14

Inglenook: A Cozy Place by the Fire

Robert Pritchard and Robert Rennick

Inglenook ("a cozy place by the fire") Community High School is located in historic Corktown in the oldest continuously operated building of the Toronto District School Board (TDSB). The school founders were Richard Haney, the school's first coordinator, and several families who were members of the Karma Co-op. They were inspired by the counterculture thinking of the 1960s, and wanted an alternative school that both invited the community into the school and used the resources of urban Toronto to create McLuhan's idea of "a classroom without walls."

Parents, students, and teachers were equally involved in decision-making at "the Nook," as it is affectionately called. Through our Outreach program, students engage with the community, exploring academic and personal interests, and through volunteering, they give back to the community. Now in its forty-first year, the Nook continues to offer a comfortable family-like atmosphere for students desiring an alternative to oppressive, unchallenging, textbook-driven learning, and to the anonymity of many large mainstream schools.

R. Pritchard (✉) · R. Rennick
Inglenook Community High School, Toronto, Canada

© The Author(s) 2017
N. Bascia et al. (eds.), *Alternative Schooling and Student Engagement*,
DOI 10.1007/978-3-319-54259-1_14

179

HISTORY

Teachers and parents started Inglenook as a private school for students unhappy in mainstream schools. It was located in a Theosophical church basement on MacPherson Avenue in downtown Toronto. Parents were deeply involved, and the school charged tuition to pay the "volunteer" teachers. Needless to say, it was exciting to be involved in the creation of a school, and there was a strong sense that experiments in education and the creation of an alternative school were part of the larger zeitgeist and a feeling that, as Dylan's anthem put it, "the times they are a changin'."

Over time, the costs of the Nook escalated and with it tuition, and there was a growing concern that the school was in real danger of becoming an elitist enclave for disaffected upper middle-class students and their affluent parents. What to do? After much discussion and agonizing, the decision was made to approach the Toronto Board of Education and see whether it would be possible to join the Board as an official alternative school. This would secure a permanent location and secure funding to pay the teachers, and it would make the school open to all students who wanted an alternative education but did not necessarily have the funds to pay the high and escalating tuition of a private school. A proposal was drawn up for a school from grades 9 through 13, sent to the Toronto Board of Education, and finally accepted. Inglenook Community High School was born.

The model that was presented to and adopted by the Board included these key features:

- **Democratic decision-making**: (to include students and community members). There were weekly "town hall" type meetings and evening General Membership meetings that included students, teachers, parents, interested community members, and administrators.
- **CEASA**: (Committee for the Evaluation of Academic Standards and Admissions). All prospective Nook students were interviewed by this committee composed of students, parents, and teachers to determine whether there was a good fit between what the school could offer in terms of both courses and the Nook culture (e.g., teachers called by their first names, a student lounge, and an expectation that students would work co-operatively and responsibly to keep the school clean and safe) and the needs and expectations of the potential student. This committee also served as a sounding

board for student, teacher, and parent concerns. For example, a teacher could "take" a student to CEASA with concerns about attendance, classroom behavior, lack of progress, and incomplete assignments. A student could "take" another student for concerns about bullying or sexist behavior. A student could "take" a teacher with concerns about course work, course direction, or other issues. CEASA was not seen as a punitive body but as a safe space where students and teachers could resolve problems with the help of their peers. CEASA was also responsible for trying to maintain the key features of the original model and Nook culture.

- **Outreach**: This was a program that ran every Wednesday, when regular classes were suspended, and allowed students to go out into the community as volunteers or to explore potential career options, for example, volunteering in a gallery, a seniors' residence, an elementary school, a photo studio, and the Humane Society. Because initially many Nook students were quite privileged, there was also a sense of "giving back to the community." Over the history of the Nook, many students did find successful career paths and Outreach was and continues to be one of the most distinctive features of the Nook.

- **Pedagogy**: Nook courses were taught in an interdisciplinary manner. The courses were constructed around modules and often teachers would "trade" modules if they had a particular interest or expertise in an area. For example, a geography teacher would come into a history course and provide the geographic context for an historic event; an art teacher might come into a film course to help students develop storyboards for a film that the students were working on in the course; a math teacher might offer a unit in a visual arts course that demonstrated the many deep connections between art and geometry. An attempt was always made to relate each course being offered to the other courses in the school and to pay attention to how key concepts and issues were fundamental to the various courses. Courses were also refracted through the lens of social justice and critical thinking that challenged the dominant paradigm.

- **Innovation**: The Nook was also seen as what today would be called an "incubator" for new and novel courses. The Nook pioneered a number of "firsts," for example, being one of the first Ontario high schools to offer Philosophy as a credit course. At the time, there was a special protocol for Ministry approval for what were deemed "experimental" courses. After jumping through many hoops, the Nook was granted permission to offer the Philosophy course. Other innovative courses at the time were Film Studies, Media Studies and later Afro-American History, Queer Studies, and more.

- **Community**: As the name suggests, Inglenook Community High School teachers, parents, and students were concerned with, and worked hard to build, a safe and exciting community within the walls of the school and connect with the larger community outside the school building. There was a strong sense that, located as the Nook was in downtown Toronto, the school should utilize and engage with many of the resources that this location had to offer. Visits to art galleries, museums, historic buildings, cafes, other schools, universities, theaters, parks, and so on were a regular feature of the early days of the school. People from the community who had expertise in relevant areas were often brought into the classroom to offer lectures, seminars, and a range of activities, and there were special conference days focused on issues such as human rights, music, and health.

TEACHERS

Who were the teachers at the Nook and why would a teacher want to teach in an alternative school? One of us (Rob Rennick) was there from the beginning of the Nook as a private school as a seemingly paradoxical "paid volunteer" who later joined the Board and became an "official" Board teacher. One of us (Bob Pritchard) was the first "official" board teacher. He came to the Nook from Contact School, another alternative school in the Toronto Board.

Teachers who were interested in teaching at the Nook and other alternative schools were typically, and stereotypically, seen as living a counter-culture or alternative lifestyle. At one time, it was the case that four out of four teachers had been to India, which was seen as a counter-culture "hot-spot" and proof that one was an "alternative" teacher. Many teachers were artists and musicians in the community outside the school and brought these interests and skills to their courses at the Nook.

The teachers shared a world-view that was focused on critical thinking, social justice, and the use of the arts across the curriculum to enhance students' learning experiences. The teachers also typically believed in what is now called a "flattened hierarchy," a belief that the traditional top-down organizational style that dominated the Toronto Board and mainstream schools was not desirable. The core belief was, and still is, that all the members of the Nook community who would be affected by decisions should be involved in the decision-making process. The Nook received recognition for these pedagogical and community efforts by being chosen as an Exemplary School by the Canadian Education Association in 1994.

SHARED SPACE

The Nook shared space at 19 Sackville Street in an historic building origin-ally designed by William George Storm in Corktown. When the Nook started, that area was what might, without exaggeration, be called an industrial wasteland, located across the street from an automobile fender repair shop, near a salvage junkyard and, depending on which way the wind blew, often treated to the unpleasant odor of a nearby meatpacking plant.

We shared space with Wandering Spirit Survival School, the first aboriginal school in the Toronto Board. There were many wonderful connections and synergies between the two schools, as well as some sig-nificant challenges. Many Nook students did their Outreach Placements at Wandering Spirit, and it was delightful to have young children in the building and the fragrance of the sweet grass ceremonies, which were a frequent feature of WSSS.

The Nook has always had a shared operating kitchen where students could store and prepare food. In order to keep the kitchen clean and safe, student "hoppers" were chosen whose role was to clean the kitchen and student lounge, of course, working alongside the caretaking staff. Serving on CEASA, keeping the school clean, and generally looking out for each other were considered fundamental expectations of all students and teachers at the Nook and a key element of Nook culture.

As mentioned, music, visual arts, and theater were considered integral to the Nook experience. The school was decorated—according to one Board inspector "over decorated"—with student art, photos, and pro-jects. There was a designated photo wall recording student activities, Nook events, and famous alumni. Additionally, there were hundreds of videos made by students documenting the various aspects of Nook life and culture, many student newspapers, student sculptures, and so on. Many courses included seminars and projects that were based on visual arts and music; the arts generally were an integral part of the interdisci-plinary approach to pedagogy.

The (in)famous Nook Coffee Houses, which initially ran a couple of times a month and now run three or four times a year, were a forum for student bands, musicians of every style from punk to classical, from jazz to rap and hip hop, to spoken word, and so on for a long list. Teachers often performed, and Rob and Bob's group Postmodern Thieves is still going strong after forty years!

The Nook community wanted and needed a more permanent space for student, teacher, and community art. Eventually, the Inglenook Art Gallery, which was started by students and which the Board officially recognized, was created and remains a lively space for a wide variety of art and fashion installations, along with various course projects. Often, members from the larger community contributed shows such as an exhibition of quilts, and an eco-exhibit that saw the gallery and the first floor decorated with hand-made wooden trees. For one year, a notorious "punk Christmas" with a blackened, upside-down Christmas tree and cans of Campbell Soup (à la Warhol) dominated the front hall to the delight and consternation of many.

A student project featuring a "crucified alien" at a Toronto Board student art show became a media event, resulted in a call from the Director of the Toronto Board, and occasioned a lively discussion on what was acceptable art for students to produce in high school and what role censorship could and should play in the arts and education.

From its early years, the Nook also had a functioning darkroom and there were many courses on various aspects of photography. For many students, the darkroom was almost a home away from home, and often students had to be asked to leave at the end of the day lest they work on their prints overnight! For at least one student who ran the darkroom, this led to a successful career in photography. For several students, photography became their main artistic practice and resulted in shows in Toronto art galleries. Often, students who return to the Nook for a range of events including reunions, comment on how photography remains a vital part of their life.

ADMINISTRATION

In its early days as a Toronto Board school, the Nook was under the wing of a superintendent who was supportive and took a *laissez-faire* attitude toward the school. This attitude and the fact that the Toronto Board knew almost nothing about the school—often calling it

Inglewood—allowed the Nook to grow in an unfettered way and develop its own unique Nook culture and pedagogy.

Eventually, the Board and the Ministry worked hard to limit the freedom that the Nook enjoyed, and this resulted in a great deal of pushback and several protests. One of the most notorious was when students chained themselves to the playground structures in protest over the Board proposal to level all Board playgrounds over alleged safety concerns. The playground was part of the heritage of the school building, dating back to the time when it had been Sackville Public School. It became a quiet place for students to "hang out" and seemed to pose no danger to high school students.

The Nook was eventually placed under a principal, and in due course, a vice-principal was added. This model had limitations and depended a great deal on how simpatico a particular principal was to alternative schools and their philosophies. Now, the Nook is part of an administrative model of a principal and two vice-principals for nine alternative schools in the Toronto District School Board.

THE PRESENT

Where is the Nook today? Fortunately, because of the commitment of students, teachers, parents, and alumni, many of the original features of the Nook model, such as the Outreach Program, The Inglenook Gallery, the shared kitchen, special events like Culture Days, and field trips including trips to Stratford, New York, Buffalo, and elsewhere have remained intact. Some, like CEASA, have been greatly reduced or eliminated through decisions made by the Toronto District School Board and Ontario Secondary School Teachers' Federation (OSSTF). For example, it is unthinkable today that students could be part of an interview process to select teachers for the school or that they could "take" a teacher to CEASA for perceived problems with teacher behavior or the nature and progress of a course.

The demographics of the school have also changed significantly. Initially, the Nook offered grade 9 to grade 13 courses until grade 13 was abolished, and the Ontario Academic Credits (OACs) were added. Because of staff reductions at the school—again the occasion of student/teacher/parent protests—the Nook is now only a grade 11 and 12 program.

In the past, many students were highly academic, and their expectation along with the expectation of their peers and parents was that they would continue on to university. A number of alumni have earned PhDs. Currently, many Nook students are so-called "high-risk" and are dealing with anxiety and other health and emotional/psychological challenges. This change has resulted in necessary adjustments to the curriculum. Needless to say, the prime function of the Nook is still to be a safe inclusive space in which students can succeed academically and socially and deal with the myriad issues that are part of being an adolescent in our contemporary society.

THE FUTURE: THE NOOK AT FIFTY

Whither the Nook? Now celebrating forty-one years of success what might the future look like? What might the Nook look like at fifty years? We would suggest that there are four major developments/issues that will shape the future of the Nook and, we would argue, education generally.

- **Technology**: The ubiquitous role of technology and social media in students' lives and, of course, in the wider culture is a major factor. Most students are "wired" most of the time and gigabytes of information are continuously available at their fingertips. No need to argue now about who wrote a particular book or when a pop star was born, or wonder what the latest images of Pluto look like. A few taps and swipes and the information is right there. It seems obvious that teaching and learning must change in fundamental ways to prepare students for their future role as engaged citizens and workers in this information-rich, always-connected global village/mall. There is clearly no need any longer for the "sage on the stage," but rather there is a need to help students learn how to find relevant reliable information and how to critically process that information.
- **Emotional/Psychological Issues**: An epidemic of anxiety, school-phobia, and a wide range of emotional/psychological and health challenges, which seem to cut across socio-economic groups, give rise to concerns in both alternative and mainstream schools. What then is the role of the school? Is it not more than an academic space? Is it not also a "therapeutic" space? What does that mean for teaching and learning and the role of teachers? What would it mean for altered courses and the styles of teaching? These are ongoing challenges that must be sensitively thought through for necessary changes to be implemented.

- **Work**: The profound changes in the world of work both locally and globally will deeply affect all of our students. Ironically, as more citizens are able to pursue post-secondary education (although this may change if tuition continues to escalate), there are fewer "traditional" jobs available for which a university or college education used to prepare students. With the exponential increase in algorithms, roboticization, and outsourcing to so-called Third World countries, it is difficult to predict what types of jobs there will be five years from now, let alone ten or fifteen. Think of the role of disruptive algorithms such as the UberX app and the impact it is having on the taxi industry in many locations, and the many ethical, political, and economic issues/debates this has engendered. The only constant seems to be the increasing dominance of "smart" technology in students' lives and in the larger community.
- **Staff and Administration**: A key challenge for any school and especially for small alternative schools is finding dedicated qualified teachers who share a common vision of what constitutes an alternative school. This is a major concern with all schools generally and the Nook specifically as the "old guard" retires and moves on. Of what have been called the "four pillars" of the original Nook Staff— Rob, Bob, Gretchen, and Irene—three have retired and sometime sooner rather than later, the fourth will also retire. What will this mean for the Nook?

There have been times in the Nook's history when some teachers who either chose to teach there or were "bumped" in did not "buy into" the Nook alternative philosophy or the necessity of key elements of the school. They resented and resisted the long hours and hard work that are critical to build and maintain an effective alternative community school. Some of these teachers saw their work at the school as "just a job," and one teacher even went so far as to say that she only taught to "pay the mortgage." The Nook like all alternative schools grew and grows from a shared vision and the dedication of staff in working hard to maintain that vision, so finding and retaining committed staff who share that vision is a sine qua non.

The Nook and alternative schools generally also need administrators who understand the unique needs of small alternative schools and appreciate the underlying philosophies of alternative schools. Fortunately, the Nook has had a number of such administrators but also some who just "never got it" and did not offer the kind of support at the school or Toronto Board level that the Nook needed on issues such as funding, staffing, and pedagogical freedom. Even with the best will, principals and vice-principals are of course subject to the demands and directives of the superintendents, all the way up through the hierarchical chain to the Ontario Ministry of Education and its many directives. The framework of OSSTF around staffing also, of course, places certain constraints into the mix.

A key element that will determine the continued success of the school will be finding dedicated staff and supportive administrators who share a common vision of Nook culture, the basis of alternative philosophy and pedagogy, and even the very need for alternative schools. Without these, the name Inglenook Community High School would remain, and the building would appear the same, but the experience for both students and teachers would be markedly different from what it has been. That in our view would be a tragic loss.

The future of the Nook, of course, is not automatic. It has to be created through human endeavor and choices. Our hope and expectation is that the Nook will continue for many more years as a safe, inclusive, academically challenging "cozy place by the fire," where students can learn to think critically and take responsibility for their lives as both citizens of Canada and denizens of our fragile small blue planet.

AUTHORS' BIOGRAPHY

Robert Pritchard taught at two Toronto Board alternative schools, Contact for three years and Inglenook Community High School for twenty-seven years. As a teacher at Inglenook, he introduced several then innovative courses including media studies, film studies, and philosophy and served as Inglenook's Coordinator and Curriculum Leader for ten years. For fifteen years, he was also an adjunct professor in distance education at Nova Southeastern University in Florida. He is currently retired and among his many community activities/projects, he is a volunteer at College Montrose Children's Place and the Events Coordinator for his neighborhood park. Along with Robert Rennick, he is a member of the band Post-Modern Thieves.

Robert Rennick is currently a teacher and Curriculum Leader at Inglenook Community High School. He has taught at the school for forty years. He is a practicing visual artist and along with Robert Pritchard a member of the band Post-Modern Thieves.

CHAPTER 15

The Name Unspoken: Wandering Spirit Survival School

Sharon Berg

Five elements combined in September 1976 to establish a model for the way to educate First Nations youth in urban settings. One, co-founder Pauline Shirt lived in the Bain Co-op in Toronto, a Housing Co-operative with a collection of people ready to volunteer and help Wandering Spirit Survival School (WSSS) take root and grow. Two, Eddie Benton-Banai's orange and white Volkswagen van had a big sticker across the back, announcing, "You are in Indian country." It gave notice of an Aboriginal re-visioning of the colonial land grab that corralled First Nations on tiny, inadequate, reserves and forced them to endure the Residential Schools system. Three, Eddie founded the Red School House (RSH) in St. Paul, Minnesota, in 1972 as the first of the American Indian Movement's Native Way Survival Schools. RSH modeled a return to teachings from the Old Ways in modern times. Four, the name of the school itself was recovered from a century of lies told by the Canadian government. Wandering Spirit had been labeled part of the Riel Rebellion and was hung as a traitor to the crown, but he was shunned as *a killer of his own*. After decades of his name being unspoken on Pauline's

S. Berg (✉)
UBC, Vancouver, Canada

© The Author(s) 2017
N. Bascia et al. (eds.), *Alternative Schooling and Student Engagement*,
DOI 10.1007/978-3-319-54259-1_15

reserve, he was reclaimed as a hero of First Nations people.[1] Five, the Native People's Caravan to Ottawa in 1974 called for Indian Control of Indian Education, better health services, better housing, and a litany of related demands for better treatment of First Nations in Canada. Yet, the federal government refused to meet leaders of the Caravan, resulting in a so-called riot on Parliament Hill in 1974, and their demands continued to be resisted. These days Pauline says,

> The school started, and it rippled everything about the educational system. The Native Way of life, and how we educate within the Four Sacred Colors, gave the start for all of these [First Nations] Colleges and Universities... as if Spirit said Okay, get going now. (Shirt 2016)

Pioneering a Native Way School

In 1976, Wandering Spirit was the first Native Way School established in Canada. It set a model for other elementary schools in Canada, Scandinavia, and New Zealand. A phrase that comes into Pauline's speech regularly is a concept taken from traditional teachings, "Put the child in a safe place." Her personal realization of its importance takes root in her own experience of childhood trauma at Blue Quills Residential School in Alberta. Pauline continues:

> We need... a safe environment for the children. The children cannot go through that torturous time... That's when [First Nations people] started holding our breath... We were made to feel fear, fear, fear.[2]

Pauline's vision of Native Way as a model for emancipatory education takes root in her community. She is a Cree woman who Fasted[3] for guidance and was counseled by the Good Spiritual Grandfathers to found a school. Many others, including her ex-partner Vern Harper, helped to establish the Parent Council and volunteer support that turned her dream of a safe school for urban Native children into reality. Pauline's Four Seasons Curriculum is a distinct pedagogy and the story-within-a-story for a community that, in her words, helped children and adults from Toronto's Aboriginal community recover the Good Walk through Native Way.

In 1994, I began to meet with Pauline to document the history of WSSS in the founder's words.

S: Pauline... I've got two stories on the seed for Wandering Spirit...
    that Clayton and his difficulties planted the seed, and that it was
    the Caravan[4] ...I'm wondering how they come together. Did the
    Caravan lay a ground work, and then Clayton was ... the final drop
    of water in the bucket that made it spill over?
P: He was the one that decided that. He was the deciding factor, in
    that. Yeah.
S: But you must have been talking about founding a school earlier?
P: Yeah... [during] the Native Peoples' Caravan... We used to have
    meetings over there ... in Ottawa...that was where the seeds were
    planted...We said, you go home to your own areas, to your own
    reserves, wherever you are, and start ... You know? So, we... started
    talking about the schools.
S: It sounds like a number of seeds were planted, at the same time ...
P: Yup.
S: ... education, health, and other issues, and you just picked up the
    one for education?
P: ... education was affecting my children... Clayton was just begin-
    ning his Kindergarten and he hated it ...he used to get beaten up...
    You listen to the spirit of your.child and say...this is unsafe territory
    for my child, so what can we do? ...we started... talking to some
    people in [the Bain Co-op] ...some parents, and we said, 'Okay,
    why don't we start our own school? (Shirt and Berg 1994)

The beginning was more difficult than might first be imagined. Pauline
started the school in her living room. Many parents worried that they
would lose their children in a raid by the Children's Aid Society (CAS).
This was not a far-fetched notion. A disparity study that reported in June
2016 indicates that "Aboriginal and Black kids are far more likely to be
investigated and taken into care than White children" (Contenta et al.
2016). Indeed, 126 per 1000 Aboriginal cases continue to be investigated compared to 75 per 1000 of Black cases and 54 per 1000 of White
cases. Native children have been "scooped" by the CAS from the 1960s
onward and lost by their families, for perceived infractions of neglect and
abuse.

    In its first year, WSSS struggled to be recognized by the Ontario
Ministry of Education as a private cultural school. It survived six months
without funding, and applied for adoption by the Toronto Board of
Education (TBE) as an Alternative School. It also changed location twice

and more than doubled its student roll. The perseverance of WSSS "was a testimony to the commitment of the parents and volunteers," and its difficult beginning proved to be "a year when many stereotypes were broken down" as WSSS gained respect from numerous trustees on the Board of Education. (Novak: 6)

NATIVE WAY PEDAGOGY: A STRATEGY FOR RECOVERY

As a spokesman for WSSS, Vern Harper took up the role of War Chief, dealing with the public, in a moiety system operating as a gynocracy, with Pauline holding the role of a Peace Chief who dealt with the community itself. One of the original complaints of First Nations community is that colonizers were blind to the social roles of Aboriginal women. WSSS was founded on the idea that the path toward Aboriginal self-determination begins with Native education. The proposal that Native Way education was a radical trend is cause to point out that Native control of Native education was not a new idea but a very old one.[5]

Alex MacKay, the Ojibway language teacher, reported that parents sent their children to WSSS "to make them aware of their native culture and their language, and the kids are really receptive to it" (DiManno 1988). While earlier communities lost continuity with tradition through forced acculturation (through residential schooling, out-of-community adoption, and relocation), the founders of WSSS recognized that the metaphoric symbology embedded in Aboriginal languages continues to tie spiritual teachings to pragmatic lessons of survival. In other words, to speak an Aboriginal language is to speak of sacred teachings within an environment that involves the entire community. Language encompasses storytelling and directed lessons, in addition to the specialized narratives of songs, dances, and rituals.

It may look like fun in contrast to the lessons delivered in regular schools, yet among First Nations, dancing, drumming, and singing are regarded as serious work demanding reverence, practice, and intense concentration. In the National Film Board documentary of WSSS, Jim Dumont takes the proposal that Native people heal through a return to traditions to another level, insisting,

> Unless we know the legends and stories of Creation, unless we know the songs and ceremonies, we don't really know who we are…That is really the center of the school, the basis of the whole Native Way school.

Even seemingly utilitarian tasks such as cooking, sewing, or preparing Feasts are layered with story and protocol through cultural analogs that guide students to discover meaning in both their social interactions and their place in the natural world. The tenets of Aboriginal pedagogy articulate their regional relationship to the land in a thematic progression through the Four Seasons.

Robert Regnier identified WSSS as part of an Emancipatory School Movement.[6] The pedagogy of the Survival Schools Network unified the many indigenous nations of North America in the 1970s through the articulation of shared moral principles and values, signified by common metaphoric analogs. Through the participation of respected Elders, WSSS made a conscious return to traditional social patterns in transgenerational delivery of creation stories, caution tales, legends, and histories. However, Pauline stresses their culture classes were not simple history or sociology lectures.

WSSS offered an immersion program. Culture was articulated through social activities directly linked to seasonal themes or special events. For instance, boys learned to make a Water drum not as a craft activity, but so they would have it to use in specific situations. The making of the drum was preceded by teachings about its significance, including the protocols guiding its use in certain ceremonies. Traditional outfits made by the children were created to use at social events held at the school, such as the monthly Feasts or seasonal ceremonies. They made their own outfits and learned a variety of dances to go with each outfit. A fancy dancer made an outfit with beautiful quilt patterns and long-fringed shawls for the women or brightly colored feathers on a bustle backboard for the men. Yet, a girl who made a dress ornamented with curls of metal, sewn so close they could touch and jingle as she moved, learned the jingle dance. The orientation of the school was lived traditions, and gender differences in those traditions always communicated balance and respect. This addressed students' notions of personal identity through markers of their roles in the community. Placing the stress on living culture tied the curriculum to the thirteen moons of the natural world. As one reporter observed, the school year at WSSS was different,

Summer excursions to wilderness camps and visits to the school by resource people, such as a native herbalist or survival expert, reinforce the lessons. (Brydon 1979)

Just as there were after-four classes and monthly Feasts in the evenings, the calendar year at WSSS extended far beyond the regular school calendar.[7]

SYSTEMATIC CHALLENGES/COMMUNITY ISSUES

Pauline reports that staff at WSSS were always working around visiting academics, yet the most abundant sources of literature about the school are interest pieces or profiles in newspapers and magazines of the day.[8] They offer glimpses of the school in action through comments on a child's activity or the mention of study topics, but reconstruction of educational experiences for WSSS students is often frustrated by oversimplification. Therefore, the interviews featured in the 1978 NFB documentary, *Wandering Spirit Survival School*, offer an important treatment of the school's history. The NFB short *The Man, the Snake, and the Fox* (1979) also sheds light on WSSS's project-oriented program by presenting an actual storytelling event at WSSS featuring the students with their Ojibway language teacher, Basil Johnson.

Still, the newspapers highlighted important political issues faced by the WSSS founders.[9] For instance, there was the controversy following their refusal to start the day with the Lord's Prayer according to the policy of the Ontario Ministry of Education at the time (Dutton 1979). Journalism also identifies specific issues that confused Aboriginal children in dominant school settings through their history classes. For instance, in regular schools, children were taught that Big Bear and Wandering Spirit participated in the Northwest Rebellion and, like Louis Riel, were traitors to Canada. Even the school's name was met by political resistance,

> The Mounties were unsuccessful in their bid to change the school's name, yet the irony of the situation is not lost on the Indians. They are expected to attend schools named after such white heroes as Sir John A. MacDonald... [though] it was his government that quite simply stole the Indians' and Metis' land in the West. (Brydon 1979)

As Pauline explains, Riel was posthumously declared a Father of Confederation, yet, Aboriginal leaders, jailed or executed as his co-conspirators, remain labeled as traitors to the Crown. This continued misrepresentation confuses students and continues to demoralize Aboriginal people.

As a spokesman for WSSS, Vern often grounded his comments about the purpose of the school in issues of concern for the greater Aboriginal community, "One of the biggest problems for native people is a John Wayne mentality" ... (Horgan 1979). Yet, the issues of identity WSSS addressed were more convoluted than this. At a national conference addressing the prospects for children in 1979, Vern identified a "rift that separated families when children left home and adopted the white man's city ways" saying WSSS "helps children to deal with their double heritage" (Farrell 1979). The resurgence of Native Way allowed Aboriginal playwright Tomson Highway to announce, "I came back to the dream"(Marchand: 41). However, despite a strong contingent of activist support for WSSS,[10] opinions in Toronto's Aboriginal community in Toronto differed about how—and if—their stolen heritage could be recovered. The acculturative forces of more than 100 years pitted those who chose to forgo their heritage to adopt a white lifestyle against those who resisted the status quo and returned to traditions. Thus, the most hurtful resistance came from some of those whom the school was designed to serve. Vern Harper, reports,

> Many of our people, because of oppression, have developed a back-of-the-bus mentality, and are afraid not only to make demands, but have such low self-esteem that they don't believe in their own rights...considered too militant and radical... many Indian people ... saw no benefit in a separate school and wanted their children to "make it" in the regular school system. (Novak: 5)

As a result, the WSSS community was met with a realization that "one's most dogged and slippery opponents are often found in one's own community." (110) In a moment of frustration, Vern would ask, "Why try to be an imitation white man?" (Brydon 1979). Native Way pedagogy approached the issue of a student's poor self-image and the low status of Aboriginals in dominant society, first, by affirming the student's difference and, second, by fostering an inclusionary experience in a Native context. As Vern said, "At Wandering Spirit we are lucky to have the four races ... One race cannot survive without the other three" (Reid 1978).

NATIVE WAY EDUCATION INCLUDES FAMILY AND COMMUNITY

WSSS's project to extend the influence of its activism was frustrated by the primary reason for founding WSSS, namely, centuries of trauma and frustration that Aboriginal people have suffered in the name of education under the Indian Act (Truth and Reconciliation Commission 2016). Traditional culture stresses the involvement of extended families in raising and educating children, but family networks were fractured by generations of Residential schooling. Almost overnight, First Nations were expected to resume the responsibility for parenting, with little acknowledgment that their models for adult–child interaction were nuns and priests or that their experience was rooted in the trauma of Residential Schooling (Alcoze 1988).

WSSS was significant in carving the way for a national network of Native-directed schools. Yet, the trauma experienced by the school community often eclipsed the social and spiritual dynamic inherent in Pauline's vision. As Laura Reid (1978) says, it took fifteen years to dismantle the Residential Schools system.[11] "Unfortunately, the original stigma attached to the Native Canadian didn't disappear with the schools" (16–19). Even today, the Residential School experience continues to affect the generations of First Nations who were "…systematically intimidated into forgetting they were Indian" (Marchand: 41).[12] The Native Way schools emerged to address this phase of Indian education in Canada. Indeed, if each new generation is cradled in the arms of 18-year-old mothers, between the Indian Act of 1876 and the final year of the residential schools, 6 generations were stripped of continuity in traditions and world view. As prophesied, the Native Survival Schools welcomed a 7th generation with a revival.

The focus of Native Way education rests on the idea that "children are the future." At WSSS, the children could not be separated from the social reality of urban Natives. Aboriginals comprise less than 5 percent of the Canadian population, yet their future is more compromised than any other group living in Canada (Regnier 1994: 135).

> The suicide of about 5000 Canadian Indians under the age of 25 each year is at a rate six times higher than for non-Indians. Some researchers believe the true rate is twelve times higher than the Canadian average. (133)

Regnier found between 74 and 94 percent of Aboriginals were sexually abused in childhood and "fifty percent of the federal prison population is

Aboriginal," rising to a 70 percent incarceration rate by the age of 25 in Saskatchewan (135). The Office of the Correctional Investigator (2016) indicates little has changed. The school dropout rate is just one expression of discouraging statistics for self-perpetuating, destructive social patterns evident in the Aboriginal population. From the beginning, WSSS addressed two other compelling facts: 1) "Sixty percent of Toronto's native families ... are headed by only one parent, almost always a mother" (Marchand 1980) and 2) the personal despair experienced in relation to brokenness of family was often expressed through alcoholism.

In line with the goal of providing a secure environment for learning, WSSS addressed the home environment of its population. Students were encouraged to escape self-destructive patterns witnessed in their community by making a commitment to non-violence and adopting First Nations values, traditions, proper nutrition, and by abstaining from addictive substances, as modeled by their teachers.

> A tall man with a salt-and-pepper braid that falls to the middle of his back, [Vern] gathers up a rambunctious child in his long arms and hugs him, and the child becomes easy and quiet. [They] show them spirituality and love and try to teach by example. (Singer 1980)

Modeling and demonstration are gentle, forgiving, and powerful methods of teaching and learning. This is foundational to Native Way education.

In an extension of this logic, families were welcomed into the school,

> The idea of the afternoon sessions is to have parents attend classes with the students ... This is all part of a plan to get parents more involved in the education of their children, a plan taken so seriously by the school's executive council that direct parental involvement is one of the criteria required to enroll a child (TBE 1977 cited in TNT 1977).

Many families at WSSS were desperate for crisis intervention, so WSSS adopted an additional principle responsibility. Parents were encouraged to assume the responsibility for the model they set by earning their children's respect, even as they found their healing. In the WSSS documentary, Vern says,

> Already we see the home life changing...parents who maybe are drinking will quit drinking ... It does affect our children. If our children are seeing

fighting and arguing at home, they cannot come to school and concentrate on what they're trying to learn.

The children learned to see themselves differently through their experiences at WSSS, in part because they began to see their parents differently. Vern's insights on the subject were based in years of addiction counseling,

> When an alcoholic or an addict leaves his bottle or his addiction … it leaves an empty space. And if he doesn't replace that emptiness with something else, chances are he will go back to his alcohol or drugs. So, the last state… is worse than the first. The answer for native people is spiritualism…Men and women can grab that pipe, and it will carry them through anything. (Marchand: 113)

At WSSS, teachings delivered through the Sacred Circle each morning suggested social and physical illnesses are caused by an imbalance in the physical, emotional, intellectual and spiritual aspects of being. Elders taught the brokenness of families and criminal activity among urban youth were caused by being raised with a paucity of stories (teachings) and the scattering of communities (Aken 1993; Lightning 1993). In general, the pedagogy of healing "proceeds in phases of belonging, understanding and critical reflection," which are cyclical (Regnier 1994). Having good health means living with a meaningful vision of one's wholeness, connectedness, and balance in the world, whereas illness is a loss of meaning that results in weakness, fragmentation, and isolation resulting in lack of purpose and direction (135).

Among Aboriginal nations, the pipe is a channel for counsel with the Good Grandfathers and Creator.[13] Living by the Pipe means walking the Good Walk, holding a sense of purpose invested with meaning. Sacred Circle rituals are an affirmation that individuals can return to "*harmony with the whole*" (138). Indeed, Regnier suggests, the harmony of reintegration developed through the Sacred Circle ceremony assumes a prior brokenness and the potential for reconciliation in a process "that recognizes individual limitations," while stressing inclusion.

WSSS became an extension of the students' homes, reflecting a traditional social pattern that knit family and community members in mutually supportive relationships. Not only did the school embrace parents through their participation in morning circles, afternoon cultural classes, monthly Feasts, and seasonal camping trips to ceremonies,[14] but it established what Bill Lewis refers to as a buddy system. Each child was partnered with an adult (other than a parent) who offered support on a 24-hour-a-day basis in the style of a Big Brother or Big Sister. Just as the pedagogy and curriculum were "indigenized," the school welded facets of dominant culture social activism with Aboriginal pedagogy in the belief that "schools were centers of healing and teachers were healers … [who] move beyond personal needs to become servants of the community" (Regnier 1994: 136). While Vern Harper admits they walked a fine line in recovering traditions to re-infuse cultural pride in their students, he also declared, "It is up to us to do something different. No one out there is going to do it for us" (Hughes 1979). Aboriginal students can only turn their attention to academic success when they have discovered pride in their identity, healing in their families, and belonging in their community.

In the NFB documentary, parents' evaluations of the success of WSSS are expressed in their comments on the changes they noticed in their children after they started to attend WSSS. One woman insisted,

> They're a lot more self-assured … A lot of them were very turned-off school because they've had a lot of bad experiences, and now … most days they're eager to come to school and learn about their culture.

Another said,

> They're becoming more, you know, proud of themselves, being Indian. And I'm really happy about that because I want them to … respect themselves and hold their heads up, wherever they go.

The language teacher, Alex MacKay, also saw the school's success in the enthusiasm of his students. Culture is not something pulled out for special occasions. Rather, it is the constant expression of being in relationship to the social, spiritual, and physical world.

LOOKING TOWARD THE FUTURE

Now, in 2016, Pauline believes she must reclaim the original story of the school, stressing the roles members of the collective assumed in relation to community. The story changed through renaming the school.

Though it still exists in the Toronto District School Board (TDSB) as First Nations School, and continues to positively influence First Nations children, it is not the same place. In January 2016, Pauline and her son, Clayton Harper (now working as a Traditionalist, Spokesman, and Healer in Toronto) began work as part of the Aboriginal Education Centre. They are talking to the TDSB about founding a second Native Way School, starting with Kindergarten and adding a grade with each year until the school has Kindergarten to Grade 12.

In a January 2016 interview, Pauline said,

The spirit is still with me. No one took up care for the spirit ...The old men said, tobacco will be given to help get the school back. The Aboriginal Education Centre has taken it up and asked me to help them move it to another school.

Upon its election, the new Trudeau Liberals vow the Canadian government will help First Nations to rewrite the approach to Native education. Time will tell.

NOTES

1. When Pauline named WSSS, she had no idea that Wandering Spirit was her relative.
2. Telephone conversation, January 2016.
3. Fasting is also called a Spirit Quest. It usually involves 4 days and nights of isolation on the land without food or water, under the care of a Medicine Man.
4. This refers to the Native People's Caravan to Ottawa (NPCO) in 1974.
5. Pauline calls the program at WSSS Four Seasons Curriculum, but refers to curriculum in the Survival Schools network as Native Way.
6. Robert Regnier taught in the Education Department at University of Saskatchewan. He also served as Principal for the Saskatoon Native Survival School at one point. In 1987, Regnier interviewed Pauline and she invited me to sit in. I had a telephone consultation with him about using his transcripts in 1995.
7. The name of each moon is tied to the biotic community in both its seasons and its regions.
8. The majority of these pieces cover the period from 1977 to 1980, which Pauline refers to as 'the heydays of Wandering Spirit'.

9. I obtained access to Pauline's personal archives in 1997. The archives proved an especially valuable source of information about specific incidents surrounding the decision to found WSSS.

10. In terms of chronology of participation, Nancy Woods was the first teacher. Pauline ran the school from the beginning and Vern (who worked elsewhere) joined the school after a year and a half. Ken Tobias was an early cultural consultant who acted as a teacher briefly after Nancy left. When the school was adopted by the TBE, Wendy Beatty, Kathy Sims, Elizabeth Thompson, Fay MacKenzie, and Mark Machida all spent time at WSSS as certified teachers. Initially, Pauline taught Cree language classes. The Elder Kasper Solomon and Basil Johnson both taught Ojibway language classes and acted as cultural advisors and storytellers. George Kenny participated as a storyteller. In the school's *heydays*, Ken Tobias, Sam Moosecamp, Joe Sylvester, Dawn Smoke, Mark Philips, and Clarence Kaachagee were among the many cultural program advisors.

11. In fact, the Truth and Reconciliation Commission Report (2016) indicates the last residential school closed in 1998, some twenty years later, making a total of thirty-five years.

12. Marchand (1980) refers to people in their 20s and 30s, placing them in their 50s and 60s now. The last school closed in 1998. Yet, because local provincial schools were not legally required to open their doors to them, some Indian children were shipped hundreds of miles to be billeted in Residential school buildings while attending public school.

13. The pipe is at the center of the Sacred Circle and the Four Seasons curriculum.

14. The Four Seasons are marked by ceremonies occurring at the summer and winter Solstices and spring and fall Equinoxes, no matter the weather. Ceremonies are held over four-day periods at various locations (often on reserve) in Wyoming, Michigan, or northern Ontario.

REFERENCES

Alcoze, Thom. 1988–1989. *The Original People of North America*. Class lectures, Sudbury: Laurentian University.

Aken, Linda. 1993. Pimosatarnowin Sikaw Kakeequaywin: Walking and Talking, A Saulteau Elder's View of Native Education. *Canadian Journal of Native Education* 19 (2): 189–214.

Brydon, Joan. 1979. Wandering Spirit School. *Seven News* (Ward 7, Toronto), February 10, 3.

Contenta, Sandro, Laurie Monsebraaten, and Jim Rankin. 2016. CAS Study Reveals Stark Racial Disparities for Blacks, Aboriginals. *Toronto Star.com*, June 23.

DiManno, Rosie. 1988. Cultivating a Spirit at Wandering Spirit: Native Way a Priority at School for Indian Kids. *Toronto Star*, June 5, B6.

Dutton, Don. 1979. Indian Kids Start Day with Ancient Ritual. *Toronto Star*, September 18.

Farrell, Ann. 1979. Programs Help Native Child: Year of the Child. *Toronto Star*, June 13, C14.

Horgan, Denys. 1979. The Sacred Circle: School in the Heart of Toronto keeps Native Spirituality Alive. *The Globe & Mail*, Last modified May 19–20.

Hughes, Margaret (Sion). 1979. An Alternative School for Native Children. *New Times*, July 15, 7.

Lightning, Walter. 1993. Compassionate Mind: Implications of a Text Written by Elder Louis Sun-child. *Canadian Journal of Native Education* 19 (2): 215–253.

Marchand, Philip. 1980. The Native Dream: The Painfully Fragmented Inheritance of Urban Indians, Haunted by Spiritual Loss. *Toronto Life*, October.

Office of the Correctional Investigator. http://www.oci.bec.gc.ca/cnt/rpt/oth-aut/oth-au20121022info-eng.aspx. Accessed 26 Jan 2016.

Reid, Laura. 1978. Going Home to the Red Path. *Hourglass: Magazine of Concern for Community Education*, November 16–19, 5 (1).

Regnier, Robert. 1994. The Sacred Circle: A Hocess Pedagogy of Healing. *Interchange* 25: 129–144.

Truth and Reconciliation Commission of Canada. 2016. *A Knock on The Door: The Essential History of Residential Schools from the Truth and Reconciliation Commission of Canada/ Foreword by Phil Fontaine*. Winnipeg: University of Manitoba Press.

TNT (Toronto Native Times). 1977. *Counsellor leaves Pedahbun*. Toronto: Toronto Native Times, December 8.

AUTHOR BIOGRAPHY

Sharon Berg M. Ed (York) D. Ed (UBC), is a scholar and book-published author of poetry, fiction, essays, and reviews. Her creative work has appeared in periodicals across Canada, the UK, The Netherlands, the USA, and Australia. She lives in Sarnia, Ontario, and is host/organizer for a Reading series, and founding editor of Big Pond Rumours Literary E-Zine and Micro-Press. She is working on a book-length history of Wandering Spirit Survival School.

CHAPTER 16

The Triangle Program: Canada's Only High School Program for LGBTQ Students

Steven Solomon

In September 1995, the Triangle Program opened its doors as a program of Oasis Alternative Secondary School in the former Toronto Board of Education (TBE). Having reached its 20th anniversary in 2016, Triangle continues to be Canada's only high school education program serving lesbian, gay, bisexual, trans, and queer (LGBTQ) identified students. For many of its students, Triangle offers an opportunity to escape the experiences of homophobia, biphobia, and transphobia endured in their previous schools. Once they landed in Triangle students found a safe space and time to reconnect to school through curriculum that reflected more of who they are, if not more of who they wanted to be. With a queer lens on subjects such as history and English, educators at Triangle (out lesbians and gay men) offer a learning environment where being your authentic self is just as important as what you are studying. This chapter, written by Triangle's former school social worker (1997–2011), explores the Program's earliest beginnings, aims, goals, challenges, and triumphs. It will discuss and highlight the circumstances, key players, and political framework that gave rise to Triangle along with some key points

S. Solomon (✉)
Ryerson University, Toronto, Canada

© The Author(s) 2017
N. Bascia et al. (eds.), *Alternative Schooling and Student Engagement*,
DOI 10.1007/978-3-319-54259-1_16

in its evolution. This narrative unfolded within the shifting contexts of LGBTQ issues in education.

The ten years before Triangle opened its doors were marked by significant events that provide the context of this innovative program's establishment. The murder of TBE gay librarian Ken Zeller in High Park in June 1985 was a watershed moment for the local school board in Toronto. This vicious and ultimately fatal gay bashing, at the hands of a group of Toronto high school students, forced the TBE to confront the issue of homophobia. In 1986, school trustee Olivia Chow explored the circumstances of homophobia and began, "an ad hoc investigation of homophobia in the school system, concluding that 'considerable abuse' towards those suspected of being gay was taking place unchecked in Toronto schools" (McCaskell 2005: 93).

Early in 1988, a proposal to establish a counseling program for lesbian and gay youth emerged in what would become known as the Human Sexuality Program. Counseling services covered a wide range of concerns including support for lesbian and gay youth. In later years, it focused specifically on issues related to sexual orientation and gender identity, providing counseling support for lesbian and gay students, staff development, and classroom workshops addressing homophobia across the Board from kindergarten to grade 12. While the counseling program was being created, there were discussions about establishing an alternative school program for lesbian and gay youth. At that time, it was necessary to establish a presence within the Board. A Human Sexuality Program achieved this.

A key communilty-based player during this time was the Toronto Counseling Centre for Lesbians and Gays (TCCLG), a volunteer-based organization providing counseling support to lesbians and gay men. The TCCLG later joined with Family Services of Toronto, creating the David Kelley Services Program, named after one of the founders of the TCCLG, to offer counseling to LGBTQ communities. The connection to the school board began with two TCCLG volunteers, Tony Gambini and John Hunter, both TBE social workers. Tony observed an increasing number of lesbian and gay youth seeking out the TCCLG for support. As a school social worker, he wondered if it was possible to address this gap in service within the TBE. Tony would be the inspiration of the Human Sexuality Program.

With help from Olivia Chow and George Bielmeier, a board member of TCCLG and a Ryerson Polytechnic Institute (now Ryerson University) social work professor, respectively, and liaising with Dr. Greg

McClare, Senior Coordinator of Social Work Services at the TBE, the Human Sexuality Program began during the 1988–1989 school year with Tony as a part-time social worker. These efforts included the establishment of an advisory committee for the Human Sexuality Program, with membership from The Hospital for Sick Children, TCCLG, PFLAGE (a parent organization), and Ryerson. Membership also included Olivia Chow and other Board departments and staff.

In 1992/1993, I was a fourth-year social work student from Ryerson doing my practicum/internship placement with the Human Sexuality Program. My main task that school year was to develop a proposal for an alternative school program for lesbian and gay students. At that time, there was a dearth of research and writing on school issues facing lesbian and gay students. During this time, a support group for lesbian and gay students was running at the TBE, facilitated by Tony and staff from the TBE Equity Studies Centre. In 1992, Tony became a full-time employee in the Human Sexuality Program (HSP). Krin Zook, who worked with students in need at Rosedale Heights Secondary School, offered classroom workshops addressing homophobia. Recalling Tony Gambini's earlier inspiration for a counseling program, McCaskell (2005) points out, "Tony Gambini's experience as the human sexuality counsellor had given him ample experience of the devastation that was occurring in the lives of many gay and lesbian students as they struggled to get an education in homophobic secondary school settings. In response Tony came up with the idea of a school for gay and lesbian youth." (p. 215)

In January 1995, the Zeller Program Planning Committee (ZPPC) formally proposed the establishment of a school for LGBTQ youth. The ZPPC consisted of three teachers from Oasis Alternative Secondary School, a TBE trustee, and an advisor from the Human Sexuality Program. The family of Ken Zeller was approached to seek permission to name the school in memory of Ken. The family declined. Shortly thereafter, the school was named the Triangle Program and added to offerings of Oasis Alternative Secondary School, a long-standing alternative school in the TBE. Consistent with the philosophy and mission of Oasis, Triangle offered a full-time academic program for the "at-risk" youth who were casualties of homophobia. Some had dropped out of school and other were on the verge of doing so. In keeping with Oasis's mission, each student was offered an individualized course of study. Students stayed as long as they needed. The program was intended to promote "transition back to the mainstream". These students now had the opportunity to re-engage with school, receive support in response to their experiences of homophobia and transphobia, and then re-enter a mainstream school to complete their studies. In many cases, students moved on to other gay positive alternative schools.

Some criticisms at the time declared that the program was "segregating" students. The use of such a provocative term overlooked that students dropping out of school was the ultimate form of segregation. The Metropolitan Community Church of Toronto (MCCT) was approached to house Triangle and senior pastor Brent Hawkes agreed, at no rental cost. School board trustee John Campey played an important role in Triangle's beginnings. Given the political climate of the early 1990s regarding lesbian and gay issues in general and education in particular, he "proposed establishing Triangle as a satellite program to the downtown Oasis Alternative School... establishing one more such program would be an administrative rather than a political matter" (McCaskell 2005: 216).

In September 1995, the Triangle Program opened its doors on the 2nd floor of MCCT, with its first full-time teacher, John Terpstra, who had previously served as head of the English Department at Jarvis Collegiate, a large academic downtown secondary school. Tony Gambini became the first social worker for Triangle, offering counseling support as part of his work in the Human Sexuality Program. At the very same time as Triangle opened its doors, it is important to note that the first Black focused high school program, Nighana, also began, though it would not be housed as a program of an existing school (like Triangle), but housed within Davenport Perth Neighbourhood Community Centre. Similar to the Human Sexuality Program, Triangle had an advisory committee made up of program staff (teaching and social work), Oasis staff, and community-based organizations serving LGBTQ youth. The advisory committee provided crucial support to Triangle especially to advocate for the resources within the TBE. Triangle is Canada's only high school program for LGBTQ students. It is the second in North America after Harvey Milk in New York.

TRIANGLE 1995–2005

In the first couple of years, the Triangle curriculum developed with individualized math studies and group classes for English (with a lesbian/gay focus), among other subjects. Enrollment in the 2nd year was approximately 22 students, 7 returning from the inaugural year, with students earning about 45 credits in total. Media attention on Triangle was keen in these early years, with positive stories written in local newspapers and magazines (Toronto Star, Toronto Life). There were some less charitable stories printed, specifically the Alberta Report (McGovern 1995: 33) on Triangle entitled "Reading, Writing, and Rimming." Community support was tremendous, with a multitude of volunteers coming forward to contribute. A nutrition program was launched and tutors volunteered their time to work one on one with students in the classroom. These supports endure to this day.

In June 1996, the idea of a community-based prom called "Over the Rainbow, The Prom You Never Had" became a reality. The following year, Triangle began what has become a long tradition of sponsoring "The Pride Prom," a student-only prom. The advertising poster read "On 11 June 1997 all lesbian, gay, bisexual, and transgender students and their friends are invited to the first Board-sanctioned lesbigay prom in Canada." Nearly 150 high school students celebrated both Pride and the end of the school year. In later years, Supporting Our Youth, a community-based organization serving LGBTQ youth, became a co-sponsor of this event.

Against the backdrop of a significant right wing shift at the provincial government level, including the amalgamation of local school boards in the metro area, Triangle went from serving TBE students to becoming the Triangle Program of the newly established Toronto District School Board (TDSB) in January 1998. In 1998/1999, following the retirement of its first full-time teacher, Triangle was led by two out lesbian teachers, Vanessa Russell and Patty Barclay, and Triangle moved from the 2nd floor into the aptly named "Rainbow Classroom" in the church basement. Vanessa came to Triangle as an experienced Board equity worker, and Patty was a long-standing teacher and coordinator at Oasis. Together, Vanessa and Patty further developed the LGBTQ content of Triangle's curriculum. Triangle students engaged in courses that incorporated coming out stories, community, homophobia studies, wellness, Holocaust curriculum, and even a quilting unit. An end-of-year video unit was instituted for students to work alongside community artists and videographers (including the late, award-winning Melissa Levin) to create a visual project. During this time, Triangle students were given free 10-month fitness memberships at a local gym. Students were achieving some of their first high school successes. For many, this was their first positive experience with school.

Given that Triangle students were escaping homophobic and transphobic violence in their previous schools, the safer space of Triangle was critical for their success, but their non-academic lives continued to present them with challenges. As the school social worker, with assistance from a series of social work placement students, my work at Triangle included addressing issues such as precarious housing, family conflict, peer relationships, and social assistance for those living on their own, to name just a few. Krin Zook and I organized regular individual check-ins with students to provide support.

Triangle students came with years of homophobic experience, often from earlier than high school. The impact of such trauma and its relationship to learning was noted in an article Vaness and I co-authored that discussed homophobic bullying in elementary schools. For one student in particular who suffered horrendous homophobia, both verbal and physical, before showing up at Triangle, the impact on learning was manifested during Vanessa's one on one work teaching him math.

> When she [Vanessa] sat down with the student to begin some work in math, she started with a review of integers knowing that he [the student] would have already learned about them in elementary school. Vanessa believed it would be a safe space to start. She was astonished to find that this student had no recollection of ever learning negative and positive numbers. She started to put the pieces of the puzzle together and she realized his experiences of harassment began precisely at the time he would have begun learning integers. He had just stopped learning (Solomon and Russell 2004: 24).

In June 1999, the Toronto District School Board adopted its Equity Policy. Published in 2000, the Equity Foundation Statement alongside the commitments to equity policy implementation, included Anti-homophobia and Sexual Orientation Equity, which states,

> A curriculum that strives for sexual orientation equity provides a balance of perspectives. The TorontoDistrict School Board acknowledges that inequities have existed in the curriculum; therefore, the Board is committed to enabling all lesbian and gay students and students who identify themselves on the basis of sexual orientation and gender identity to see themselves reflected in the curriculum. (TDSB 2000: 14)

In many ways, the Triangle Program had already been doing this for nearly four years. In 2003, the lives of three Triangle students were captured on film, in the School House Production, "Class Queers." Directed by Melissa Levin and Roxana Spicer, the documentary follows the joys- and challenges-facing Triangle students. Melissa had a long-standing relationship with Triangle as our invited videographer for the popular video unit. As Telefilm Canada writes, "*Class Queers* is an intimate and compelling documentary about three teenagers and how the homophobia they encounter in the high school educational system has had an impact on their lives in the classroom and at home" (Telefilm Canada 2004). In many ways, *Class Queers* captured the breadth and depth of many Triangle students' lives and showed how their varied experiences had led them to Triangle.

By 2005, Triangle was humming along registering and graduating more and more students. From 2005 onward, former Triangle Program volunteer tutor Jeffrey White became the full-time teacher, and Triangle added its second full-time teacher, Les Tager, continuing the critical role of having gender parity in the teaching roles. While I continued in my social work role, Triangle did face its own staffing cut and Krin's position had been eliminated in 2003. For its tenth anniversary, the program published "Triangle Writes: Out of the Margins and into the Light." This anthology of Triangle experiences was an opportunity for current and former students as well as staff to reflect on Triangle at this significant milestone. Up to that point, Triangle had registered close to 275 students.

TRIANGLE 2006–2016

During my leave of absence in 2005/2006 to begin doctoral studies, the Triangle teaching staff retained its full-time teachers and its gender parity with Jeffrey White and Les Tager. Upon my return in the spring of 2007, former teaching intern Anthony Grandy had joined the program, replacing Les Tager. During the next few years, Triangle would increase its full-time teaching complement to three (Emily Wadsworth followed by Susan Magerman). In 2012/2013, Jeffrey and Anthony remained as the full-time teachers. This second decade of Triangle would see further renovations to our classroom space, and after a year-long stint upstairs on the main level, we had three separate classrooms and one open space for Triangle.

During this time, Triangle began to attract younger students. While many were registering to complete their senior year of high school, others coming for intake interviews had only just begun high school. An increasing number of students came to intake interviews with parents/guardians. The first such interview (in fact the father had made the initial call) occurred in 1997. I recall that meeting fondly. I found myself apologizing to the father for staring—up until that point, parents/guardians had been far more in the background lives of our students, if not completely absent. With more students out and living at home, the Triangle staff now found themselves supported by partnerships with parents and guardians active in the daily lives of the students.

During this past decade, a substantial number of social and legal shifts have occurred, not just in Toronto, but also in other parts of Ontario and across Canada. In June 2005, federal legislation was enacted to make the definition of marriage inclusive of same-sex couples across Canada. In the run-up to this legislation, strides were made toward equal access to government benefits and adoption rights for same-sex couples. In June 2009, the Ontario government passed Bill 157, the Keeping Our Kids Safe at School Act, which among other things required school boards to address homophobia and gender-based violence. In 2012, in Ontario, Toby's law was passed, resulting in an updated provincial human rights code. This added gender identity and gender expression to the list of prohibited grounds for discrimination.

In many ways, the Triangle Program championed, through its daily efforts, the same issues now being undertaken across Ontario. Triangle had originated as a result of the glaring absence of meaningful policy and practice to support Lesbian, Gay, Bisexual, Trans, Queer, 2 Spirit (LGBTQ2S) students. The issue of safe and accessible washrooms has been a moot point at Triangle. In her 2011 ethnographic study involving Triangle, Dr. Doreen Fumia of Ryerson University, and chair of Triangle's Community council, noted in one of her interviews, the following student's remarks on Triangle's significance,

> So I went with my mom and I fell in love with [Triangle] because I was like, oh my god, I can be myself and they have single bathrooms! I don't have to worry about people beating me up. And that's how I ended up going to the Triangle program. But yeah, I'm really happy that I went and when I chose to go there I kind of thought that I was never gonna graduate and never gonna go anywhere with my life, so it's kind of a big deal that I did and actually got a lot more opportunities because ... I wouldn't have ... if I had stayed at a random mainstream school. (Fumia 2011)

The recent campaign to guarantee that students have the right to access washrooms that correspond to their gender identity continues.

The TDSB now has an explicit policy and commitment to have gender-neutral bathrooms in all its schools. At a broader level, however, these changes seek to promote and affirm action and make all schools safer and more welcoming to LGBTQ students. Today, more and more elementary and secondary schools have active and growing Gay Straight Alliances (GSA). In fact, a few years ago, the TDSB Board of Trustees voted to identify themselves as a GSA. Former school trustee Kathleen Wynne, an out lesbian, is now the Premier of Ontario. Put another way, these changes reflect the very real issues that made Triangle necessary in the first place.

More than 30 years ago, Ken Zeller, a Toronto librarian, was murdered in High Park. Ten years after that fatal gay bashing, a small transitional alternative school program for lesbian and gay youth began operating as a "one room school house" on the second floor of MCCT. In June of 2016, Triangle celebrated its 20th anniversary, bringing together the current and the former students, staff, volunteers, and community partners. Over the past two decades, nearly 600 students have registered at the Triangle Program, many with the goal of successfully finishing their high school diploma. Some of these graduates have gone on to post-secondary institutions, while others have pursued aims outside of formal education, confident in their success both at school and in their larger social lives. Times have definitely changed, but students continue to seek out Triangle for its original mission and aim—providing a safer space for LGBTQ2S students to learn, grow, and build community.

REFERENCES

Fumia, Doreen. 2011. Desiring and Doing Equity: The Triangle Program for LGBTIQ2S Youth. *Federation for the Humanities and Social Sciences* (blog), December 20. http://www.ideas-idees.ca/blog/desiring-and-doing-equity-triangle-program-lgbtiq2s-youth.

McCaskell, Tim. 2005. *Race to Equity: Disrupting Educational Inequality.* Toronto: Between the Lines.

McGovern, C. 1995. Reading, Writing and Rimming. *Alberta Report/Western Report* 22: 33.

Solomon, Steven, and Vanessa Russell. 2004. Addressing Homophobic Bullying in the Elementary Classroom. *Orbit* 34 (2): 24–26.

Toronto District School Board. 2000. *Equity Foundation Statement and Commitments to Equity Policy Implementation.* http://www.tdsb.on.ca/_site/ViewItem.asp?siteid=15&menuid=682&pageid=546.

AUTHOR BIOGRAPHY

Steven Solomon Ph.D., MSW, is a full-time contract lecturer with the School of Social Work at Ryerson University. Prior to full-time teaching, Steven was a school social worker with the Toronto District School Board (TDSB) for 15 years offering counseling support to LGBTQ2S students and families, facilitating anti-homophobia and anti-transphobia workshops across the board, kindergarten to grade 12, and providing social work support to the Triangle Program of Oasis Alternative Secondary School Steven received his PhD in social work from the Factor-Inwentash Faculty of Social Work at the University of Toronto. His doctoral research investigated the prevalence of homophobic and sexist language use among middle school students in the TDSB.

CHAPTER 17

Credit Factory or Alternative Education for Adults? Student Re-Engagement Through Multi-Media Arts and Social Justice Education: A Transdisciplinary Pilot Project

Vanessa Russell and Cheryl Mootoo

During a period of political changes that affected education in profound ways and caused upheaval, a new program was born at the Toronto District School Board (TDSB). We write this chapter and situate ourselves as two teachers working in a non-alternative school setting for a population of young adults still eligible for full student funding—18- to 20-year-olds who have not yet graduated in year 4 of their high school careers. We believe that many of the challenges we face in our school emerge from this non-alternative school designation. As such, we have

V. Russell (✉) · C. Mootoo
Ontario Institute for Studies in Education at the University of Toronto, Toronto, Canada

© The Author(s) 2017   213
N. Bascia et al. (eds.), *Alternative Schooling and Student Engagement*,
DOI 10.1007/978-3-319-54259-1_17

created a critical practitioner inquiry pilot project embedded in alternative education traditions to address some of these difficulties.

Our school is one of the five TDSB Ed-Vance Programs. In the TDSB's course selection and planning guide, Ed-Vance is described in the following way.

> Ed-Vance programs allow students ages 18 to 21 years old to complete a high school diploma in a flexible, personalized program in an adult environment. The program focuses on strengthening literacy skills, accumulation of credits (2 to 3 in a nine-week term and 8 to 10 in a full year) and valuable work experience through cooperative education. Students who are eligible have achieved a minimum of 5 credits, have been out of school, but have demonstrated dedication to earning their diploma, and can attend regularly. (Choices 2015–2016, 23)

Given deep cuts to adult education during the time of political upheaval, the school boards wanting to continue to offer adult education were stuck between a rock and a hard place. The Ed-Vance program and its other iterations across the province are important because they make possible the funding required to keep school buildings that house adult programs operating and boiler rooms running.

Our school offers students an accelerated credit delivery model to complete their Ontario Secondary School Diploma (OSSD). Individual Ed-Vance school Web sites highlight this feature: "a great opportunity to earn credits fast—up to 12 credits in just one year"[1]; "we offer 4 quadmesters (quads) a year, with the opportunity for learners to earn up to 3 credits in 9 weeks".[2] The promise of more credits in less time is a carrot used to entice older adolescents back to school when they have been out of school for a period of time, a criterion for eligibility to the program. This promise, however, falls short of the reality. Although student success manifests itself in different ways in our school, including the ultimate—graduation—our experience is that very few students achieve the expected three credits per quad.

Our school receives a diversity of students, many with gaps in their learning and achievement levels. We believe there are ethical and equity considerations in bringing together an accelerated curriculum via a nine-week credit delivery model with a transient, constantly shifting student population, some with special education requirements and some who are English language learners, new immigrants, and/or refugees. These are some of the many reasons our students have not graduated by year 4.

A significant challenge for Ed-Vance Programs is student disengagement. A report about Student Success Indicators (TDSB 2013) suggests that "the dropout rate of students increases as students become older ... and increases dramatically during years 5 to 7" (p. 2). For example, according to this report, during the 2011–2012 academic year, dropout rates for year 4 were 7%, increasing to 16% for year 5, and spiking to almost half of the number of students leaving before graduating by year 7. For many teachers in Ed-Vance, this statistic is shocking. An accelerated credit delivery model creates a perfect storm of problems that undermines opportunities for our students to maximize their learning.

In 2016, in recognition of our growing concerns, we (the two authors) applied for and received funding from the TDSB and support through the Ontario Ministry of Education (Teacher Learning and Leadership Program) to develop and implement a pilot research project to address some of these challenges through pedagogical and curriculum approaches rooted in alternative education traditions: student centered; inquiry driven; project based; and grounded in the arts, technology, and equity. We (the two authors) are delighted with and gratefully acknowledge this important institutional support. In preparation for our pilot project, Vanessa interviewed several teachers across three Ed-Vance programs and facilitated a roundtable discussion with our school colleagues on student absenteeism as part of her "student success" portfolio in the Guidance Department during quad 4 (Spring 2016). Three broad and interconnected areas of concern emerged from these discussions: curricular content; pedagogical approaches; and building community.

Our colleagues, both within our school and beyond, share a discourse of Ed-Vance as an alternative program, NOT an alternative school. What this means for us is that it was envisioned, created, and implemented by bureaucrats and school personnel rather than students, parents, and community—from the top-down versus bottom-up. To many of our colleagues this also means that "we do not have as much flexibility as is advertised" and that curricular content must meet the Ministry's curriculum expectations even though we have only 9 weeks to accomplish this. More often than not, our students are overwhelmed by "juggling three courses" over the time span. Full funding per student comes only with at least a two course timetable. The push for students to take three courses is advantageous to the school rather than to the student. If a student drops a course when taking three, the school still receives full funding. However, if the student starts with two and drops to one, they are recognized as part-time and the Ministry of Education per-student funding is reduced. Some of our students are young and sole-support parents with work obligations; many are employed full-time. Our efforts to cover the curriculum become "a mile wide and an inch deep," only scratching the surface of difficult and complex issues. Nine weeks allows little time for deep reflection for teachers as well as for students, but for those students who have learning difficulties, the pace becomes much too fast. Collectively, these issues exacerbate student disengagement and absenteeism. Students vote with their feet and leave.

Pedagogical approaches to teaching and learning are often hindered by student absenteeism. Missing a week of school in a regular program is one thing, but in nine-week courses of two-hour classes, curriculum integrity begins to unravel. It is not a rare occurrence for some students to register up to two weeks after the start date. Two-hour classes in themselves are a challenge with adolescent learners. As one colleague said, "It's the worst thing we can do to our students, the adult model sucks." Support from teachers to help students "catch up on the work" can be experienced as pressure. This can create a tension between teachers and students. Many Ed-Vance teachers create rich learning opportunities with diverse activities, discussions, films, guest speakers, field trips, and so on. It becomes impossible for students missing weeks of school to "catch up." However, pressure from administration, guidance departments, and the students themselves leads some teachers to rely on worksheets, thus intensifying student disengagement while allowing time for students to catch up and pass their courses. Accelerated credit delivery by any means necessary, at the expense of rich pedagogy with the sole objective of credit accumulation, has become known as a "credit factory" by almost all of our colleagues within our own school and across the other Ed-Vance programs.

Community building at the classroom level is paramount in the development of positive teacher–student and peer–peer relationships. This takes time, energy, and careful planning. Trust is built upon a safe and caring community. One Ed-Vance program began a "Pod System" to enhance student learning across subjects by attempting to create meaningful community. It consisted of teams of three teachers working together delivering three credits to the same group of students. The program fell apart because it was imposed by administration with little teacher buy-in, with subjects not aligned according to the curricular content, and no time allotted for teachers to plan or work together.

Once again students were overwhelmed by the work. However, this system had a positive impact on student retention. Students felt connected to peers and to their teachers. Indeed, in our experience, many of our students do not like the end of quad because they feel like they are just getting to know their peers and teachers and all of a sudden it is over. We, as teachers, also feel the tug because we know that it often takes longer than one quad for our students to develop the readiness and willingness to learn.

At the school level, other challenges to community building are the inequitable conditions between the Adult Day School (students 21 and above) and the Ed-Vance Program (students 18–20), which are housed in the same facility. Literally, this means that in classrooms across the hall from each other, breakfast is provided for one group of 20 adolescent learners who have a full-time salaried teacher with benefits, but there is no breakfast for the other group of 40–50 adult students who have contract instructors paid solely for each hour of instruction. Students constantly see, hear, and feel these differences.

It is a misrepresentation to paint a picture of Ed-Vance solely as a site of struggle for the students. All of our colleagues interviewed agree that the so-called "victory lappers" do extremely well with an accelerated program. These students have finished all or most of their credits and come back for an extra year to upgrade or take specific courses for post-secondary studies. However, the victory lappers are far outnumbered by the sort of students we have described. Some of the teachers interviewed see Ed-Vance as a place—despite its challenges—for second chances and a teacher's role as catching those most vulnerable "in a kind of support net." While some students "miss the net and go splat," most Ed-Vance teachers are strongly motivated to build positive relationships with their students, meet their pedagogical needs, and provide them with meaningful learning opportunities. These are some of the key ideas undergirding our pilot project.

A Story from the Classroom: One Illustration of the Impact of Accelerated Credit Delivery

Vanessa landed at our school in 2015–2016. Over several decades of university secondments, school district equity positions, and doctoral work, Vanessa supported in-service and pre-service teachers and administrators to understand more deeply the intersected nature of schooling, oppression, diversity, and poverty. This work gave way to the development of innovative curricular and pedagogical practices to further reduce teaching and learning barriers.

By the beginning of quad 2, having been out of the classroom for many years, Vanessa was finally finding her place and pace in school. Two weeks after the start of the quad and to her utter surprise, a student she had never met walked into the classroom one hour late in the middle of a discussion. He was a tall young Black man in a parka, heavy boots, with earbuds leaking loud music. He clomped across the classroom and found a vacant seat, sat down, and pulled out his cell phone to text someone-something-somewhere. Vanessa was flabbergasted. She went up to the student and kindly asked him to take off his coat, put away his phone, and turn off his music. After reviewing his timetable, she introduced him to the class. She assured him that as soon as students began their independent projects, she would sit down with him to introduce him to the work he had missed and help to prioritize next steps. Returning to the discussion, the class was interrupted once again after a few minutes with the thrum of loud music. Once again, Vanessa calmly turned to the new student to ask him to turn it off. This happened several more times before Vanessa "lost it." She went up to the student and said, "Gimme your phone." He was immediately on his feet glaring down at her. Vanessa's first thought was, "What the hell am I doing getting into a power struggle with a student I don't know?" Her second thought, "OMG, the power differentials: young Black man, White woman of a certain age, nightmare." And then she paused and thought, I know better than this. She asked herself this question. What would a good teacher do right now? This pause left a tiny crack for intuition to flood in. It felt like the words came from someone else, "Listen, I would never ask a student to do something that I wasn't willing to do myself. So if you give me your phone, I'll give you mine and we'll see who starts jonesing[3] first." For the first time, the student looked down and into her eyes, the scowl morphing into a smile, "Yah, I'm game."

From that moment on, teacher and student began to develop a relationship based on trust. The student's Somali name is Dalmar but he gave Vanessa permission to call him by the name his friends use, Dal[4]. They exchanged their cells each class almost as a game at first, but it did help Dal to focus on his work. His engagement increased, and he did very well completing projects and participating in classroom discussion.

Dal's attendance was spotty because he worked full-time. He talked to Vanessa about how to strategize and prioritize his school work alongside his job. He told Vanessa a bit of his life story, like the time he went to the dentist and had a headache for three days following his appointment.

With two and a half weeks left to the end of the quad, Dal came to Vanessa very upset. He was taking physics and wanted to drop the course because he was failing. Working full-time made the juggling of two nine-week courses impossible for him. When he registered, Dal was already accommodated because of his job and enrolled in two rather than three courses. When he tried to drop the course, he was told that Ed-Vance could not support part-time students due to funding. He decided to drop both courses in order for his physics mark not to appear on his transcript and reduce his post-secondary decisions. All the work he did in Vanessa's course became inconsequential. He was already 19 years old, and his motivation to complete his OSSD was quickly diminishing. His frustration and anger came through loud and clear as tears ran down his cheeks. Dal did not want Vanessa to "rock the boat" and intervene because he wanted to reapply in a future quad. She too was frustrated and angry with all the work the two of them had done to build a strong pedagogical relationship. The voice of her colleague came back to her. It is one thing to hold out a "support net" and have a student "miss the net and go splat" because of their own choices, inability, or lack of readiness to learn. However, it is quite another when the institution creates circumstances and barriers that allow students to free fall into the abyss.

THE FALLOUT

As young adults, our students are expected to self-manage their time, personal and family responsibilities, and employment, as well as their education goals. Many have jobs, some are young parents, and others are dealing with challenging family matters. Sadly, some have physical and mental health issues, or substance abuse and addiction issues. And while the Ed-Vance program provides a second chance for students beyond year four to complete their high school education, the current structure can be a barrier for struggling students. The accelerated program leaves little time to accumulate knowledge in a meaningful way. The three-course requirement, combined with an early start and long class periods, adds additional stress. Each class is two hours long with no breaks. A brief 40-minute lunch is all that breaks up the day. Many arrive late, and others leave early for work and personal commitments, or because they are unable to maintain their focus for the entire day. Individual siloed subjects can add to the work load and limit the integration of knowledge. As a result of these cascading factors, students can become demotivated and disengaged. In response to personal experiences with our own students in the Ed-Vance program, we began to think about how we could re-engage students to facilitate their success in the classroom. In a survey of some of our students, we noted a discord between their preliminary expectations and their actual experiences.

School administrators are pressured to maintained school funding and staffing allocation levels. In turn, teachers are expected to motivate student attendance. This creates the ongoing tensions between the school administration and the teacher, as well as between the teacher and student. The crux of the matter is that the program itself is fallible. Contacting students to get them to return to the classroom is a bandage solution to a systemic problem. Despite good intentions by both teachers and administrators, the current program does not explicitly address student engagement on a fundamental level that helps them connect to their interests and to their lives in a meaningful way. For these students, an alternative solution is required—not just an alternative schedule.

Our concern about attendance issues, poor credit accumulation, and lack of classroom community became the impetus for discussion and the basis for our proposal to the TLLP program. Underpinning these conversations was a common belief in alternative education as an avenue to re-engage students and to revitalize our teaching.

THE PILOT

Our proposal, *A Transdisciplinary Pilot Project: Student Re-engagement through Multi-Media Arts and Social Justice Education,* was initially channeled through the Ministry of Education's Teacher Leadership and Learning Program (TLLP) and later supported by our school board. It seeks to improve attendance and credit accumulation by providing a new focus for student learning and re-engagement. The intent is to provide a holistic, integrated curricular approach to learning that is project based, with an arts-and-technology focus and social justice orientation, to help students find meaning in, and develop connections to, peers, teachers, school, and community. We hope to inspire new ways of creating knowledge for and with students, so they may empower themselves. In alignment with these goals, are a number of strategies and pedagogical approaches that we will be integrating into the pilot.

Alter the Pace and Schedule

To slow down the accelerated pace, the intent is to provide students with an extended study over two quadmesters (making up a semester of study) and provide an altered daily schedule to fill a four-hour block. The day will begin with a late start to allow students more time to manage their personal schedules and responsibilities. The first hour will focus on an exchange of ideas, a "conversation café," where both students and teachers present concepts and share findings. Lessons on specific concepts will be introduced and students will participate through a series of collaborative and individual activities. Demonstrations, workshops, and tutorials will take place to assist students in developing required skills for their projects. These range from digital imaging, animation, motion graphics, video performance, to installation-based media artworks. Though teaching is organic, providing students with a structure for the day will help them manage their time and will assist us in our teaching methods and planning.

With more time, we will be able to create more opportunities for processing and reflection of course material. The potential also exists to establish meaningful connections with students and build a positive classroom culture. And while there is more time committed to the program, the day itself will be shorter, requiring students to attend only four hours of class rather than six hours as in the regular Ed-Vance program. The trade-off is that students will only receive two credits per quadmester instead of three credits offered in the regular program. We are currently looking at how to integrate a separate e-learning course to complement the bundle of courses offered to allow for an additional credit.

Integrate the Curriculum

Throughout the pilot, we will explore whether team teaching an integrated curriculum, focused on breaking down siloed subjects prevalent within the secondary schools, will re-engage students in a meaningful way and positively affect their success. This transdisciplinary approach will be taught collaboratively, using curriculum from Social Sciences, Visual Arts, and Communications Technology. Collectively, these courses will provide students with the opportunity to work more efficiently among subject areas.

Within this integrated curriculum, we will aim for a reduction in the duplication of skills and concepts in a range of subject areas and will increase relevance for the learner. It is our hope that the student will see the big picture, rather than just the fragmented parts.

Increase Self Awareness

Strengthening awareness of the "self" in context with the "other" is an important aspect of student re-engagement and will be woven throughout the pilot. It begins with facilitating meaningful student-centered inquiry. We acknowledge student interests, experiences, and perceptions. In this way, we allow students to direct their own learning, and we expect that this will both demonstrate and manifest our understanding that individual perspectives matter. Through guidance and mentoring, we hope students will build the confidence to share who they are as individuals and reflect this awareness through their project work and relationships with peers and teachers.

There will be various opportunities for students to investigate, experiment, and analyze themselves and the world they live in. Students will explore interests related to identity, equity, and social justice using digital media applications and artistic practices to express their ideas and perspectives creatively.

Provide Authentic Learning Opportunities

In context with building a strong sense of the self, we intend to integrate key concepts through a project-based learning model. Project-based learning (PBL)[5] will allow students to apply their knowledge to authentic real-world scenarios strengthening and extending connections outside the classroom. To facilitate this, we work on establishing community partnerships with social justice-oriented and art-focused organizations to promote activism, along with technical and artistic skill development in our students. This will include access to art and digital media workshops, guest speakers, and field trips. Focus will be on active, open-ended problem solving, and real-life contexts.

As an extension to the program, we intend to promote experiential learning by establishing optional co-op placements related to the pilot focus. Through opportunities for authentic learning experiences and autonomous choices outside the classroom, we hope that students will develop motivation and set new goals for themselves.

Provide Access to an Online Classroom

Integrated into the courses offered in the pilot will be access to an online classroom where students can remotely access course content both in and out of the classroom. This will provide opportunities for students to track their progress and stay on top of assignments. The blended learning model is not intended to replace classroom learning but will augment it by helping connect students to course material, assignments, descriptive feedback, and evaluations. This will build flexibility into the program by extending access to course content for students who are absent or unable to attend the full day. This should work for young adults whose lives require flexible hours to further their education.

THE INQUIRY

The pilot was designed to begin in the 2016–2017 academic year. It is based on critical practitioner inquiry and teacher reflection. We intend to demonstrate the challenges and possibilities of the pilot project, through evidence-based data related to student retention, credit accumulation, and a study of student profiles.

Beyond the pilot project, we hope that the result might spur further the creation of viable school programs at Ed-Vance and other secondary schools to support disenfranchised students and transform traditional and siloed approaches to teaching. A number of key questions will guide our work:

1. How might restructuring the program day and duration help to improve student attendance and retention? In what ways does increased time to process and reflect positively affect student success?
2. How does a transdisciplinary teaching approach help to integrate knowledge in more meaningful and efficient ways, to create new transformative ways to attain and share knowledge? Does an integrated curriculum encourage student engagement?

3. Will a project-based learning model rooted in community connections help to re-engage students? Are students motivated to set goals for their future?

4. How might an Alternative School designation or a hybrid model make possible the structural changes—late start, de-siloed subjects, bundled credits across a semester of study, and the development of community partnerships—to fully meet the diverse needs of adult learners under the Ed-Vance umbrella?

These and other questions will likely surface throughout the duration of our work. We anticipate that there may be some aspects that are difficult to fit within the framework of the existing Ed-Vance model. We have already had to negotiate to keep key components intact. However, we are determined to move forward and advocate for the successful components of this pilot to provide an alternative education model for supporting disenfranchised young adult students who may be left to linger beyond their fourth, fifth, and even sixth year of their high school education.

NOTES

1. http://yorkdale.net/secondary/?page_id=8
2. http://www.tdsb.on.ca/Findyour/Schools.aspx?schno=2832
3. Withdrawal from addiction
4. Dalmar is not the student's real name, but pseudonym.
5. Buck Institute for Education, Project Based Learning, http://www.bie.org/

REFERENCE

Toronto District School Board Facts. 2013. *Student Success Indicators Year 4 (Grade 12) Student Outcomes*. Issue 4: 5.

Spring, Joel. 2016. *Deculturalization and the Struggle for Equality: A Brief History of the Education of Dominated Cultures in the United States*. Routledge.

AUTHORS' BIOGRAPHY

Vanessa Russell completed her PhD in 2009 at the Ontario Institute for Studies in Education at the University of Toronto (OISE/UT) and has worked as a teacher educator at both York University and OISE/UT. She has held a number of leadership positions at the Toronto District School Board's Equity Department and has taught at the Triangle Program, Canada's only dedicated classroom for queer students "at-risk." Vanessa has published extensively in the areas of anti-oppression education, embodiment, and ethics. She currently works in an Ed-Vance program teaching young adults returning to secondary school to complete their Ontario Secondary School Diploma. Vanessa co-authors a chapter focusing on a research-based pilot project that she developed with a colleague to re-engage students. This pilot is rooted in alternative education traditions—student and community driven; art, equity, and technology focused; transdisciplinary; project-based learning.

Cheryl Mootoo came into teaching after twenty years of professional experience in a variety of interdisciplinary creative and technical fields related to architecture, interior, graphic, retail, and exhibit design. She has dual degrees in Environmental and Architectural Studies from the University of Waterloo and received her Bachelor of Education from University of Toronto (OISE/UT). Cheryl applies her industry experience to various courses in the Visual Arts, Technological Design, and Communication Technologies subject areas at the high school level. She is currently assigned to an Ed-Vance school within the Toronto District School Board supporting students who are beyond year 4 of their high school education. Cheryl is also an active member of the Digital Lead Learner (DLL) network for the Toronto District School Board providing mentoring, workshops, and training to colleagues and teachers on the Integration of Technology in the Classroom. She is currently collaborating with Vanessa Russell on a pilot project providing a transdisciplinary team teaching approach within the Ed-Vance model to promote student re-engagement through media arts and culture, equity, and social justice studies.

CHAPTER 18

Resistance: Student Activism, SEED Alternative School, and the Struggle Against Streaming

Katheryne Schulz A.

INTRODUCTION

This chapter uses my early experiences as a high school student activist at SEED Alternative school to explore the overlapping organizing campaigns for student rights, equity, and de-streaming that were underway in the late 1980s at the Toronto Board of Education. It combines personal reflection with the recollections of other social justice activists, and uses media reports, Toronto Board of Education archive materials, and key texts to unpack the role of SEED and other alternative schools as catalysts for broader education reform efforts.

Throughout this chapter, I refer to poverty-and working-class people separately although the critics of streaming usually lump them together. This is not the kind of local and specific understanding of poverty-class people that is needed to organize successfully. In reality, the working and the poverty classes are populated and spatially located in ways that shape

K. Schulz A. (✉)
Ontario Institute for Studies in Education, University of Toronto, Toronto, Canada

© The Author(s) 2017
N. Bascia et al. (eds.), *Alternative Schooling and Student Engagement*,
DOI 10.1007/978-3-319-54259-1_18

227

their political organization differently. For example, being working class is generally identified with the attachment to the workforce and political organization through workplace trade unions. Being poverty class is closely identified with precarious work, unemployment, and welfare. Due to systemic discrimination, poverty-class people are more likely to be single mothers, Indigenous, racialized, disabled and/or recent immigrants (Khosla 2003). In urban spaces like Toronto, they are often tenants living in neighborhoods with high levels of poverty (United Way 2004). In my conclusion, I discuss the neighborhood-based organizing that poverty-class people do in more detail.[1]

GROWING UP "STREAMED"

My mother, Pat Schulz, used to say, "it's not the meek who inherit the earth, it's the organized." She was a Marxist Feminist from a working-class Dutch/British family with strong Socialist leanings. As a (barely) paid Trotskyist organizer in the 1950s and 1960s, my mother honed her political analysis and her organizing skills in Toronto, Montreal, and Ottawa. Shortly after my father's death in 1971, she did unpaid community organizing with other single mothers in a public housing project called Moss Park in downtown Toronto. At the local school, they ran a pre-school child care program and created a hot breakfast and lunch program. My mother and other single mothers also successfully fought the welfare administration that refused to allow them to enrol in university while trying to "redirect" them to hair dressing school. She ultimately got her Master's degree.

When we moved out of Moss Park to Bain Co-op in 1975, we traded better member-run, cooperative housing for worse schools. Neighborhood residents at the time were predominantly white, Black, Chinese, or Greek families from the poverty or working class. The poorest families lived in the Regent Park and Blake Street housing projects. A 1976 teacher survey for my school district described it as "the worst area in the city."[2] The overwhelming majority of teachers said they did not want to teach in our schools. Teachers from outside of our district, who had never actually taught any of us, said they thought we had discipline problems, we were on welfare, we came from "disorganized families" and we were "culturally deprived" (Area Four Work Group).

Having come from a school where poverty-class kids were treated well, my next elementary school was a shock. Some teachers spoke sarcastically to students and belittled them in front of the class. I watched my fifth grade teacher chase a student down the hall and then punch his fist through the glass window in the stairway door while trying to grab him. Racist language among students was common.

School streaming policies meant that after my elementary and middle schools, kids in my neighborhood labeled "vocational" went to Castle Frank High School to learn a trade. Castle Frank students were poor and its student body was a mix of White and Black students with a small minority of Chinese. Most of my Bain Co-op friends remained in these authoritarian, streamed classrooms until they dropped out or graduated.

In order to avoid streaming, my mother lied and said we lived inside the catchment area for the middle class, predominantly White, academic stream Jesse Ketchum Junior and Senior Public School. This meant leaving my neighborhood and traveling for 45 min on public transport every morning. I was alone in classrooms where my clothes were wrong, my lunches were wrong, I swore too much and I was not "cool."

Just before my fifteenth birthday, my mother lost her battle with breast cancer. By then, I had attended a number of different schools, so my high school transcript was a mess when I finally landed at West End Alternative school. West End was specifically geared to working-class and minority kids who had reached "the end of the line" academically and were at high risk of dropping out.

There I met my first teacher mentor, Harry Smaller. Harry is a jeans-wearing, bearded, hippy looking guy and a legendary organizer. He is also an excellent student activist recruiter. Harry built a relationship with me over a couple of years and although I left West End and actually finished high school at SEED Alternative, Harry (See Chap. 13) saw I was interested in politics and he found ways for me to get involved as a young activist.

The Struggle Against Streaming

Streaming is a practice of dominating poverty-class and racialized communities through control of their children. Canfield write that streaming is "a form of institutionalized violence that works to convince many working-class and racialized students, as well as their parents, that they belong in dead-end programs with stunted curricula, which almost always lead to insecure, low-paid employment." (p. 361) Students who are streamed into vocational and even general level programs experience education in a way that is different from the experience of affluent children. For example, Anyon's (1981) study in U.S. schools assessed differential outcomes for students from poor vs. affluent schools. She found that for poor students the focus was on following rules, learning by rote, limited explanation of the course material, and lots of copying from the blackboard. In affluent schools, "teachers were polite to children, did not make nasty or sarcastic remarks, and gave few direct orders" (p. 82). These classroom experiences teach poverty-class children to expect authoritarianism and to accept it.

By the late 1980s in Toronto, parents and progressive educators had been campaigning against streaming and racism in schools for years. Spurred on by the Board of Education's School Community Relations Committee, parents demanded more involvement in curriculum and programming, and on school committees (McCaskell 2005). Other activists focused on establishing school programs for specific student populations. In 1976, Indigenous activists Pauline Shirt and Vern Harper mobilized their community and successfully established Toronto's first Native Survival School for grades one to eight, called Wandering Spirit. Toronto's West End Alternative School and Contact Alternative were both established to assist marginalized students at risk of dropping out, and their students came primarily from poor, working-class and racialized populations.

On the one hand, resistance to de-streaming was entrenched among privileged parents and educators, which made it difficult to de-stream the entire school system. On the other, setting up pilot schools was labor-intensive and could only provide a small number of students with a positive alternative learning experience. Furthermore, the very folks that alternative pilots aimed to serve might view them with suspicion because they were not part of the mainstream system. Separate services for the wealthy are usually higher quality while precisely the opposite is true for poverty-class people. One of the founders of Wandering Spirit, Vern Harper describes this experience:

> Many of our people, because of oppression, have developed a 'back-of-the-bus' mentality, and are not only afraid to make demands, but have such low self-esteem that they don't believe in their own rights ... many Indian people ... saw no benefit in a separate school and wanted their children to "make it" in the regular school system." (Berg 1998: 217) (See Chap. 15 by Berg)

SEED Alternative School

In 1986, when I enrolled in SEED Alternative School to finish grades twelve and thirteen, I was initially unaware of these larger struggles at the Toronto Board of Education. I found school oppressive and I just wanted to do my time and graduate. SEED was located in a second floor office space at the intersection of College and Yonge streets in downtown Toronto. SEED pioneered the catalyst model of learning that meant students could decide what they wanted to learn and then seek out community members willing to share their expertise by teaching on a volunteer basis. The inspiration for SEED came from the ideas of Jean Piaget and A.S. Neill's Summerhill. Accordingly, the SEED philosophy emphasized democratic decision-making, critical thinking, and collective action.

At SEED, it was not weird to be left-wing or to disagree with teachers; it was encouraged. Students negotiated individual learning contracts. We chose courses or independent study and got credits by doing workshops, writing papers, or producing artwork. Students had direct control over the learning process. Our relationships with our teachers were also a lot more equal and democratic than in "straight" schools. SEED attracted teachers who were interested in sharing power with students. Both West End and SEED relied on a combination of student self-evaluation and teacher evaluation. This was the first time I was exposed to the idea that I should assess the value of my intellectual work and set my own goals for improvement. It was light years away from the authoritarian vocational education offered in my neighborhood. Furthermore, alternative schools did not have on-site principals to impose discipline. SEED Student Lilian Radovac remembers,

> There were lots of ways of being active that SEED nurtured. Nobody cracked down; nobody came and acted worried that you were doing what you were doing ... Just having the general meetings was also huge. A lot of what I learned about organizing I learned at SEED because you could practice and not just study (L. Radovac, personal communication, February 13: 2016).

SEED was a supportive space for me, but I also had to confront some contradictions. There was no way for me to be in this great learning environment without reflecting on the fact that none of my poverty-class friends had access to it. This was because SEED was an advanced stream school, and its students were mostly white and affluent. I was at SEED because I had escaped the schooling trap by being labeled "exceptional." But I knew that these labels were biased and that my first class education really came from my mother and the Marxist Feminist social movements we belonged to. Furthermore, while most of my fellow students came from progressive families and that created a bond among us, unlike most of them, I was living on my own and working part-time. I decided to get involved and do something about things such as streaming and poverty and discrimination against youth that really made me mad. So I reconnected with Harry Smaller and he helped me connect with a youth advocacy legal clinic called Justice for Children.

SOCIAL ASSISTANCE REVIEW COMMITTEE AND THE TRESPASS TO PROPERTY ACT

The first thing Harry and I worked on together was a submission to the province's Social Assistance Review Committee (SARC). We worked up a survey for students on welfare and I got SEED students to approve it at the weekly General Meeting. Then I sat in the SEED smoking room and conducted the survey with sixteen students on welfare who agreed to participate. I used the report to make a deputation at the SARC hearings. As a result, I was able to connect with students at the school who did not have money, and we learned that there was a legal clinic specifically geared to children and youth that we could go to for help.

I had negotiated independent study credit for my student activist involvement, so that my schoolwork and my activist work did not conflict. So, when Harry Smaller asked me to convene another SEED student group and to submit our comments to the provincial Trespass to Property Act review, I agreed. Lawyer Raj Anand was investigating widespread complaints against shopping mall owners because their security guards were profiling and harassing poor and racialized people, especially youth. With the approval of the SEED student body, we documented the harassment that students were experiencing at the College Park shopping mall across the street from our school. We argued that there had to be a transparent complaints process that youth and other marginalized groups could use to report guards who were guilty of harassment.

The final report released by Raj Anand included a series of recommendations aimed at reining in mall authorities.

In 1989, after I graduated, SEED student Lilian Radovac remembers that there was another crackdown at College Park against young people and she, Cory Doctorow, and Michael Moya were harassed and thrown out. Cory recalls: "I got a campaigning law firm to get us into a hearing at the City to complain about it. The (SEED) faculty backed me all the way." Cory also recalls receiving independent study credit for this and the organizing he did against the Gulf War while studying at SEED (C. Doctorow, personal communication, January 10, 2016).

CAMPAIGNING AT THE TORONTO ASSOCIATION OF STUDENT COUNCILS

Later that year, I met school board Trustee Olivia Chow for the first time at one of our SEED General Meetings. Olivia was a vibrant young organizer, committed to making Toronto schools more democratic. She was going from school to school, alerting students to the fact that the Board of Education was making plans to close alternative secondary schools and consolidate programs in response to declining enrolment, without consulting students or parents (O. Chow, personal communication, February 9, 2016). There was also a proposal around the same time to consolidate English as a second language programs into one school. With Olivia's encouragement, I was elected the SEED delegate to the barely functioning Toronto Association of Student Councils (TASC). TASC was an informal group at the Toronto Board of Education where student leaders were supposed to meet and put forward student concerns to Trustees. Olivia's plan was to get students to join together through TASC and to push for greater student involvement at the Board.

In May 1987, we held our first TASC leadership conference and identified what would become a very committed and articulate group of students including Noah Novogrodsky from Northern Secondary School, Brian Good from Jarvis Collegiate, and Kyla Tompkins from City Alternative. We nominated Noah to re-write the TASC constitution, so students were put firmly in charge of running our own meetings and setting our own agenda without going through the Board administration.

That fall we reached out to student council presidents at "straight" schools such as Jarvis and Northern, as well as alternative schools, and asked them to push the Toronto Board to consult the community about declining enrolment. We were successful and public hearings were held. Noah remembers that combining forces made for a potent combination:

> The alternative schools used TASC to get outsized influence at the Board by uniting with progressives from more established schools like Northern and Jarvis. It gave the alternative schools more clout. We developed an inside/outside strategy where students from the mainstream schools worked on reforming the structure. And the alternatives would agitate from the outside because they had the moxy to make demands and mobilize around them. (N. Novogrodsky, personal communication, February 11, 2016).

Solidarity between staff and students at SEED also helped. When the issue was brought to SEED's general meeting, students and teachers came up with the brilliant idea of extending a field trip planned for the same day as the hearings, and unanimously voted to bring their school bus straight to the Board of Education in time to participate.

As a result of our organizing efforts, on 19 November 1987, two hundred students crowded into the Toronto Board of Education to make their voices heard. The unprecedented number of students took the Trustees by surprise. *Now Magazine* reported that the deputations turned into "something of a sit-in as students packed the Board's College Street auditorium." (Suhanic 1987) What followed were impassioned deputations demanding broader public consultation on the proposals that many felt deliberately targeted marginalized students. By opening up and slowing down the process, we successfully forced the Toronto Board to consult broadly and to make compromise recommendations. This provided an important opportunity for community members to mobilize around what new programs would be established in their neighborhoods.

Part of the difficulty in sustaining TASC lay in its lack of institutional support because TASC had no formal standing at the Board. Olivia Chow worked with us to strengthen TASC, and we won an office, a small budget and a half-time staff position. Ultimately, TASC was linked to the Board's Students Affairs Committee. As word spread about the possibility of real involvement, student participation grew.

A big breakthrough for student rights came in October 1994, when TASC successfully submitted a proposal for a Student Trustee position to be created at the Board (J. Haverhall, personal communication, February 5, 2016). In January 1995, the Royal Commission on Learning report recommended that Ontario school boards have at least one Student Trustee. By the late 1990s, student representatives existed in most of the seventy plus school boards across Ontario.

DE-STREAMING CASTLE FRANK

While campaigns for greater student and community participation were successful, struggles around deeper systemic issues such as streaming met with much greater resistance. The issue of streaming in Toronto schools came to a head with the release of the 1987 *Ontario Study of the Relevance of Education and the Issue of Dropouts.* Conducted by George Radwanski, the study found that a stunning 31% of high school students in Ontario were dropping out. While only 12% of students in the academic stream left school before graduation, the dropout rate was 62% among general level students and 79% per cent among vocational level students. Poverty, citizenship, and ethnicity/race were cited as the key determinants to dropping out.

Adisa S. Oji was a poverty-class student activist in the struggle against streaming in the mid-1980s. In 1985, Adisa met Olivia Chow and became involved in doing media interviews and speaking at the Toronto Board about his experiences as a student who confronted both racism and streaming. In 1974, Adisa and his family had come to Canada from Jamaica. In grade nine, Adisa went into an academic level five program. Adisa started having difficulty at school that year following his parents' divorce. When he went to a guidance counselor for advice, the counselor advised him to drop out of the academic stream into a level three vocational program, even though Adisa had demonstrated the ability to do level five work and was actually struggling with family issues. Adisa went to a level three program for grade ten and realized it was a dead end, but when he wanted to return to a level five program, he was told he would have to "work his way back up." Adisa did just that and graduated with honors from an academic program. However, Adisa's situation was so outrageous that his story became synonymous with the injustice of streaming (A. S. Oji, personal communication, March 9, 2016).

By 1988, it looked as if persistent campaigning against streaming might be having some effect. The declining enrolment that had led us to mobilize around Task Force IV for broader consultation about the closure and consolidation of basic level schools had led to unexpected results. Castle Frank High School was chosen as the site for a new non-streamed pilot school named Rosedale Heights. Just as I was graduating, the de-streaming struggle came full circle back to my old neighborhood.

Toronto's current Deputy Mayor Pam McConnell was a school board trustee for the area at the time, along with her colleague Fran Endicott, one of the Toronto Board's first Black Trustees. She recalls that Castle Frank was highly stigmatized and that Black moms in Regent Park were complaining to Fran about the education their kids were getting,

> Girls who went to that ECE program were basically looking after Rosedale children part-time. Students were also taught to launder and press baby clothes. It was a nanny program. The boys went to the culinary program or shop. The culinary program was cooking the school lunches for students and teachers. Teachers had a dining room with tablecloths and students were taught to be waiters, cooks and dishwashers. So instead of having to pay cafeteria staff, it was providing free labor to the school. It had no connection to future employment

> (P. McConnell, personal communication, March 10, 2016).

Harry Smaller (See Chap. 13) was involved in the Comprehensive Work Group that organized to end streaming. He recalls intense institutional resistance to de-streaming, including the Rosedale Heights pilot (H. Smaller, personal communication, February 11, 2016). Pam McConnell remembers that both the Castle Frank principal and many of the teachers were not supportive of the transition. Eventually a new, more supportive principal took over, but even then, the majority of students were not coming from neighborhood middle schools:

> We never called (Rosedale Heights) an alternative school but it was based on those principles. We had to work very hard to promote it. We used school concerts and the music program to do community outreach.

> (P. McConnell, personal communication, March 10, 2016).

The de-streamed program was phased in starting with Grade 9 as the Castle Frank program was phased out. Sean McIntyre, a Rosedale Heights student whose father was very active in founding the school, observes that the poverty-class student population that formed the majority of students at Castle Frank, declined over time:

Maybe one quarter of the student body was local and the rest were attracted from out of district because it had a progressive reputation and a strong arts program. It appealed to those who could not get into Etobicoke School for the Arts. We needed to attract students from Regent Park and St. Jamestown, but they were less and less over time. The parents at Rosedale Heights were primarily more well-to-do progressives (S. McIntyre, personal communication, March 10, 2016).

The successful takeover of Castle Frank and its transition into a school for the arts was not accompanied by organizing in local poverty-class neighborhoods to demand access to the school and to prevent the more affluent from pushing out poorer families.[3]

Pam McConnell sees Rosedale Heights as an experiment that pushed principals and teachers to re-examine their assumptions. She points out that it highlighted the need for better teaching methods and pathways to education programs in poor neighborhoods and that schooling in Regent Park did improve. Overall, however, Harry Smaller reflects that attempts to connect poverty-class and racialized students to better schooling were largely unsuccessful:

The neighborhoods that could have benefitted most were not organized. Also alternative schools, with the exception of Contact, are very middle class. In my experience, it was tough to convince working class and minority parents that alternative schools were a viable alternative. At the same time, trying to mobilize parents in the regular school system to fight for education that was radically different was a big challenge.

CONCLUSION

Taking on an activist role at SEED brought with it some positive short-term gains. Students on welfare were connected with a legal clinic that could help them, and the Trespass to Property campaign helped us make the connections between profiling and violence against poor and racialized people, especially youth.

By mobilizing a large number of students, we entrenched student participation within the Board structure. However, the degree to which this benefited poverty-class students directly is questionable. Generally, affluent students participate disproportionately because they have more resources and time to participate, and they do not experience the kind of violent backlash against collective organizing that marginalized communities have to confront.

Alternative schools played an important role in these organizing efforts because they encouraged students to learn in more equity-focused and democratic ways, and to practice their insights through direct political action. Moreover, mentors, such as Harry Smaller and Olivia Chow, are crucial because their support "grows" the young organizers that are needed if social justice organizing is to be sustained.

Alternative schools acted as incubators for students, teachers, and parents who were critical of the education system and willing to challenge the authority of the school board. Schools such as West End Alternative and Contact specifically focused on working-class and racialized students, offered not only much more positive spaces for learning but also for political engagement. However, as Harry Smaller noted, the majority of alternative schools continue to serve predominantly middle-class families.

In their very thorough examination of streaming in Ontario, Clandfield et al. (2014) argue that while streaming today is done differently, the outcomes for less affluent, special needs and racialized students remain substantially below average. Although vocational schools have been closed, children continue to be streamed according to the biased perceptions of their abilities into vocational, general, and academic courses. Affluent parents continue to dominate the discourse around schooling and enjoy access to more resources than marginalized parents do.

Furthermore, while my student activist experiences were mainly positive, this is because I was organizing with students from affluent schools such as SEED and Jarvis Collegiate. For example, when we organized our protest at the Toronto Board, trustees listened to our deputations and nobody called the cops. For students from poor and racialized communities, institutional violence works to foreclose upon democratic participation in their own schooling including democratic protest. The point of institutional violence is to discourage collective resistance. One only needs to attend a heavily policed Ontario Coalition Against Poverty or a Black Lives Matter rally to see that this is so.

Indigenous people, many of whom are from the poverty class, appear to be the most successful at cross-class organizing through Native Friendship Centres, their band councils, and more recently, the Idle No More movement. Challenges to residential school violence and the establishment of Native survival schools are examples of successful collective organizing. In general, however, poverty-class people in urban areas do not have many resources to self-organize and therefore existing groups generally function within neighborhood boundaries. Nevertheless, poverty-class neighborhoods are organized in very important ways primarily through the unpaid community work that poverty-class women do. These women, many of them racialized mothers, need allies to help sustain the tenants' associations, community kitchens and gardens, food programs, after school spaces created to support kids, welfare rights groups, and neighborhood social or cultural associations that are all examples of their self-organizing (Naples 1998; Schulz 2012).

Organizing against streaming in their neighborhoods is an important way to inoculate poverty-class children against the authoritarianism they are subjected to in the classroom, and to grow the practice of resistance. My mother's teachings and my early experiences helped me to resist inadequate schooling. I could compare my experiences and see that although in Moss Park we were equally poor and even more racially diverse than at Bain Avenue, our mothers' collective organizing resulted in better schooling for us.

Moving beyond pilot projects and small-scale programs for marginalized students so that every student can access a de-streamed education will require an enormous collective effort. We have many workable ideas and examples to build upon. Allies interested in organizing against streaming would do well to abandon elitist thinking about who is capable of social movement organizing and leadership, respect indigenous political networks, and learn how to effectively support poverty-class people's collective self-determination.

There are important lessons to be learned from the de-streaming struggles of the 1980s. Poverty-class people need access to de-streamed, neighborhood education. This means winning a fair share of resources within the larger education system, and when resources are won, mobilizing to hold on to them. Poverty-class parents must organize collectively if they are to successfully support their children in taking control of their own learning.

Notes

1. The fact of limited mobility between classes has never stopped anyone from naming the working or middle classes for who they are, and yet there is reluctance to acknowledge poor people as a class precisely because doing so might lead to collective resistance. However, class misrecognition is a serious barrier to organizing particularly when people repeatedly identify as middle or working class although they

obviously are not. As Adisa S. Oji rightly observed to me, "self-defini-
tion is a pre-requisite to self-determination." One way to kick-start this
process is to articulate and share a collective history of resistance.
2. The Area Four Work Group was struck in 1974, and it consisted of three
staff from the area four school district that is in the east End of Toronto.
According to the survey authors, area four vice-principals were frustrated
by staffing problems and convened the work group to find ways of countering the "bad image" of the area, starting with a teacher survey.
3. In her work, scholar and activist Susan Parkison Stern (1998) uses the
term "push-out" to describe how Black parents are blocked from participating in their children's education by school officials.

Acknowledgements Thanks to the activists who shared their insights, Melinda
Vandenbeld Giles, Tim McCaskell, and the editors of this book for their support.
Any errors are my responsibility.

REFERENCES

Khosla, Punam. 2003. *If Low-Income Women of Colour Counted in Toronto.*
Toronto: Community Social Planning Council of Toronto.
United Way of Great Toronto and the Canadian Council on Social
Development. 2004. *Poverty by Postal Code: The Geography of Neighborhood
poverty, City of Toronto, 1981–2001.* Toronto: Authors.
Anyon, Jean. 1981. Social Class and School Knowledge. *Curriculum Inquiry* 1
(1): 3–42.
McCaskell, Tim. 2005. *Race to Equity: Disrupting Educational Inequality.*
Toronto: Between the Lines.
Berg, Sharon. 1998. Wandering Spirit Survival School: Native Education and
Emancipation through the Four Seasons Curriculum. Master's thesis, York
University. http://www.collectionscanada.gc.ca/obj/s4/f2/dsk2/ftp01/
MQ39172.pdf.
Suhanic, Gigi. 1987. Board Report Stirs Protest. *Now Magazine*, November 26.
http://nowtoronto.newspaperdirect.com/epaper/viewer.aspx.
Naples, Nancy. 1998. *Grassroots Warriors: Activist Mothering, Community Work
and the War on Poverty.* New York: Routledge.
Schulz, Katheryne. 2012. It's Not the Meek Who Inherit the Earth: Low
Income Mothers Organize for Economic Justice in Canada. In *Mothering
in the Age of Neoliberalism 2012*, ed. Melinda Vandenbeld Giles, 355–372.
Bradford, Ontario: Demeter Press.
Parkison Stern, Susan. 1998. Conversation, Research, and Struggles over
Schooling in an African American community. In *Community activism and*

feminist politics: Organizing Across Race, Class and Gender 1998, ed. Nancy. A. Naples, 107–127. New York, NY: Routledge.

AUTHOR BIOGRAPHY

Katheryne Schulz is a community organizer and political strategist who is currently completing her doctorate in Social Justice Education at the Ontario Institute for Studies in Education, University of Toronto. Her research focuses on the political organizing done by activist poverty class women within their communities.

PART V

Epilogue

CHAPTER 19

Some Last Words

Esther Sokolov Fine and Ellen Manney

This book rises out of a deep sense of social responsibility and out of a conference held in Toronto in November 2012. We want the wider world to know about the early days of public alternative schools, what they continue to accomplish, and some of their hopes for the future. Like a good wine, our stories have been maturing for many years. It is time to decant them. Observation and instinct tell us that there is a contemporary readership thirsting to discover and re-discover what alternative public schools can offer students.

In this chapter and the epilogue that follows, voices of former alternative school teachers and students leave us with praise and gratitude along with some warnings, critique, and serious questions. We begin with our own voices:

Esther Fine: My own awareness of alternative public schools began in Toronto in the early 1970s with formative Alpha Alternative School discussions that preceded the opening of the school. This was some years

E.S. Fine (✉) · E. Manney
York University, Toronto, Canada

© The Author(s) 2017
N. Bascia et al. (eds.), *Alternative Schooling and Student Engagement*,
DOI 10.1007/978-3-319-54259-1_19

before I became a teacher, at a time when my daughter Keira was still too young for school. I went to the meetings with neighbors. There I met educators like Roger Simon, Malcolm Levin, and others who later became important to my life as a teacher, an academic, and as a parent. I still have a vivid picture in my mind of Roger's daughter Kim running around in her size 3 OshKosh pants with bouncing red curls and a big smile on her face (see her reminiscences below in this chapter). I hadn't thought to bring Keira with me, but I learned right from the start that even our toddlers were welcome at such meetings. Some years later, Kim and Keira met in kindergarten and later became friends at Spectrum, the first alternative middle school in Toronto.

Speaking of Spectrum, during my early years of teaching and union activism, when I was a vice-president of the Toronto Teachers' Federation (TTF), I was anticipating a long meeting—4:30 TTF office—where I first met Ellen Manney. Ellen was one of the three teacher-founders of Spectrum. I asked Ellen about Spectrum's waiting list for 1981. She said there was still plenty of time. No list yet for '81. I asked her if she would start the list and put Keira's name at the top. She agreed do that.

When the time came, I had to persuade Keira to attend an alternative school. She said she would try it out, as long as she could change her mind before the winter semester began. Our arrangement was that if she wasn't enjoying Spectrum by January, she could leave, choose a different school—perhaps return to the Kensington neighborhood of her elementary years.

As it turned out, Keira's experience at Spectrum was mixed, but she decided to stick it out. She graduated from there in 1983, not regretting her decision to stay, but flatly refusing to attend an alternative high school. I so wanted her to go to City School. She wanted the much larger Northern Secondary. We were considering alternatives and children's rights in a city where we were, and still are, fortunate enough to have so many good options. Keira made her own choice.

As an adult Keira is a strong person with a powerful voice who knows when and how to express her opinions and take a stand when it really matters. She remembers doing so on at least one occasion at Spectrum during a noisy chaotic class meeting. She has done so since in some highly difficult situations where no one else had the "guts" to speak up. Sometimes she writes it out first, sometimes she rises to the occasion in a powerful and spontaneous way. Spectrum gave her some early opportunities to find her courage and her voice.

My next experience with alternative schools was at Downtown Alternative School (DAS), where I worked with wonderful teachers including Joan Baer and Ann Lacey. I accepted an offer to job share there, despite mixed feelings about leaving my work with kids in the housing project areas of the city. It was the right move for me. As a community, DAS was exploring a problem-solving approach that the children named "Peacemaking." I worked there for 4 years and learned a great deal. When I left to take up a position in the Faculty of Education at York University, I applied for and received funding (from the Social Sciences and Humanities Research Council of Canada) to engage in video research at DAS. That research done with filmmaker Roberta King has continued for more than 22 years and is the subject of my recent book *Raising Peacemakers* (Garn Press 2015). Edited films from that project can be seen at www.childrenaspeacemakers.ca. What a privilege it has been for me as a researcher to have had such deep access to alternative school students and teachers for such a long time. Only in an alternative school could this have been possible.

Ellen Manney (Spectrum, a Founding Teacher): In September 1978, Spectrum School opened its doors to 70+ families, no furniture, few supplies, and became the first grades 7 and 8 alternative school in the Toronto Board of Education. I was one of the founders and stayed there for 10 years. That was one of the very high points in my career. It was a rich and gutsy time. There were a number of Canadian progressives and American draft dodgers whose kids had reached 12 and 13 years of age, living in Toronto. They were looking for an individualized, exciting, creative way of educating their kids, a school where they thought their kids would flourish. And flourish most of them did. The student population was gifted in all kinds of ways; the parents were full of energy wanting to make this school the best it could be. This was a school that was teacher driven, with kids and parents having input. The final decisions were made by the teachers. "This is not a free school," we said when we explained the philosophy.

Being basically unfettered by principals, so-called accountability, and in the middle of the progressive culture of the time in education, I was able to really use my brain creatively to invent projects that I knew many kids would love and be enticed by as they developed skills connected with these ideas. For example, every kid in the school, all 74, had to do a multidisciplinary project called "Be an Expert." They had to choose whatever they wanted to learn about, from how to make a skateboard to Freud on the unconscious, you name it. They had to research the topic by reading, interviewing an expert in the field (which meant learning how to make use of the telephone before computers), how to set up and interview, and how to make the oral presentation as interesting as possible to other students.

I took delight in hearing that a kid was interested in somebody or something, and I would try to get someone in to talk or demonstrate— or we would go somewhere to find more information. We worked with the Young People's Theatre on the plays, "Whale, and The Secret Garden." The kids made parts of the stage sets for the plays. What fun for everybody, and the learning was fantastic.

Of course, for me teaching visual art was always a treat. One time, the kids made self-portraits with papier mache and fabric. We called it "Class Meeting" and set it up in the lobby of the Toronto Board of Education, all 74 sculptures. We painted murals on the walls of the rooms we used. What a fight with the principal. Now every school has murals!

We played jug band tunes at Mariposa Folk Festival, where the kids met lots of famous folk singers and musicians. We had many panels with experts to talk about their fields, many trips to all kinds of places where most schools would never go. We were very brave, hopeful, creative and we were risk takers.

REFLECTIONS FROM STUDENTS

Rachel Fulford (Spectrum, excerpted): My 2 years at Spectrum had a profound impact on me, much of which I can't put into words, but there are three areas that I can focus on:

1. **Calling teachers by their first names.** This was important for me and emblematic of the alternative school experience. Instead of distant figures of pure authority, we had human beings who we could relate to and who seemed to be more at eye level which, paradoxically, allowed us to idealize them even more. They weren't so far above us that they couldn't see us. We could confide in them. They had feet of clay and they were OK with this. Realizing that teachers could be like this was a tremendous relief. Pre-teens/early teens are at a pupa stage—not caterpillar, not butterfly; they need to individuate from their parents but also need adults to guide them.

It's important to have adults you can respect while you undergo this metamorphosis, but who also feel attainable and trustworthy; you can look up to them without feeling below them. This helped me understand what kind of adult I wanted to be, that I could emulate the fairness and compassion of Spectrum's teachers, who seemed genuinely interested in us without wanting to exploit, humiliate, or take anything away from us. Our growth and our successes felt like ours, and we could also take stock of our regressions and our failings, because we had non-judgmental adults who could hear us not as children, not as adults, but as human beings at a liminal stage who need to be taken seriously but are [were] growing and changing and therefore vulnerable.

2. **Wednesday afternoon self-guided field trips.** I came to love the city where I was born. At Spectrum, we were invited to explore it. We were given the freedom to do what we wanted with field trip time, which made us feel grown-up ... with this freedom came responsibility: We had to write and present a brief report on what we had done, even if all we did was study at the Reference Library. The opportunity to relate our afternoon adventures to genuinely interested teachers was crucial. There is a lot of talk these days about "mindfulness." We were practicing this, in a very concrete way, by sharing our experience and our thoughts with teachers who did not make us feel judged ...

We developed a taste for freedom alongside a capacity to endure it, to channel it and to reap its benefits ... I learned that you can be a tourist and see your city with fresh eyes if you open your mind to the different cultures and worlds all waiting to be discovered within the place we take for granted. Cities have cities within them, cultures have cultures within them, and this is something I learned on my own time, so I never forgot it.

3. **Morning meetings.** When we all met as a group, all 74 students and three teachers, we had the chance to experience democracy in action. We learned when to be passionate and brave in raising our concerns, and when to be tactful. We learned to speak up and we learned to listen, realizing with wonder each day that there were more than 70 subjectivities in the room, each with a unique perspective on the day and on the experience of having lived another

day (their own day) in the school. It was eye-opening, to say the least. This has influenced my ability to listen without pre-judging. It has left me receptive to the other-ness of the other, while also trusting that there is a way we can work toward common ground, through open, respectful conversation and listening.

Kim Simon (Spectrum): Writing this makes me feel a bit old. It was a long time ago that I was educated in the Toronto alternative school system, both in grade seven and eight at Spectrum and then in grades ten through twelve at City School. And feeling old, I don't have a particularly detailed memory of classes or lessons; what I do have is more like flashes or murky vignettes. I have a deep memory of a vibe, an ideology even. I have a few friendships that will last a lifetime, and I have the feeling, when I bump into someone I went to alternative school with, that I still sort of understand who they are, that they maybe "get it." And by get it I mean, what it means to be an active participant in this world.

I wouldn't exactly say my alternative school education made my life easier. I learned what critical thinking is at such an early age, even if I didn't know how to name it until later. I learned not to take for granted given truths, I learned to ask a lot of questions and decide what the truth is for myself. I learned there are a lot of different opinions in the world and that I need to be aware of them. I learned that people have different learning styles and ways of being and that these differences should be embraced by the systems we learn and work within. People kept asking me what I thought at such an early age and though it took some time, eventually this forced me out of excruciating shyness. I learned I really had to speak up for what I believed was right.

Having learned that I needed to take an active role in deciding what I think and feel and am passionate about, underscored by the support of incredible parents, I actually had a pretty hard time when I wasn't in alternative schools. In grade nine I decided to go to a high school with a bigger range of arts programs. It wasn't an alternative school. I remember a class trip to a museum where the woman leading us on a tour of an exhibition was explaining what the artist felt and intended in making a certain painting. I raised my hand and asked how she knew what the artist had been feeling and thinking. I hadn't yet learned that what I was really asking about was the tour guide's methodology for analysis, and so I was perceived simply as a disruptive pain in the ass and asked to be quiet and stand aside from the group. I went back to the alternative school system for grade 10. I wasn't prepared yet for the real world.

My "normative" high school, undergraduate and graduate school experiences were full of moments where I felt like the "problem child," perceived as criticizing the program, the teacher, "the system." I was always the student in the room questioning what the teacher said and why, trying to get some debate going, always attracted to the other problem children. I was certain I was being productively critical, not negative. Just asking questions. I'm still working on my delivery frankly. I left many university degrees in search of others for the right fit. I couldn't bear to play the game just to get through it and get a job. I was always looking for the right community of thinkers where we might productively challenge each other rather than sit quietly in our silos, absorbing givens and patting ourselves on the back.

Now, as a curator of a contemporary art gallery, I'm still looking for that community, only now I'm trying to actively create it through my work. I have no doubt that what I do now is informed by these early experiences in alternative education. I often talk about the inherent ideology of my curatorial work as invested in pedagogy, a pedagogy that is a necessarily creative and experimenting practice. It's a hopeful pedagogy that wants to understand the gallery as a productive civic space, a place for people to think and experience in public together, whether through solidarity or debate.

Tamar Drushka (Spectrum Founding Year/City School): In her grade 8 year Tamar moved from a "regular" school to Spectrum, which was in its first year of existence. She transferred again after her grade 9 year in a conventional school, an "experience in hell," to City School, which had been established by a concerned group of parents, teachers, and students. Tamar writes as follows:

> This was where I really learned the most about participating in my own education. I asked a friend recently who had also attended City School about his experience there and he said he would not have lasted in the regular high school, that it was City School (where he had to travel all the way across the city every day to be there) that had kept him in school until he graduated

> I would say that the most significant way that my experience with an alternative school education affects me in my adult life is that I generally take a much more proactive approach to most situations, especially at work and my life as an entrepreneur. I know that I can have much more of a say in the process, that my voice is important and that I can have an impact

and be a part of the decision-making process in any venture I am involved with. It is small groups of people working together who can and do change the world.

It has been a somewhat odd experience for me, sending my four children through the public school system in Nova Scotia. A lot of it seems very backward compared with my educational experience in Toronto, which I now see was quite ahead of its time. I was very fortunate to have had this experience.

I recall saying to my kids here in NS when they were in high school, "Speak up about this; you can change it! It's your education, you have the right to speak to the principal, the student union, etc. about this." I recall being somewhat dumbfounded when my own kids just looked at me and shook their heads. They said, "No Mom, it's not like that, we can't do that here." And I realized in that moment that somehow, I had not passed it on to them. It was a moment of great disappointment and even some shock for me, and it caused me to wonder about the why of it.

I am currently working on a business survey project for a town in Nova Scotia that wants development. One of the comments I hear repeatedly from business owners, is that we need to teach kids entrepreneurial skills in high school. My own four children were taught these skills, and this has definitely set them apart and given them a whole other set of skills that most of their peers simply do not have.

So I would say that my experience at Spectrum gave me a decided advantage, mostly because it was so small and such a unique group of people that came together in a very thoughtful way. It provided us with a much richer experience than most kids get at that age. I realize now how very rich it was, that there are people who never experience that kind of thinking and approach to learning.

Having Ken Whiteley as our music teacher was only one of the many gifts that were given to us by the team of teachers at Spectrum. Throughout the whole thing, I learned that we could have a say, that we could be responsible, indeed we are responsible for what and how we chose to learn and create in this world. We learned about things that were "outside the box" of mainstream thinking. We learned and lived the value of "Small is Beautiful." We learned that we could make our own instruments, create our own projects, and speak to adults as equals. We learned how to be responsible for our own choices.

A few years ago, I began to reconnect with people from my high school years, and I think it is a very worthwhile project to examine how that experience has affected and even governed our lives. I look forward to reading this book when it is completed. I do think that we could be doing a bit more to try and bring our experience forward into the education system because if there was ever a time when that kind of thinking was needed, it is now.

To that end I am currently considering how I can put together some type of course to take into the school system to teach kids more of the kinds of thinking and skills that have been so useful to me and my own four +2 children.

Ben Whiteley (Delta Senior Alternative School, Grades 7–8):

At Delta, I was given a framework to explore and develop my interests. Our curriculum was organized into 6 week blocks or contract periods where we were given a major project to be completed and handed in on the last week of the period. The amount of work was agreed upon by the student and teacher and we signed our contract. We were given a lot freedom to pick projects within a given broad topic. This opportunity allowed us to explore different learning styles. We either had to write a piece or a make a presentation, and you could work in a group or by yourself. The last project of the year we could pick any topic. As a last project in our grade 8 year, a few friends and I wrote, arranged and recorded our own CD. We easily spent a hundred hours on it. It just goes to show you, if you are engaged and feel ownership of your learning, you will be inclined to put more time and effort into it and ultimately get more out of it. The school didn't have a music program but had a supportive environment where if you wanted to do or learn something, you got positive encouragement and support. That philosophy has stayed with me.

Rosemary Richings (excerpted): tells us that she eventually left DAS because of some bullying issues, evidence that our best efforts are never perfect. Nevertheless, she wrote quite positively about her time at the school:

My significant other grew up in a small town, so his only options as a student were Catholic and Public schools. The first time I told him about Downtown Alternative School (DAS) he had a lot of questions. One day we sat on a bench facing the DAS playground as I talked about what DAS was like. When I look back on that conversation, I realize that I forgot to mention something important. Thanks to DAS I have an unlimited amount of patience for people's misunderstandings. One of my fondest memories of DAS was its inviting, communal vibe. We helped each other out. We listened compassionately. Most important of all, we respected each other's differences. Early on in my DAS years, my doctor diagnosed me with a permanent disability. I felt so lucky to be in an environment where differences were openly celebrated. Post-DAS, my choices reflected my love of communal, welcoming environments. In high school, I started getting heavily involved in theater and writing groups. After high school, I decided to do my BA at a liberal arts college with a small town vibe. In college, I was heavily involved in the school paper and the drama club. After college, I started a web content writing business. I fell in love with the web and its ability to bring people together.

My last peace circle[1]: was such a long time ago that I don't remember what it was about. At an early age, our teachers taught us how to handle conflict like mature adults, which is awesome. If a little girl was in tears in the classroom after recess, it was time for a peace circle. If someone wasn't sharing their toys like they promised, it was also time for a peace circle. If anyone had a problem we'd work towards a solution together. It never involved violence, screaming, or name-calling …. I blame DAS for making me a good friend, girlfriend, daughter, etc. If I ever have children, I hope their problems are never deemed unimportant. That was one of the best parts of DAS that I'll always remember. Every problem is worth a lengthy discussion with loved ones and peers, no matter what.

Zak Smith (DAS):

I would consider myself to be a "product" of Toronto alternative schools. Almost all of my elementary, middle, and secondary experience took place in alternative public schools, and therefore it's safe to say that I am who I am as a direct result of only having the alternative school experience.

Our earliest school experiences come at a time when our minds are developing rapidly, open to absorb everything the world offers us. In the alternative elementary school, I attended during this critical developmental period, my teachers not only understood how important it was to teach to the whole child, but they felt that informing their teaching with this understanding was their obligation to each child, and to the society in which those children were finding their place. When I speak of teaching the whole child, I am talking about teaching self-regulation, building social-emotional and mental wellness, practicing social skills, encouraging individual autonomy and celebrating uniqueness. There was a strong emphasis on building healthy relationships with our peers, the adults in our lives, and with the communities in which we live. My "whole" health was intentionally and thoughtfully fostered and supported through this framework, and everyone in the school community was engaged with it, correction, lived by it.

Now I am proud to say that I too am a professional educator, entrusted with the shared responsibility to help in shaping the next generation as my teachers once did. My earliest educational experiences now inform my teaching practice, and there is no lesson I plan in which the whole child has not been considered, and not one day goes by in which I don't reflect on how I can better meet the needs of the whole child the next day.

I've heard before that teaching is the only profession that creates all others, but I would take it a step further. School communities help us shape our unique identities, shared value systems, hopes, aspirations, and, probably most important, our compassion for others. It was my early alternative school experience that taught me the invaluable lessons needed by every child so that one's true potential can be realized. I am who I am because of it, and I like who I am.

Nataleah Hunter-Young (DAS, quoted with permission from *Raising Peacemakers* **(pp. 22–23):** DAS socialized me in a way that was so organic, honest and authentic that I found the follow-up school environments confusing and often hurtful.

Why do I have to call you 'Miss?

What do you mean I have to walk on the right side of the hallway?

Oh, you mean you don't care much for my point of view or my sense of humor?

My questions, if not directly concerning whatever we are being taught, are irrelevant? I see.

DAS taught me to question everything, that there was never just "one side." Most important, I learned that my feelings were truths. MY truths. And that if we each had truths then there was no "right way," there was only ever the way that worked best for you, at that time, in that moment.

In an extensive bio that she wrote for *Raising Peacemakers* (pp. 24-27), Nataleah tells us that she was born in Toronto to a Jamaican father and

Guyanese (raised British) mother who were both very "community minded" and political in nature. She speaks about her education both during and after DAS, including her degree in sociology and her experiences as a Master of Social Work student that led her a graduate assistantship with Stephen Lewis (former Canadian ambassador to the United Nations) who was teaching a course on the United Nations Millennium Development Goals as a distinguished visiting professor in residence.

Nataleah writes, "Having the good fortune of listening to one of the world's greatest speakers on a weekly basis for four months led me right back into the world of international development following graduation." Nataleah has done anti-racist and social justice work in Burkina Faso, Jamaica, and here in Canada. She is now a doctoral student at Ryerson University.[2]

NOTES

1. Rosemary remembers experiencing "peace circles" and "peacemakings" from her time at DAS. See *Raising Peacemakers*, E. Fine, Garn Press, 2015.
2. Publicly Funded Alternative Schooling in the GTA: A First Ever Conference! held in Toronto in November 2012 and funded by the Social Sciences and Humanities Research Council of Canada (SSHRC), the Faculty of Education at York University, OISE, the Toronto District School Board, and the Toronto Catholic District School Board (see Chap. 12 by Rodrigues).

REFERENCE

Fine, Esther Sokolov. 2015. *Raising peacemakers*. Garn Press.

AUTHORS' BIOGRAPHY

Esther Sokolov Fine is Professor Emeritus and Senior Scholar at York University in Toronto, Canada. Prior to her work in the York Faculty of Education, she was an elementary teacher with the Toronto Board of Education, where she taught in downtown public housing communities and alternative programs. Her latest book, *Raising Peacemakers* (Garn Press 2015), tells the story of her 22 years of research with a community of students at a small alternative school, beginning when they were very young and interviewing them as they grew up. Her research has been funded by Social Sciences and Humanities

Research Council of Canada (SSHRC). Research interviews filmed by Roberta King can be seen at www.childrenaspeacemakers.ca.

Ellen Manney was born and raised in Brooklyn, New York, where she developed a deep love for the natural world, art, and music. Her interests were nurtured at the Brooklyn Botanical Gardens and by her parents who were educators, her mother a visual artist, and her father a classical pianist. She graduated from Pratt Institute (B.A) and the University of California, Berkeley (M.A.) and is a retired visual art teacher of children from kindergarten to grade 8 (Toronto District School Board). She was a founder of Spectrum School, the first alternative grades 7 and 8 school in the Toronto Board of Education. From the beginning of her career to the present, she has been a strong advocate for children, having been influenced by her sister, who has special needs.

EPILOGUE

Braxton Wignall was in his third year of high school at SEED when he decided to attend the 2012 "First Ever" conference on public alternative schools in the Greater Toronto Area. As a direct result of his participation in the discussion, he led the movement that resulted in an alternative Student Led Conference, hosted by SEED Alternative School the following May, and every May since that time (see Chap. 12 by Rodrigues).

Braxton Wignall:

For a long time—most of my grade school and high school years—I was convinced that something was terribly wrong with me. Authority figures in these educational and religious institutions couldn't quite put a finger on what was wrong with me, but they had many ideas, most of which my family and I did not agree with. I got used to altercations and stand-offs with authority figures; they and I couldn't see eye-to-eye. Eventually I ended up spending more time in the office, at home, or in the hallways. School wasn't helping me; it was trapping me in a state of mind that made me feel incapable of being "normal" like the rest of the students. This mainstream institutional pipeline was not for me, and before I had the words to explain I knew I needed an alternative to what was going on.

I was no stranger to alternatives. I spent multiple years in behavior programs, small classes, and alternative learning centers. My reason for being there was not the best, however the forward thinking progressive nature was amazing. For once I didn't feel like walls were closing on me and that

© The Editor(s) (if applicable) and The Author(s) 2017
N. Bascia et al. (eds.), *Alternative Schooling and Student Engagement*,
DOI 10.1007/978-3-319-54259-1

I was helpless. So, after years of trying to convince myself that I needed to fix what the institutional leaders said was terribly wrong with me, I realized I needed an alternative of my choice. I found one.

There is this idea that says you can't advance in any field by trying to fit a structurally different way of dealing with things in the old framework, rather than looking at it as a fundamentally different thing. Mainstream schooling does exactly what this idea suggests not to do. I agree with this idea, and the reason why I decided to find an alternative of my own choice is because I knew alternative schools operated on different fundamentals that were better suited for me and my style of learning.

I am 21 years old now, and a large part of who I am is because of alternative schools, specifically SEED Alternative Secondary School located in the Riverdale community of Toronto. I was sixteen years old when I began going to SEED and had no idea of the positive impact it would have on me.

Every alternative school has its own unique culture. I'll be speaking to my experience at SEED and not making generalized statements. SEED is a space that encourages student voice and choice, fosters healthy relationships, and encourages critical thinking and informed decision-making—necessary components of well-rounded education. The ability to exercise choice is very important, even more important it is crucial to make informed decisions. On my first day at SEED I experienced something I've never experienced before. Liam Rodrigues, our English teacher left the room after telling our class to make a list of things/topics we'd like to explore and the books or pieces of literature we'd like to read. He informed us of the Ministry expectations–number of essays, types of essays, novel studies, etc. and left the rest to us, the students, to choose the way we'd like our curriculum to be set up. This was a huge learning point for me in understanding that if I want to see something happen, I must engage in the decision-making process (See Rodrigues - Chap. 12 in this book).

Community is an essential part of the SEED culture. All members of the SEED community—teachers, students, parents, volunteers, etc.—are big supporters of community and building healthy relationships. Prior to attending SEED, I was not aware of the fact that the relationships I had built in my community weren't genuine and were not opening my mind up. It became apparent as the community dynamic at SEED grew on me. I started appreciating diversity beyond race, and began openly accepting and genuinely caring for my community and people from all walks of life and all lived realities. I made close friends at SEED. Some were gay, bisexual, trans, and many other intersections of the human race. This was a big revelation for me as a young Black male raised in suburban ghettos and low-income neighborhoods my entire life, where the kind of openness I experienced at SEED was frowned upon.

The diversity of this community and my part in it made me feel more human. All of these unique members of our community were accepted and valued, and for the first time in my life I too, felt accepted. The relationships built at SEED were very healthy; the most important relationships I built were the ones with teachers and school board administrators who gave me opportunities to develop leadership skills and truly believed in the things I had to say and wanted to do. The dynamic of this community and the relationships influenced how I think.

Prior to attending SEED I was being fed the same boring information that wasn't updated to keep up with the evolution of society and people's realities. The information and content wasn't outdated; however, it wasn't reflective of the demographic and the various cultures in our schools. Other students and I who were not White, rarely ever had any connection to the content and experiences in our curriculum. It was frustrating enough being fed all these dead White guys' values and beliefs, but what made it worse was being suspended and disciplined for acknowledging the fact that the curriculum wasn't reflecting my culture or reality and for not being afraid to go head-to-head with teachers about my feelings about this. I was beginning to think critically at the age of ten when I noticed these things.

My current self would now advise my 10-year-old self to find better ways of dealing with the frustration upon acknowledging the gaps in my education. What I needed was an articulate voice, a way to speak and be heard. I developed that voice while being at SEED, while continuing to think critically and peel back layers of understanding, I was able to confidently express frustration and concern and to advocate for myself and my peers. It is because of this voice that I don't fear challenging the status quo and challenging those authority figures in institutions I find myself in. It is important for us as humans to understand that information will be presented to us at all times, and we have to think critically about that information before we believe it to be fact. If need be we should be equipped with the necessary tools to confront and stand up against things that don't sit right with us. I developed this critical lens while being at SEED. It has allowed me to uncover many understandings of myself, navigate difficult situations, and most important of all stand up for myself and others who remain voiceless.

The work I do now was never on my radar. It naturally came to me as I understood that I am a catalyst for change. The initiation of this awareness came during the Public Alternative Schools Conference put on by York University. During the conference, I realized that only adults, educators and professionals in related fields were speaking to the public and students about education—about how to make it better, about gaps in curriculum and many other topics pertaining to the quality of education, specifically alternative education. None of this made sense to me. If students are the primary stakeholders in education, why weren't we involved in speaking about our lived experiences in alternative learning spaces? At the end of day one, Esther Fine, a professor I respect a lot, (who has in many ways supported and given my voice listening ears and respect), opened the floor for comments and discussion. I took the opportunity to voice my concern.

In retrospect, I would like to have made my statement a little more controlled, and I regret not apologizing to Dr. Fine at the time. Many students, myself included, were frustrated listening to adults speak all day about the quality of our education without even inviting us to be part of the discussion. I declared in that moment I was going to get my peers together and plan a conference led by students and organized by students to have these discussions about alternative education. This conference has been running annually for three years, and it has shown me that students care about their education if they are involved in the decision-making.

For so many years, the planning and organization of education has been done with a top down approach that has shut kids out and silenced their input. I wanted this conference to break that cycle and put students, the primary stakeholders in education, at the front of the discussion and be the driving force behind the decisions. I wanted students, like me, to begin reimagining education.

In 2013, the inaugural year of the conference, I was asked to join a team that was going to write and publish the first Hip Hop Curriculum in accordance with the Ministry of Education's Standards. I was a grade twelve student on a team of Toronto District School Boardand Toronto Catholic District School Board teachers, principals and superintendents, as well as local community members who worked closely with communities and youth. This experience was refreshing for me. I was developing curriculum that would be available to my peers and younger students I hoped to reach, inspire, and spark change in. Even more important, it was a curriculum that is rooted in my culture. It was relevant to me. This was my calling, to influence change and engage in the decisions that affect me and those in my community.

Since the conference and since finishing the curriculum, I have been blessed to work with kids ages six to eighteen, delivering the curriculum; involving kids in the annual student led conference; and engaging with the Provincial and Municipal governments. Working with kids is the only way I feel able to help solve some of the issues that often plague youth in society. Equipping kids with the tools and understandings to handle what life throws their way is my goal.

SEED provided me with the right tools to get my feet planted in society and move toward the type of work I do. The one thing I will value the most and share with people, is the impact community has on an individual. The feeling of being accepted and a contributing member of a larger group can create so much positivity for people. Advocacy will always remain with me. I will always be ready and willing to advocate for the voiceless and stand up for myself when needed. Finally, I am always thinking critically and examining situations frequently as I aim to land myself in the best situation. Ultimately the alternative school system in Toronto has affected my life positively and prepared for me the world beyond school.

David Lewis Stein (Spectrum Parent Late 1970s):

The following lines are excerpted (with permission) from a letter written to Ellen Manney by Spectrum parent (and Toronto journalist) David Lewis Stein nearly 40 years ago in response to an evaluation of Spectrum "for the advisory council." David is the father of Kate and Ben, two of Spectrum's early graduates, and grandfather of Emma McQuiggan—a much more recent (2011–2013) Spectrum grad. In a letter to Ellen all those years ago, David wrote:
My two children, Ben and Kate, have been at Spectrum for four of the five years the school has been in operation, and I am very pleased with the education they have received there, intellectually, socially, and spiritually. I think it is very difficult to start a school like Spectrum and to maintain it...In my experience, Spectrum stresses two kinds of development, individual achievement and group responsibility. I am thrilled that my daughter can spend a good part of grade eight working through a grade nine

French book. But I think it's just as important that she has found a group of friends at Spectrum that I think she will have all her life and that they have participated together in such things as the bike hike and the Mikado and the school trips and the auction. They have shared experiences and shared responsibilities, and they will have experiences that they will always be able to look back [on].... They have memories now that they will share all their lives. The teachers respect this emotional growth and provide time and room for it. I have profound respect for their patience and their sensitivity and for their endurance. In an alternative school, there is not a rigid system of education for people to put their confidence in. One cannot look forward in an alternative school to seeing things done the same way every day so that people emerge at the end with the same ideas and polished to the same high gloss. This kind of school obviously has certain advantages. The advantage of alternative school is that the teachers meet the children at their own emotional level and try to encourage them to work and grow as individuals and learn to be part of a community.

Emma Mcquiggan (Spectrum. David Lewis Stein's Granddaughter 2016):

I went to Spectrum Alternative School. At my elementary school, another small alternative school, I was badly bullied and socially ostracized. I was very quiet, always scared, and my grades were never great, but when I went to Spectrum, it was much better. My teachers were more encouraging and understanding. I was never good at visual arts, but my art teacher never expected me to be Da Vinci. She expected my best work, even if it looked like it was drawn by a six-year-old. She taught me how to balance color, how to examine art critically, and actually be proud [of] my work. It helped my then poor, self-esteem immensely.

I had never been good at math either, but my teacher at Spectrum actually made it understandable. I finally got it. Numbers made sense for once. But the most important factor at Spectrum was my ability to grow. I became more confident. The [kind of] close knit environment that I hated at my previous school [now] worked in my favor. I was close with lots of people. I made great friends. My grades went way up. I was finally happy. For that, I'm eternally grateful to Spectrum. My experience there changed my life.

Ellen Manney, a Founder of Spectrum School (Founded 1978):

If it wasn't for the Toronto Board of Education endorsing public alternative schools, there would be none in this city. They deserve a giant thank you. I never imagined that I would ever think in these terms. They endorsed us grudgingly, gave us practically no support, fought us in so many petty ways hoping that we would fail, and look what happened. We not only blossomed but bore many different kinds of seeds. Those seeds were planted; they grew into new schools and were nurtured by parents, teachers, and kids. So thank you, Toronto Board of Educationand Toronto District School Board, for being brave enough to allow creative minds to put big ideas into practice.

There wouldn't be alternative schools if there weren't kids and parents who believed in these big ideas, fought for them, embraced them, and were brave enough to buck conventional school. Many of those Spectrum kids, 38 years ago, are now artists, writers, musicians, actors, doctors, lawyers, teachers, journalists, etc. What a gift for me to participate in helping to shape this population, now in their 40s, some of whom have children of their own. What a pleasure! Thanks!

FURTHER READING

The ALPHA Community. 1988. *The ALPHA Parent Handbook*. Toronto.

The ALPHA Community. 2009. *Minutes of ALPHA Parents Meeting*, March 12. Toronto.

The ALPHA Community. 2014. *The ALPHA Parent Handbook*, Vol. 2. Toronto.

Anastakis, Dimitry (ed.). 2008. *The Sixties: Passion, Politics, and Style*. Montreal: McGill-Queens.

Bannerji, Himani. 1995. *Thinking Through: Essays on Feminism, Marxism, and Anti-Racism*. Toronto: Women's Press.

Bascia, Nina, and Rhiannon Maton. 2016. Teachers' Work and Innovation in Alternative Schools. *Critical Studies in Education* 57 (1): 131–141. doi:10.10 80/17508487.2016.1117004.

Barnes, Dean Spencer. 1997. The Viability of Publicly Funded Alternative Secondary Schools in Ontario. Master's Thesis, Queen's University.

Bedard, George J., and Stephen B. Lawton. 2000. The Struggle for Power and Control: Shifting Policy-Making Models and the Harris Agenda for Education in Ontario. *Canadian Public Administration* 43 (3): 241–269.

Benton-Banai, Edward. 1988. *The Mishomis Book: The Voice of the Ojibway*. St. Paul, MN: The Red School House, Indian Country Press.

Blanc, Suzanne, and Elaine Simon. 2007. Public Education in Philadelphia: The Crucial Need for Civic Capacity in a Privatized Environment. *Phi Delta Kappan* 88 (7): 503–506.

Cable, Greg. 1973a. *After SEED*. Toronto: Toronto Board of Education.

Cable, Greg. 1973b. *Alternatives: Strategies and Stumbling Blocks*. Toronto: Toronto Board of Education.

© The Editor(s) (if applicable) and The Author(s) 2017

N. Bascia et al. (eds.), *Alternative Schooling and Student Engagement*,

DOI 10.1007/978-3-319-54259-1

Campbell, Lara, Dominique Clement, and Gregory Kealey (eds.). 2012. *Debating Dissent: Canada and the Sixties.* Toronto: University of Toronto Press.

Cheng, Maisy, G. Tsuji, M. Yau, and Sue Ziegler. 1989. *The Every Secondary Student Survey, #191.* Toronto: Research Services, Toronto Board of Education.

Cremin, Lawrence. 1973. The Free School Movement: A Perspective. In *Pygmalion or Frankenstein,* op. cit 1973, eds. John C. Carr, Jean Dresden Grambs, and EG Camp-bell, 223. York City: Columbia Teachers College. (First published in *Notes on Education 2*).

Csanady, Ashley. 2015. Ontario Premier Says It's Time the Province Started Analyzing Policies Through a 'Race Lens.' *National Post.* http://news. nationalpost.com/news/canada/ontario-premier-says-its-time-the-province-started-analyzing-policies-through-a-race-lens. Accessed 25 Nov 2015.

Dewey, John. 1916. *Democracy and Education: An Introduction to the Philosophy of Education.* New York: Macmillan.

Fielding, Ariel and Michael Barker. 2016. Seed Part One: Breaking the Rules Without Shame. *Notes from the Field.* Last Modified January 13, 2016. http://notesfromthefield.ca/talking-with-teachers-in-alternative-schools/seed-part-one/.

Four-Level Government/African Canadian Community Working Group. 1992. *Towards a New Beginning: The Report and Action Plan.* Toronto: The Working Group.

Freedman, Michael, David Quinlan, and Michael Tabor. 1980. *A Brief Look at Public Alternative Schools in Ontario.* Toronto: Consortium of Ontario Public Alternative Schools.

Free School Handbook. Toronto: 1972 Pamphlet.

Gaskell, Jane. 2014. Review of the Restacking the Deck: Streaming by Class, Race and Gender in Ontario Schools, by Canfield, David, Bruce Curtis, Grace- Edward Galabuzi, Alison Gaymes San Vicente, David Livingstone, and Harry Smaller. In *Our Schools/Ourselves Special Issue,* Vol. 23, no. 2. Ottawa: Canadian Centre for Policy Alternatives.

Gillborn, David. 2015. Intersectionality, Critical Race Theory, and the Primacy of Racism: Race, Class, Gender, and Disability in Education. *Qualitative Inquiry* 21 (3): 277–287.

Goodman, Paul. 1962. *Compulsory Mis-Education.* New York: Knopf.

Hagen, John. 2001. *Northern Passage: American Vietnam War Resisters in Canada.* Cambridge: Harvard University Press.

Hall, Emmett M., and Llyod A. Dennis. 1968. *Living and Learning: The Report of the Provincial Committee on Aims and Objectives of Education in the Schools of Ontario.* Toronto: Ontario Department of Education, Provincial Committee on Aims and Objectives of Education in the Schools of Ontario.

Henderson, Stuart Robert. 2011. *Making the Scene: Yorkville and Hip Toronto in the 1960s*. Toronto: University of Toronto Press.

Holdway, Les, Marvin Midwicki, and Christopher Wilson. 1978. *Wandering Spirit Survival School*. Toronto: National Film Board of Canada.

Holt, John. 1964. *How Children Fail*. New York: Pitman.

Ieraci, Jason. 2006. Pendulums and Paradigms: Educational Reform in Ontario. Master's thesis, University of Toronto.

James, Royson. 1989. Panel Backs Mall Customer's Rights. *Toronto Star*, September 26, 1989. http://myaccess.library.utoronto.ca/login?url=http://search.proquest.com/docview/436020632?accountid=14771.

Janovicek, Nancy. 2012, Spring. 'The Community School Literally Takes Place in the Community:' Alternative Education in the Back-to-the-Land Movement in the West Kootenays, 1959 to 1980. *Historical Studies in Education/Revue d'histoire de l'éducation* 24 (1): 150–169.

Kostash, Myrna. 1980. *Long Way from Home: The story of the Sixties Generation in Canada*. Toronto: James Lorimer.

Levin, Ben, Jane Gaskell, and Katina Pollock. 2007. What Shapes Inner-City Education Policy? *Canadian Journal of Educational Administration and Policy* 61: 1–22.

Levin, Malcolm, and Olga Dimitri. 1980. A.I.S.P. Alumni Survey. Alternative Schools Follow-Up Project.

Martell, George (ed.). 1974. *The Politics of the Canadian Public School*. Toronto: James Lewis & Samuel.

Martell, George. 1995. *A New Education Politics: Bob Roe's Legacy and the Response of the Ontario Secondary School Teachers' Federation*. Toronto: James Lorimer.

Memon, Nadeem A. 2006. Contextualizing Hall-Dennis, The Rise of Progressive Educational Practices in Ontario, 1968–1972. Master's thesis, University of Toronto.

Myers, Douglas (ed.). 1973. *The Failure of Educational Reform in Canada*. Toronto: McClelland & Stewart.

Myers, Douglas. 1972. Where Have All the Free Schools Gone: A Conversation with Bob Davis, Satu Repo, and George Martell. *Canadian Forum*, October. Also in Myers (above), 1973.

Newmann, Richard. 2003. *Sixties Legacy: A History of the Public Alternative Schools Movement, 1967–2001*. New York: Peter Lang.

Novak, Bill. 1981. *Towards Indian Control of Indian Education in Ontario*. Toronto: York University. (Unpublished Paper).

Novak, Bill (Uncredited Editor, Assisted by Rosemary Moffat and Other WSSS Staff). 1983. *The Wandering Spirit Survival School Information Handbook*. Toronto: Self-published by WSSS.

Novak, Mark. 1975. *Living and Learning in the Free School*. Toronto: McClelland and Stewart.

Nygreen, Kysa. 2006. Reproducing or Challenging Power in the Questions We Ask and the Methods We Use: A Framework for Activist Research in Urban Education. *The Urban Review* 38 (1): 1–26.

Ontario Federation of Labour. 2001. *The Privatization of Ontario's Education System: 1995–2001*. Ontario, January, 2001. http://ofl.ca/wp-content/uploads/2002.01.01-Report-EducationPrivatization.pdf.

Ontario Ministry of Education. 1986. *Provincial Review Report Number 3: Alternative Schools and Programs in the Public System*. Ontario.

O'Rourke, Debra L. 2009. Defining and Defending a Democratic Public Education Site. Master's thesis, York University.

O'Rourke, Debra, and Caroline Nash. 2016. *Sharing Education*.http://alphaschool.ca/about/history/. Accessed March 2016.

OSSTF Issues. 2002. *Budget Cuts and Adult and Special Education Opportunities Issues in Ontario Education*, September, 2002. http://www.ossft.on.ca/www/issues/edfi/cuts.html.

Owram, Doug. 1996. *Born at the Right Time: A History of the Baby-Boom Generation*. Toronto: University of Toronto Press.

Palaeologu, Athena (ed.). 2009. *The Sixties in Canada: A Turbulent and Creative Decade*. Black Rose: Montreal.

Palmer, Bryan. 2009. *Canada's 1960s: The Ironies of Identity in a Rebellious Era*. Toronto: University of Toronto Press.

Questions and Answers on Adult Education. (n.d.). http://fcis.oise.utoronto.ca/~daniel_schugurensky/faqs/qa14.html. Accessed 30 Sept 2016.

Radwanski, George. 1987. *Ontario Study of the Relevance of Education and the Issue of Dropouts*. Toronto: Ministry of Education.

Rainford, Lisa. 2012. Cuts to Teaching Staff at Alternative School 'Catastrophic': Toronto District School Board to Axe 200 Positions in Effort to Balance Budget. *Bloor West Villager*. Last Modified May 10, 2012. http://www.insidetoronto.com/news-story/77655-cuts-to-teaching-staff-at-alternative-school-catastrophic-/.

Regnier, Robert. 1987. Survival Schools as Emancipatory Education. *Canadian Journal of Native Education* 14 (2): 42–53.

Rousseau, Jean-Jacques. 1979. *Emile or On Education*, trans. Allan Bloom. New York: Basic Books, 1979. (Earlier trans. Barbara Foxley. London: Dent, 1911).

Rushowy, Kristin. 2012. Toronto and Peel School Boards Prepare for Biggest Cuts since Harris Years. *The Toronto Star*, June 13, 2012. http://www.thestar.com/yourtoronto/education/2012/06/13/toronto_and_peel_school_boards_prepare_for_biggest_cuts_since_harris_years.html.

School District of Philadelphia. 2016. http://www.phila.k12.pa.us. Accessed 15 June 2016.

School Profile. (n.d.). http://yorkdale.net/secondary/?page_id=8. Accessed 30 Sept 2016.

TDSB. (n.d.). *Burnhamthorpe Collegiate Institute.* http://www.tdsb.on.ca/ Findyour/Schools.aspx?schno=2832. Accessed 30 Sept 2016.

Shuttleworth, Dale. 2010. Creating Alternatives in Education. Campaign for Public Education. *Playing Fast and Loose with Public Education* 77–84.

Shuttleworth, Dale. 2012. History and Politics of Alternative Schooling in Toronto: 1965—1990. In *Presentation at the Publicly Funded Alternative Schooling in the GTA Conference,* November 17–18, 2012.

Shulman, Lee S. 1986. Those Who Understand: Knowledge Growth in Teaching. *Educational Researcher* 15 (2): 4–14.

Shulman, Lee S. 1987. Knowledge and Teaching: Foundations of the New Reform. *Harvard educational review* 57 (1): 1–23.

Silberman, Charles. E. 1970. *Crisis in the Classroom.* New York: Random House.

Simon, Roger, Malcolm Levin, Marto Fieldstone, and Ann Johnston. 1973. *The Development and Evaluation of an Alternative High School: A Report on SEE (School of Experimental Education). Phase 2.* Toronto: Ontario Institute for Studies in Education.

Slinger, Joey. Circa 1980. A Salute to Native Kids Unlocking Spirits of the Past. *Toronto Star.*

Snowsill, Tony. 1978. *The Man, the Snake, and the Fox.* Toronto, Ottawa: National Film Board of Canada.

Telefilm Canada. 2014. *Class Queers,* August 10, 2016, https://www.telefilm. ca/en/catalogues/production/class-queers.

The United Nations. 1948. *The Universal Declaration of Human Rights.* http:// www.un.org/en/documents/udhr/. Accessed 19 Sept 2008.

Tiberio, Amanda. 2010. Alternative Schools Advisory Committee. *Toronto District School Board.* http://www.tdsb.on.ca/Portals/0/ Community/CommunityAdvisory committees/ICAC/Subcommittees/ AchievementGapReptDraftMay172010.pdf. Accessed 19 January 2010.

Toronto Board of Education Area Four Work Group. 1976. *A Study of the Image of Area Four.* Toronto: In the Castle Frank school file, Toronto District School Board Archives.

Toronto District School Board (TDSB). 2012. *Alternative Schools. Policy P062.* Toronto. http://www2.tdsb.on.ca/ppf/uploads/files/live/91/1595.pdf. Accessed Sept 2012.

Turner Consulting Group Inc. 2015. *Voices of Ontario Black Educators: An Experiential Report.* Ontario, November. http://onabse.org/ONABSE_ VOICES_OF_BLACK_EDUCATORS_Final_Report.pdf.

Verzuh, Ron. 1989. *Underground Times: Canada's Flower-Child Revolutionaries.* Toronto: Deneau.

Why Project Based Learning (PBL)? (n.d.). http://www.bie.org/. Accessed 30 Sept 2016.

Yip, Douglas. 1971. *SEED: The First Year.* Toronto: Research Department, Board of Education for the City of Toronto.

INDEX

© The Editor(s) (if applicable) and The Author(s) 2017
N. Bascia et al. (eds.), *Alternative Schooling and Student Engagement,*
DOI 10.1007/978-3-319-54259-1

Montessori/Maria Montessori, 73, 154
Montessori school, 73, 145
Mould, Steve, 128
Multicultural education, 42, 44

N
Nataleah, 255
Native, 191, 196, 200
Native Survival School, 196, 230
Native Way, 192, 195–197
Native Way School, 190, 200
Native Way pedagogy, 195
Neil Sutherland, 74
Neill, A.S., 12, 14, 31, 73, 231
Nelson, Fiona, ix, 82, 83
New Democratic Party (NDP), ix, xi, 57, 76
New Left, 31
New School, 74
Nguzo Saba principles, 45, 46
Nighana, 206
No Child Left Behind, 32
Noonan, 65
North York, vii, viii, 137
North York Board/North York Board of Education/North York school board, vii, ix, x, 120, 137
Now Magazine, 234

O
Oasis, x, xi, 65, 206, 207
Oasis Alternative Secondary School, 205
Oasis Skateboard Factory, 65
Office of New School Models, 26, 29, 32
Oji, Adisa S., 235
Ontario Academic Credit (OAC), 60
Ontario College of Education, 96
Ontario Government, 109

Ontario Institute for Studies in Education (OISE), ix, 111, 112, 139, 161
Ontario Science Centre, 140
Ontario Secondary School Teachers Federation (OSSTF), 97, 185, 188
Open classrooms, 27
Opportunity Network: Alternative Education, The, 29
Ottawa New School, 81
Our Schools/Our Schools Ourselves, 96, 101

P
Parents, 40
Parents for a Hall–Dennis School, ix
Parkway Program, x, 27, 28, 34, 85
Performing arts schools, x
Perry, 32
Pestalozzi, Johann, 72
Philadelphia, x, 26–29, 31, 33, 34
Philadelphia's Workshop School, 34
Phillips, John, 127
Piaget, Jean, 231
Point Blank/Point Blank School, 79, 80, 82
Policy, 4, 11
Pollack-Schloss, 28, 29
Premier of Ontario, 44, 211
Principal, 6, 16, 62, 63
Principals' Association, 121
Pritchard, Bob, 182
Private school, 32, 155
Privatization, 26
Professor Malcolm Levin, 111
Program for Academic and Creative Education (PACE), 126
Progressive Conservative Party, 57
Progressive Conservative government, 64
Progressive education, 27